A Determination of the Principles and Experiments Desirable for a High-School Course of Integrated Physical Science

by

Vaden Willis Miles

*A Dissertation Submitted in Partial Fulfillment
of the Requirements for the Degree of
Doctor of Philosophy*

University of Michigan
Ann Arbor, Michigan
July, 1947

LITHOPRINTED BY EDWARDS BROTHERS, INC.
ANN ARBOR, MICHIGAN

PRINCIPLES AND EXPERIMENTS FOR COURSES OF INTEGRATED PHYSICAL SCIENCE

by

Vaden W. Miles

Wayne University

Edwards Brothers, Inc.
Ann Arbor, Michigan
1950

ACKNOWLEDGMENTS

The writer wishes to express his sincere apprecia-
tion to all those individuals whose cooperation made the
completion of this study possible.

He is especially grateful to the members of his
doctoral committee: Dr. Francis D. Curtis, Professor
of Education and of the Teaching of Science (Chairman);
Dr. Ernest F. Barker, Professor of Physics and Chairman
of the Department of Physics; Dr. Floyd E. Bartell,
Professor of Chemistry and Chairman of Graduate Study
in Chemistry; Dr. Charles R. Brassfield, Associate
Professor of Physiology, Medical School; Dr. Raleigh
Schorling, Professor of Education, Director of Instruction in the University High School, and Supervisor of
Directed Teaching; and Dr. Clifford Woody, Professor
of Education.

The investigator is especially indebted to the
following specialists in the teaching of science who
spent many hours in evaluating the principles and the
experiments: Dr. Francis D. Curtis, Professor of
Education and of the Teaching of Science, University
of Michigan; Dr. Waldo E. Blanchet, Professor of
Physical Science and Dean of the College, Fort Valley

State College, Fort Valley, Georgia; Mr. Lawrence A.
Conrey, Instructor of Physical Science, University
High School, University of Michigan, and formerly of
the Department of Chemistry, University of Wyoming;
and Mr. John C. Fisher, formerly Instructor of Physi-
cal Science, University High School, University of
Michigan, and presently at Coe College, Cedar Rapids,
Iowa, who evaluated only the principles.

Special acknowledgment is made to Dr. Francis D.
Curtis for his inspiration and helpful guidance through
a graduate program which has culminated in this experience in educational research. His friendly counsel,
clear thinking, and scholarly research shall forever
remain an inspiration to the writer as he works in
the field of science education.

Grateful acknowledgment is made to my wife,
Maxine Smith Miles, for her cooperation and help
throughout this study, including the typing of the
manuscript.

Boston   Vaden W. Miles
July, 1947

TABLE OF CONTENTS

Page

List of Tables vii

CHAPTER

I THE PROBLEM AND ITS BACKGROUND 1

Introduction 1
The Search for a Definition of an
Integrated Course of Physical Science . 1
The Introduction and Development of
Physical Science Courses in the
Senior High School 7
Investigations of the Offerings of
Physical-Science Courses in Senior
High Schools 29
Evidence Which Supports the Offering of
Integrated Courses of Physical Science
in the Senior High School 34
Research Investigations 34
Opinions of College Registrars 42
Important Reports 44
Scientific Principles as a Basis for
Organizing Materials of Instruction
in Science 51
Research on Principles as Goals of
Instruction in Science 56
Summary 64
The Need for Further Investigation 66
Statement of the Problem 67

II THE SELECTION OF PRINCIPLES FOR A COURSE
OF PHYSICAL SCIENCE 68

Statement of the Problem 68
Definitions of Terms 68
Techniques Employed 69
Findings 95

TABLE OF CONTENTS

CHAPTER   Page

III THE SELECTION AND EVALUATION OF LABORATORY
     AND DEMONSTRATION EXPERIMENTS   97

     Statement of the Problem   97
     Definitions of Terms   97
     Techniques Employed   98
       Method of Assembling Experiments   98
         Criteria for the Selection of Text-
           books and Laboratory Manuals for
           Analysis   100
         Method of Locating Possible Sources
           of Experiments Other Than Text-
           books and Laboratory Manuals   108
         Methods of Collecting, of Grouping,
           and of Refining the Statements
           of the Purposes of the Experi-
           ments   109
         Index of Reliability of the
           Analysis to Secure the Experi-
           ments   111
         Validity of the Analysis
           to Secure the Experiments   114
       Method of Assigning Experiments to
         Principles   114
         Index of Reliability of the Assign-
           ments of the Experiments to the
           Principles   115
       Evaluation of the Experiments   119
         Validity of the Assignments of the
           Experiments to the Principles ...   125
     Findings   186

TABLE OF CONTENTS

CHAPTER   Page

IV   SUMMARY, CONCLUSIONS, AND RECOMMENDATIONS   188

     Statement of the Problem   188
     Methods Used   188
     Conclusions   190
     Recommendations   192

BIBLIOGRAPHY   193

APPENDIX

   A   PRINCIPLES CONSIDERED UNDESIRABLE FOR
       INCLUSION IN AN INTEGRATED COURSE OF
       PHYSICAL SCIENCE FOR SENIOR HIGH SCHOOL .   208

   B   TABLE IV (CONTINUED)   214

   C   THE EXPERIMENTS WHICH THE EVALUATORS
       DEEMED UNDESIRABLE FOR INCLUSION IN AN
       INTEGRATED COURSE OF PHYSICAL SCIENCE ...   376

   D   THE EXPERIMENTS WHICH THE INVESTIGATOR
       WAS UNABLE TO ALLOCATE TO ANY OF THE
       214 PRINCIPLES JUDGED DESIRABLE FOR
       INCLUSION IN THE INTEGRATED COURSE OF
       PHYSICAL SCIENCE FOR SENIOR HIGH SCHOOL .   421

LIST OF TABLES

TABLE   Page

I   PRINCIPLES DESIRABLE FOR INCLUSION IN AN
       INTEGRATED COURSE OF PHYSICAL SCIENCE FOR
       SENIOR HIGH SCHOOL, IN DESCENDING ORDER
       OF THEIR RELATIVE IMPORTANCE   74

II   INDEX OF RELIABILITY OF THE ANALYSIS TO
       SECURE THE EXPERIMENTS   113

III   INDEX OF RELIABILITY OF THE ASSIGNMENTS
       OF THE EXPERIMENTS TO THE PRINCIPLES   118

IV   THE RELATIVE VALUES AND RANKS OF LABORA-
       TORY AND DEMONSTRATION EXPERIMENTS ALLO-
       CATED TO THE PRINCIPLES OF PHYSICAL SCI-
       ENCE DESIRABLE FOR INCLUSION IN AN INTE-
       GRATED COURSE OF PHYSICAL SCIENCE FOR
       SENIOR HIGH SCHOOL   126

CHAPTER I

THE PROBLEM AND ITS BACKGROUND

Introduction

Since 1930 leaders in the field of secondary education have given increasingly greater attention to
the general topic of integration of the curriculum,
with particular emphasis on the integration of closely
related areas of subject matter. According to Wise,[1]

> The field of natural science lends
> itself readily to integration, as is shown
> by the fact that two ... integrated courses,
> [general science and general biology], are
> now firmly established in our secondary
> schools.

Further illustration of fusion of the separate sciences
is found in the integrated courses of physical science
offered in the senior high school.

The Search for a Definition of an
Integrated Course of Physical Science

The literature does not reveal even one definition
which satisfactorily differentiates the integrated course

---

[1]Harold E. Wise, "An Integration of Physics and
Chemistry," Science Education, XX (April, 1936), 69.

1

of physical science from other types of science courses
in the senior high school. Featherstone[2] reminds curriculum workers that the "troublesome adjective 'integrated' ... appears to mean all kinds of things to all
kinds of people."

It seems obvious that, because of this lack of de-
finitude, workers would probably consider science
courses which cut across the subject-matter boundaries
of two or more of the physical sciences as integrated
courses of physical science. Such courses offered in
secondary schools above grade IX have most frequently
been called physical science. They have also often
been called survey of physical science, fused or integrated physical science, fused or integrated physics
and chemistry, consumer science, and senior science.

An early attempt to define "integrated physical
science" was made in 1934 by Federer[3] of West Virginia
University. He referred to "integrated physical science" as "the teaching of science in the eleventh and
twelfth years of high school from the standpoint of

[2]W. B. Featherstone, "The Place of Subjects in
an Integrated Curriculum," California Quarterly of
Secondary Education, IX (April, 1934), 235.

[3]George A. Federer, Jr., "The Teaching of
Integrated Physical Science in the West Virginia
University High School," Educational Method,
XIII (February, 1934), 271.

problems that involve both chemistry and physics."

A similar interpretation of such a course was expressed in 1937 by Slayton,[4] who, in writing of a physical-science course which he taught in the Teachers College High School of the University of Nebraska, said:

> Integrated physical science or physical science is to be regarded as the name given to a course in which a definite attempt has been made to combine physics and chemistry into an integrated pattern organized into a definite series of units of subject matter within each of which both matters of chemistry and of physics are considered and treated in a more or less related manner.

In 1944, Peterson[5] used the expression "Integrated Course in Physics and Chemistry" in the title of his doctoral dissertation. Within the dissertation and in a subsequent magazine article based upon it,

---

[4] Wilfred G. Slayton, An Evaluation of a Course in Integrated Physical Science for the Senior High School, p. 10. Unpublished Master's thesis, University of Nebraska, 1937.

[5] Shailer Peterson, The Comparison of the Achievement of Students in the Traditional High School Physics and Chemistry Courses Each of One Year's Duration With the Achievement of Students in the Integrated Course in Physics and Chemistry Over a One Year Period. Unpublished Doctor's dissertation, University of Minnesota, 1944.

he[6] used the term fused as synonymous with integrated,
but the expression "fused or integrated course in
physics and chemistry" was not defined except by impli-
cation. Some years earlier (1937), however, Peterson[7]
stated that "a fused course [of physics and chemistry
is one which] not only presents the fundamentals of
each [separate] course [or subject] but fuses or inte-
grates them, teaching them at the same time that they
may be more meaningful and may show the pupil how
they are related."

Spears, writing for the North Central Association
of Colleges and Secondary Schools,[8] defines a "fused
course [as] one that has replaced a number of subjects
previously offered in either one or a number of different subject fields, drawing heavily upon them for

---

[6]Shailer Peterson, "The Evaluation of a One-Year
Course, the Fusion of Physics and Chemistry, With Other
Physical Science Courses," Science Education, XXIX
(December, 1945), 255-264.

[7]Shailer A. Peterson, "Advocating a Fusion of
Physics and Chemistry," School Science and Mathematics, XXXVII (April, 1937), 452.

[8]North Central Association of Colleges and Second-
ary Schools, The General Education Committee of the
Commission on Curricula of Secondary Schools and Insti-
tutions of Higher Education, General Education in the
American High School, p. 183. Chicago: Scott,
Foresman and Company, 1942.

content." This definition of a fused course is in
basic accord with the one by Peterson.

In 1945, an integrated course in physical science
for the senior high school was described in the Report
of the Harvard Committee, General Education in a Free
Society.[9] Such a course would be so organized, according to the Committee,[10] as to include "a systematic
presentation of basic concepts and principles of the
physical sciences ... [with] illustrative materials
[drawn] from the fields of physics, chemistry, geology,
and astronomy." It should be noted that mention is
not made here of meteorology, a branch of physics.

Another type of physical-science course called
"senior science" was introduced in many schools during
the latter part of the decade, 1930-40. Heidel[11]
describes a "generalized high school senior science
course ... [as one] encompassing the fields of physics
and chemistry and emphasizing consumership."

[9]General Education in a Free Society, Report of
the Harvard Committee. Cambridge: Harvard University
Press, 1945.

[10]Ibid., pp. 159-160.

[11]Robert H. Heidel, "A Comparison of the Outcomes
of Instruction of the Conventional High School Physics
Course and the Generalized High School Senior Science
Course," Science Education, XXVIII (March, 1944), 88.

A somewhat different science offering is the survey course in physical science which is defined by Watson[12] as "any course of one semester or more in length which is given above Grade IX and which includes materials from two or more physical sciences and excludes materials of biological science." The same general idea is expressed by Fordemwalt,[13] who, in recommending a survey course of biology and a similar course of physical science in a proposed reorganization of science in secondary schools, says: "A survey course [is] one which cuts across conventional course boundaries and includes ... materials from several fields of learning to accomplish the purpose at hand."

The Dictionary of Education[14] includes general definitions of an "integrated or fused course of study" and of a "survey course" which are applicable

[12]D. R. Watson, "Objectives of Survey Courses in Physical Science," School Review, XLVIII (November, 1940), 685.

[13]Fred Fordemwalt, "A Reorganization of Secondary School Science," Journal of Chemical Education, XVII (November, 1940), 542.

[14]Carter V. Good (editor), Dictionary of Education, pp. 108-9. New York: McGraw-Hill Book Company, Inc., 1945.

to an integrated course of physical science for the
senior high school. The integrated or fused course
of study is defined as "a course of study in which
pupil activity is centered in themes or areas of
living and which draws upon the content of the various school subjects as mutually associated in some
genuine life relation." The survey course is defined
as "a course designed to give a general view of an
area of study, often as a means of introducing an
unfamiliar field to pupils or students before under-
taking specialized work or providing them with broad,
general concepts about an area in which they may or
may not plan to specialize."

The Introduction and Development of Physical-Science Courses in the Senior High School

As early as 1914, Caldwell[15] advocated a year of
high-school science "organized upon a broad basis involving fundamental principles of the various physical
sciences and using materials from all, if needed."

---

[15] Otis W. Caldwell, "Preliminary Report of the
Committee on a Unified High School Science Course,"
School Science and Mathematics, XIV (February, 1914),
167.

In a comprehensive investigation of the "fused or survey" course of physical science in high schools and colleges throughout the United States, Watson[16] found "the earliest such [high-school] course ... was introduced at Franklin High School of Los Angeles in 1924-25." According to Doss,[17] however, "prior to 1934 the [physical-science] course [offered in the high schools of Los Angeles] consisted of a certain number of weeks of physics [and] a certain number of weeks of chemistry, with perhaps some geology or astronomy." He further emphasized that in Los Angeles "the various branches of physical science are not now [1937] treated separately ... , [but] each branch ... is called upon as it is needed."

The change in the Los Angeles course referred to by Doss was later confirmed by Herriott and Nettels[18]

---

[16]Donald R. Watson, Survey Courses in Physical Science: Their Status, Trends, and Evaluation, p. 87. Unpublished Doctor's dissertation, University of Southern California, 1940.

[17]Charles Lester Doss, Generalized Physical Science in the Senior High School, p. 87. Unpublished Master's thesis, University of Southern California, 1937.

[18]M. E. Herriott and Charles H. Nettels, "Functional Physical Science," Curriculum Journal, XIII (December, 1942), 363.

with the statement that "Today [1942], the course [of
physical science offered in Los Angeles high schools]
is no longer merely a half year of chemistry and a
half year of physics as it once was. Instead it is a
well organized, broad course in physical science ... ."
The experience of Nettels and Herriott in the development of this course must have had a marked influence
on the organization of a textbook of physical science
by Nettels[19] and others which was first published in
1942. It is stated in this textbook that "instead of
a fragmentary treatment of chemistry or physics, a
unified presentation is made of the entire field of
the closely related physical sciences: astronomy,
chemistry, geology, meteorology, [and] physics."

The University High School of West Virginia
University is the first senior high school on record
in the published literature to have introduced a one-
year course of physical science which cuts across the
subject-matter boundaries of two or more of the physical sciences. Federer[20] reported in 1934 that "for

[19]Charles H. Nettels, Paul F. Devine, Walter L.
Nourse, and M. E. Herriott, Physical Science, p. v.
Boston: D. C. Heath and Company, 1942.

[20]Federer, op. cit., p. 273.

the past two years, [1931-32[*] and 1932-33], ...
the integrated problem has been carried out" in
this school. "Contracts" such as "What is the
relation of science to the automobile industry?"[21]
were divided into smaller problems that involved
physics and chemistry.

Evidence supplied by Watson and Ferguson does
not permit unqualified designation of the University
High School of West Virginia University as the first
senior high school to have introduced an integrated
course of physical science. Watson[22] reported on the
basis of an inquiry sent to 328 California high schools
and 81 non-California high schools, designed to secure
information concerning any fused or survey course of
physical science offered by them, that "all of the
small schools introduced their courses in 1930-31 or
later [whereas] four of the larger schools reported
such courses before this date."[23] The fused, or

[21]Ibid., p. 272.

[22]Donald R. Watson, op. cit., pp. 109 and 369.

[23]Ibid., p. 87.

[*]In a letter dated January 6, 1947 from George A.
Federer, Jr., Supervisor of Science Teaching, West
Virginia University, to Vaden W. Miles, Boston University, Mr. Federer said: "The records show that the ...
integrated course of physical science was [first] offered in the West Virginia University High School in the
school year of 1931-32."

survey, courses of physical science were merely
identified but not described by the schools reporting them. Furthermore, the year of introduction of
such courses in each of the reporting schools was not
stated by Watson,[24] except for the Franklin High
School of Los Angeles (1924-25), one other California
high school (1931-32), and a non-California high
school (1927-28). According to Doss,[25] however, an
integrated course of physical science was not offered
in a Los Angeles high school prior to 1934. Therefore,
all such courses introduced in high schools concurrent-
ly with or earlier than the one in the University High
School of West Virginia University in 1931-32 must
have been in schools outside Los Angeles.

It is altogether possible that one of the pioneer
courses in applied science referred to by Ferguson[26]
may be the first integrated course of physical science
to be offered by a senior high school in the United

[24]Ibid., pp. 87 and 112.

[25]Doss, loc. cit.

[26]William Clarence Ferguson, Instruction Problems
of Generalized Science in the Senior High School, p. 4.
Unpublished Doctor's dissertation, George Peabody
College for Teachers, 1939. [Available as Peabody
Contribution to Education No. 239]

States. According to Ferguson, "the first record of
an attempt at the new type of applied science course
was made in the senior high school of Newtonville,
Massachusetts in 1912." Similar courses were reported
by him as being introduced in Pasadena, California in
1921, Ocean Grove, New Jersey and Flint, Michigan in
approximately 1927, and Cleveland, Ohio, in 1928.

Among the pioneer courses of physical science was
one planned by Brown[27] to replace separate courses in
physics and chemistry in the Lincoln School of Teachers
College, Columbia University, "beginning in the fall
of 1934." He proposed "broad themes ... selected without regard to subject-matter boundaries across which
they cut ... [as] the objectives of an integrated
course in physical science."[28] Moreover, he expected
that "the subject matter [for such a course would] be
that material which is deemed most suitable ... ,
irrespective of the conventional classification of
that subject matter as physics, chemistry, astronomy,
or geology."[29]

---

[27] H. Emmett Brown, "Science in the New Secondary
School," Teachers College Record, XXXV (May, 1934),
706.

[28] Ibid., p. 707.

[29] Ibid., p. 703.

After experimenting with the course for 5 years in grades 11 and 12, Brown[30] presented a "tentative list of [15] units for an integrated two-year course in the physical sciences." One such unit, for example, was entitled

> Energy in the form of waves constitutes an important means by which information is received and imparted.

A major concession to college entrance requirements, which influenced the nature of the two-year course of physical science offered by Brown,[31] was that

> For certification purposes, and to assist students in their preparation for the C.E.E.B. [College Entrance Examination Board] examinations, it seemed desirable to group together in one year most of the material derived from the field of physics, and similarly in the other year, most of the material derived from chemistry.

He thought that particular grouping necessary "because students may elect to take just a single year of the two-year sequence."

---

[30]H. Emmett Brown, The Development of a Course in the Physical Sciences for the Senior High School of the Lincoln School of Teachers College, p. 31. New York: Bureau of Publications, Teachers College, Columbia University, 1939.

[31]H. Emmett Brown, "The Development of a Course in the Physical Sciences for the Senior High School of the Lincoln School," Science Education, XXIII (March, 1939), 157.

According to Craig and Lockhart,[32] in 1935 the
program of science in the Horace Mann School of
Teachers College, Columbia University, included "two
years of physical science in the eleventh and twelfth
grades." This physical-science course was "centered
around generalizations [principles]" and included
subject matter from the fields of "physics, chemistry,
geology, astronomy, and paleontology."

Therefore, the Lincoln School and perhaps the
Horace Mann School, both of which are administered by
the Teachers College of Columbia University, may in
accordance with available evidence[#] be designated as
the first senior high school or schools in the United
States to have introduced a two-year sequence of integrated physical science. The year of the introduction
of the sequence was 1934-35.

_____

[32]Gerald S. Craig and Alton I. Lockhart, "The
Program of Science in the Horace Mann School,"
Teachers College Record, XXXVI (May, 1935), 697.

[#]Unsubstantiated evidence to the contrary is presented on page 45 of Science Education in American
Schools, the Forty-sixth Yearbook [1947], Part I,
of the National Society for the Study of Education,
where it is stated: "The failure of the promising
two-year program [or course] of physical science
prepared for use throughout one of the middle-
western states about twenty years ago reveals the
difficulties encountered in carrying on such a
two-year course."

In 1935, Havighurst[33] reported "a record of 18 senior high school survey courses [of physical science] which were given in 1934-35." He also noted that "Pasadena [California] is requiring all eleventh graders to take such a course" and that "plans are on foot to establish a physical science course in all the high schools of Los Angeles." Moreover, he stated that "there is the possibility that the idea will spread until all secondary schools will offer a physical science survey course for their juniors and seniors."

A pattern for the further development of physical-science courses in secondary schools was foretold by Anibal[34] in this same year, 1935, when he said:

> The course in general physical science ... seems destined to experience the same painful stages of growth as its predecessors, [general science and general biology]. In many cases ... teachers ... have tried to fuse [only] physics and chemistry. With the whole rich environment of physical science to draw upon, there is no reason why this course should be limited to the principles of chemistry and physics. There are no barriers in nature between the principles of astronomy, geology, physics, chemistry, and other still more narrow compartments ...

---

[33]Robert J. Havighurst, "Survey Courses in the Natural Sciences," The American Physics Teacher, III (September, 1935), 101.

[34]F. G. Anibal, "Generalized Science Instruction in the Secondary Schools," California Journal of Secondary Education, X (November, 1935), 484.

A one-year course of integrated physical science, restricted to physics and chemistry, was, according to Rosenlof and Wise,[35] offered in the Teachers College High School of the University of Nebraska for the first time "during the year 1935-36." In this course, generalizations from the fields of physics and chemistry were combined into "a list of ten major generalizations which, ... when stated in problem form, became the unit problems about which the subject matter [from the fields of physics and chemistry] was organized."[36] One such unit problem, for example was:

> How may electricity be produced, and what are the physical and chemical effects of an electric current?[37]

According to Slayton,[38] this course, which was based on a Master's thesis by Wise,[39] was taught without major change in seven additional Nebraska high schools in 1936-37.

---

[35]George W. Rosenlof and Harold E. Wise, "Experimenting with a Course in Combined Physical Science," School Review, XLVI (May, 1938), 349.

[36]Ibid., p. 347.

[37]Ibid., p. 348.

[38]Slayton, op. cit., p. 5.

[39]Harold E. Wise, A Proposed Course in Integrated Physical Science for the Senior High School -- Restricted to Physics and Chemistry. Unpublished Master's thesis, University of Nebraska, 1935.

In 1935-36, Peterson[40] introduced a "physical science survey course" in the University of Oregon High School. In his course, he "attempted to survey such areas as would normally be included in physics, chemistry, geology, astronomy, meteorology, animal biology, and plant biology." The inclusion of considerable biological science in a survey course of physical science seems inappropriate.

Another digression from an integrated course of physical science was found in the proposal by Cummings[41] to introduce an "integrated science course" in the Chico (California) High School in the spring of 1935. Fusion of "physics, chemistry, [and] certain parts of biology and mathematics" were proposed.

A course in "applied science" was reported by Todd[42] as having been offered in the Oakland (California) Technical High School in 1935-36. This

---

[40]Shailer Peterson, The Comparison of the Achievement of Students in the Traditional High School Physics and Chemistry Courses Each of One Year's Duration With the Achievement of Students in the Integrated Course in Physics and Chemistry Over a One Year Period, op. cit., p. 29.

[41]Frank L. Cummings, "Practices in Fusion of Subject Matter in Various Courses," California Journal of Secondary Education, X (October, 1934), 17.

[42]Robert B. Todd, Jr., "Fusion in Practical Physical Science--An Experimental Course," School Science and Mathematics, XXXVII (January, 1937), 93.

course included "twelve units of experience, each centering about a real problem, irrespective of the subject matter" and was for "eleventh and twelfth grade pupils who ... desire some science but do not wish, or are unable to take chemistry and physics."[43] Each unit depended upon "adaptation of fundamental scientific principles as advanced by the Thirty-first Yearbook of the National Society for the Study of Education."[44]

Hogg,[45,46,*] Baird,[47,48] and Skinner[49] report

---

[43]Ibid., p. 92.

[44]Ibid., p. 93.

[45]John C. Hogg, "Science in Schools," Journal of Chemical Education, XXI (March, 1944), 132.

[46]John C. Hogg, "The Physical Sciences Course--Its Justification and Sequence," School Science and Mathematics, XXXIX (February, 1939), 175.

[47]Hal Baird, "Teaching the Physical Sciences From a Functional Point of View," Educational Methods, XVI (May, 1937), 408.

[48]Hal Baird, "A Functional Course in the Physical Sciences," Curriculum Journal, VIII (January, 1937), 14.

[49]Selby M. Skinner, "A Two-Year Physical Science Course in the University of Chicago," School Science and Mathematics, XL (October, 1940), 634.

*In a letter dated December 19, 1946 from John C. Hogg, chairman of the department of science, Phillips Exeter Academy, to Vaden W. Miles, Boston University, Mr. Hogg stated: "We introduced the integrated physical sciences course in this Academy in the fall of 1936, and it has been going strong ever since."

that their respective schools each instituted in the
fall of 1936 an integrated course of physical science
consisting of a two-year sequence. The respective
schools are: the Phillips Exeter Academy (Exeter,
New Hampshire), the Francis W. Parker School (Chicago),
and the University of Chicago represented by the first
two years of the "Four-Year College", formerly grades
XI and XII of its University High School.

According to Hogg[50] of the Phillips Exeter Academy, "In the first year [of the two-year course of
integrated physical science offered by the Academy]
emphasis is placed on chemistry and the physics is
utilitarian [in the sense that] it is designed to
clarify the chemistry." Subsequently, he[51] presented
the following 8 concepts as the major divisions of
an outline for such a course:

I. Basic Concepts of length, mass, time,
force, density
II. Concept of Pressure
III. Concept of the Molecule
IV. Concept of the Atom
V. Concept of Energy
VI. Electrical Energy
VII. Concept of the Electron
VIII. Concept of Wave Motion

---

[50]Hogg, loc. cit.

[51]John C. Hogg, "Science in Schools," op. cit.,
pp. 131-132.

The true nature of the course offered at the
Phillips Exeter Academy is, however, revealed far
better by Hogg's statement in 1939 with respect to
the course than by the titles of the 8 major divisions
of the course outline. In the words of Hogg,[52]

> There is a growing realization
> that too much is lost by the separation
> of the physical sciences.
>
> The separation of the physical
> sciences into physics and chemistry
> was, in the first place, purely arbi-
> trary and made as a matter of con-
> venience. It was never intended that
> one should be studied without the other.
> ... Physics and chemistry are the com-
> plement and supplement of each other.
> The omission of either leaves an incom-
> plete picture and, even for elementary
> students, seriously detracts from the
> value of science as an educational
> force. ... Integration of the two
> sciences [physics and chemistry]
> appears, therefore, to offer the
> solution to this vexing problem.

This same thought was again expressed in the
writings of Hogg[53] after the course had been offered
for 7 instead of only 3 years. He wrote:

> If physics and chemistry are
> taught as separate one-year courses,
> the inevitable question that arises
> is, Which should be taught first? ...
> Indeed, the only valid answer to the
> question is that neither subject

---

[52]John C. Hogg, "The Physical Sciences Course--
Its Justification and Sequence," op. cit., pp. 174-175.

[53]John C. Hogg, "Science in Schools," op. cit.,
p. 131.

should be taught first but that they
should be taught simultaneously. The
separation of the physical sciences
into physics and chemistry is un-
fortunate. The division was made
originally as a matter of convenience
and was not intended as a cleavage.
Physics and chemistry are two aspects
of the same science. Physics deals
with energy and its interrelation in
the fields of mechanics, heat, electricity, and light; chemistry deals
with the structural changes in matter
that result from energy changes. To
study one without the other is to get
an incomplete picture and the student
is seriously handicapped. These two
sciences should be integrated and
studied together for two years. Such
a course would remove many of the
difficulties inherent in the separate
courses, it would prevent over-lapping
and needless repetition, and it would
help to banish the one-year course
from the curriculum.

The two-year course of physical science offered
by the Francis W. Parker School (Chicago) was called
"The Contributions of Science to Our Life Today."[54]
In the eleventh grade the units were chosen "largely
from the area corresponding to traditional physics,"
while "in the twelfth grade the greater part of the
units [dealt] with subjects in which chemistry [was]
most apparent."[55]

---

[54]Baird, loc. cit.

[55]Hal Baird, "Teaching the Physical Sciences
from a Functional Point of View," op. cit., p. 408.

The two-year general course in physical science offered in the first 2 years of the "Four-Year College" of the University of Chicago, formerly grades XI and XII of the University High School, was "planned to include a study of those aspects of the physical world that seem important for the general education of the individual."[56] The content, according to Skinner,[57] was "drawn from the fields of physics, chemistry, geology, and astronomy, in the order of emphasis, with traces of material from meteorology, and other sciences."

The units in the course outline[58] for the first year of the two-year course were entitled:

I. The Earth, Our Home
II. The Ever Changing Face of the Earth
III. Motion, a Change Involving Force and Matter
IV. Energy, the Agent of All Change
V. The Molecular Nature of Matter
VI. Chemical Change and the Atomic Constitution of Matter
VII. Electricity at Rest and in Motion
VIII. Electricity and Matter

---

[56] Science Instruction in Elementary and High-School Grades by Members of the Faculty of the Laboratory Schools of the University of Chicago, p. 191. Chicago: The University of Chicago, 1939.

[57] Skinner, op. cit., p. 636.

[58] Science Instruction in Elementary and High-School Grades, op. cit., pp. 192-211.

The units in the course outline for the second
year were entitled:

    I.   The Chemical Reaction
    II.   The Reactions of Ions in Solution
    III.   Atomic Structure and Chemical Behavior
    IV.   Metals and Nonmetals
    V.   Carbon, the Element of Life
    VI.   The History of the Earth
    VII.   The Earth and Its Neighbors
    VIII. Waves as Carriers of Energy
    IX.   Radiation and the Nature of Stars

Peterson,[59] who had taught a survey course of
physical science in the University of Oregon High
School, administered a "fused course of physics and
chemistry" in the University of Minnesota High School
"for the first time [at that institution] during the
year 1937-38." The outline for the fused course was
altered until, during the last 3 years of its administration by him,[60] 1940-41 through 1942-43, the
material was presented in the 12 units listed below:

        Introduction
        How Can Comfort Be Increased by
            Air Conditioning?
        How Does Science Improve Our Homes
            and Office Buildings?
        How Does Water Control Our Way of
            Living?

----

[59]Peterson, op. cit., p. 34.

[60]Shailer Peterson, "The Evaluation of a One-
Year Course, the Fusion of Physics and Chemistry,
With Other Physical Science Courses," op. cit.,
p. 256.

What Should We Look for When Buying an
Automobile?
How Do We Obtain Our Gasoline?
Do We Obtain Foods and Poisons from
the Same Molecules?
Will Plastics and the New Synthetic
Textiles Make Nations Independent?
How Do We Obtain the Most Valuable Metals?
What's Wrong with This Picture?
What Has Science Done for Communication?
What Is There Left to Invent or to Discover?

The fused course of physics and chemistry was originally planned by Peterson[61] to "provide an alternate
for those students who had but one year to devote to
either Chemistry or Physics." In Minnesota's University High School, however, "the new course soon took
the place of a single year of either Chemistry or
Physics and as a result Advanced Problems courses in
both physics and chemistry had to be created for the
students who, having taken a year of Fusion, wished
to take more physical science."

Tenney of the Tower Hill School, Wilmington,
Delaware, prepared for the Progressive Education
Association[62] an outline of the unique offerings of
his school in the physical sciences. A physical-
science course, required, was followed by 1 semester

---

[61]Ibid.

[62]Progressive Education Association, Commission
on Secondary School Curriculum, Science in General
Education, pp. 477-500. New York: D. Appleton-
Century Company, Inc., 1938.

of physics and 1 of chemistry, both electives. In
an introductory note, a committee for the Association[63] said:

> The fused physical-science course
> given by Mr. Tenney is required of all
> eleventh-grade students. It completes
> the secondary-school science work of
> many. For a considerable number of
> others it furnishes the foundation of
> twelfth-year science courses consisting
> of one-half year of physics and one-half
> year of chemistry. Experience with this
> type of two-year sequence indicates that
> it prepares students for college entrance
> with the same general background in sci-
> ence as would be obtained from one full
> year's work in physics and another in
> chemistry. The two-year students there-
> fore receive the prevocational training
> in science customarily given at the
> secondary level and those taking one
> year of science get a broader concept
> of physical science than would be re-
> ceived in one year of either physics
> or chemistry. This type of organization
> seems to meet the requirements of both
> groups of students in a small school
> where only one section of a course is
> needed to include all the students in a
> given grade.

This fused physical-science course was composed
of 6 units, namely: household machines and appli-
ances, household supplies, public utilities, representative industries, the world picture, and matter
and energy.

---

[63] Ibid., p. 477.

The procedure employed in this course[64] is a notable variation from more conventional classroom procedure. In studying the unit on machines, for example, the pupils made an inventory of machines found in the home. Those pupils interested in "acoustical machines," the piano, violin, phonograph, and radio receiver devoted "work periods" to an investigation of them. Other groups worked on different problems of greater interest to their particular group. However, "one day each week was given over to class meetings during which every one did the same thing." Moreover, "the teacher stepped in when necessary to add assigned work which would clarify any points." At the end of each unit each group gave "reports" and did "demonstrations" for the class as a whole. Furthermore, generalizations or principles of physical science, and also of other areas such as economics, sociology, and history, "grew out of the work."

The final report of the Eight-Year Study (1933-1941) of the Progressive Education Association[65]

---

[64]Ibid., p. 490.

[65]Progressive Education Association, Publications Commission on the Relation of School and College, Adventure in American Education, Volume V: Thirty Schools Tell Their Story, New York: Harper and Brothers, 1943.

mentions, in addition to the physical-science courses offered by the Lincoln School, the Tower Hill School, and the University of Chicago High School, other types of physical-science courses offered in the Des Moines high schools, the Altoona (Pennsylvania) High School, and the Eagle Rock High School of Los Angeles.

In the spring of 1937 the Des Moines[66] high schools introduced "Practical Science," a one-year course intended for those pupils "who need a general knowledge of science of a less technical nature than that offered in the separate sciences." Problem materials for the course were "drawn from the physical sciences as they relate to everyday life." Biological knowledge was also "utilized if needed to understand a problem." As a "follow-up" to this applied-science course, the second semester of physics and the first semester of chemistry was "recommended."

Altoona[67] reported that in grade 11 the "elements" of physics and chemistry are studied in a nonmathematical course which "is not set up in the pre-professional spirit."

---

[66]Ibid., pp. 230-231.

[67]Ibid., p. 42.

The course of advanced physical science in the
curriculum of the Eagle Rock High School[68] (Los
Angeles) offered "an orientation experience ... in
the field of the physical sciences -- e.g., chemistry,
physics, geology, meteorology, mineralogy, etc.--
with an emphasis on the consumer rather than the pro-
ducer point of view, meeting the laboratory require-
ment for admission to the State University." Suggested broad areas for investigation were: "Water,
the Earth, the Atmosphere, Astronomy, Fuels, Light,
Transportation, Communication, Materials and Pro-
cesses, [and] Household Equipment." Specialized
courses in chemistry and physics were also available
"for those pupils who [planned] to specialize in
science or engineering in college."

In 1941, a physical-science course "intended to
help meet the needs of average boys and girls, primarily those in the noncollege group," was introduced
by Hollinger[69] and others in the senior high schools
of Pittsburgh, Pennsylvania. The content of the

[68]Ibid., p. 256.

[69]John A. Hollinger, J. Clyde Amon, Edgar M.
Hoopes, and Charles E. Manwiller, "Physical Science
in Senior High Schools," Science Education, XXVIII
(April-May, 1944), 130-135.

course was presented in 8 areas of study, 1 of them
being, for example, "applying Electricity to Daily
Living."

The physical-science course reported most recently, 1946, is that offered by the Wells High
School, Chicago. This course, required in the eleventh year except in special cases in which physics
may be substituted for it, "comprises elements of
physics, chemistry, geology, meteorology, and astronomy significant to daily living."[70] Elective courses
in physics and chemistry are also available to pupils
in the twelfth year.

Investigations of the Offerings of Physical-
Science Courses in Senior High Schools

Only 3 investigations dealing with the offerings
of physical-science courses in senior high schools
have been reported in the literature.

Ferguson,[71,72] using tabulations based upon 270
usable returns from a questionnaire sent to selected

---

[70]Virginia F. Matson and Paul R. Pierce, "Science
in the Core Curriculum," School Review, LIV
(February, 1946), 84.

[71]William C. Ferguson, "Instructional Problems
of Generalized Science in the Senior High School,"
Science Education, XXIV (February, 1940), 72-75.

[72]William Clarence Ferguson, op. cit., pp. 4,
31, and 39.

high schools in 34 states during the early part of
the school year 1938-39, reported that 13,568 students were enrolled in senior science or a similarly-
integrated science course offered by the 270 schools.
He also reported that the majority of the schools
had instituted the course in 1937-38.

During the school year 1938-39, Watson[73],[74]
made a comprehensive investigation of the fused or
survey courses of physical science offered in the
high schools and colleges of the United States. He
employed in different parts of the investigation
(1) questions submitted on post cards or on check
lists; (2) lists of textbook adoptions; (3) the serv-
ices of the California State Department of Education;
and (4) visits to 53 high schools in California. The
only physical-science courses considered were those
offered on levels "above the ninth grade" and those
"in which materials from two or more of the physical
sciences were fused in either a semester or year
course."

Watson[75] found from a study of 328 California
schools that 116 or "28.5 per cent of the [406]

[73]Donald R. Watson, op. cit., pp. 44 and 329.

[74]Donald R. Watson, "The Fused Physical Science
Course," California Journal of Secondary Education,
XV (May, 1940), 292-293.

[75]Ibid.

regular-type high schools in the state" offered in
1938-39 "a fused course in physical science." Only
14 or 10.8 percent of the 130 California schools
reporting the offering of such a course, currently
or recently, had abandoned the course. Some schools
indicated that such action was only temporary.

As part of this study, Watson[76],[77],[78] secured
responses on check lists in order to obtain data
from 250 California and non-California cities of
over twenty-five thousand population, representing
"70 per cent of the 357 [such] cities in the United
States," relative to the existence of the fused
course of physical science in the curricula of their
high schools. Of these 250 cities in 42 states, 54
or "21.6 per cent" offered such a course "in at least
one high school." Moreover, he[79] reported that "the
trend is toward a rapid expansion of such fused courses

---

[76]Ibid., p. 293.

[77]Donald R. Watson, "The Training and Experience
of Instructors in Survey Courses in Physical Science,"
Science Education, XXV (February, 1941), 80.

[78]Donald R. Watson, "A Comparison of the Growth
of Survey Courses in Physical Science in High Schools
and in Colleges," Science Education, XXIV (January,
1940), 14-20.

[79]Donald R. Watson, "Survey Courses in Physical
Science," The Junior College Journal, XI (February,
1941), 325.

[of physical science] in secondary schools."

Among the important general conclusions which may be formulated from the investigation by Watson[80] of the fused or survey courses of physical science offered in high schools of the United States in 1938-39 are:

1. There are no geographical concentrations of such courses outside of California.

2. Such courses seem to be entering curricula to a small degree in all parts of the United States.

3. Such courses exist in schools of all sizes but are more common in the larger schools.

4. Such courses are a pure elective in practically all schools offering them.

5. Sixty percent of the California high schools and about one-third of the non-California high schools reporting such a course include laboratory work as a part of the course.

6. All types of high schools consider the most important criterion for the selection of content for the course to be the relation of the content to the objectives of general education.

7. In such courses, the schools tend to emphasize an increase in scientific attitudes, the application of scientific principles around the home, and an increased understanding of the relations of physical science to health and well-being. The same schools tend to rate very low such objectives as an increase in laboratory skills, and the preparation for more advanced science courses.

----

[80]Donald R. Watson, Survey Courses in Physical Science: Their Status, Trends, and Evaluation, op. cit., pp. 8, 99, 117, 119, 122, 125, 369, 372, and 374.

8. Practically all such courses are organized on a one-year basis.

9. The high schools show a strong tendency to concentrate enrollments in the courses in the eleventh or twelfth grade.

In 1940, Hunter[81] sent a comprehensive questionnaire to about twenty-six hundred representative secondary schools of the United States in order to obtain data on trends in science. One phase of this investigation of science trends, a compilation by Hunter and Spore[82] of the physical-science offerings in high schools by states, showed that, of the 32 states which supplied data, physical science was offered in 8 states, consumer science in 6, senior science in 19, and survey science in 9. Furthermore, it was concluded that "physics and chemistry holdings, [the percentage which enrollments in physics and chemistry are of the total enrollment of pupils in high schools], are less than in previous years [but] their place is being supplemented by other advanced physical science courses."

[81]George W. Hunter, "Six Hundred Teachers Look at Science Trends," Science Education, XXVIII (February, 1944), 15 and 19.

[82]George W. Hunter and Leroy Spore, "Science Sequence and Enrollments in Secondary Schools of the United States," Science Education, XXVI (February, 1942), 75-76.

Evidence Which Supports the Offering of
Integrated Courses of Physical Science
in the Senior High School

Research Investigations

Peterson[83] did an experimental investigation of
superior quality for his doctoral dissertation at the
University of Minnesota. He compared "the achievement of students who had taken a one-year course in
which both chemistry and physics were fused, or
integrated, with the achievement of students who
had taken one or two years of other physical science
courses," namely, the more conventional courses of
chemistry, physics, and senior science.

The integrated course in physics and chemistry
taught by Peterson and student teachers under his
supervision in the University of Minnesota High
School during the interim 1937-43 was, in its final
form, presented in the 12 units which are listed on
page 23 of the present investigation.

He also prepared "a testing instrument by which
the achievement resulting from any high school physical-
science course could be compared with the achievement
resulting from another type of physical-science course."

---

[83]Shailer Peterson, op. cit., pp. 255-257 and 262.

This examination "contained 155 items, took 100
minutes for administration and included the following
13 units or sections:

Apparatus and its uses
Periodic chart and concepts relating to
  atoms and molecules
Recognizing chemical abbreviations and their
  meaning
Problems dealing with weight, volume, energy,
  and force
Associations of common names and formulas
Chemists and physicists and reasons for
  their fame
Metric system and mathematical constants
Practical problems that use physics and
  chemistry
Scientific reasoning and using the
  scientific method
Writing and balancing chemical equations
Miscellaneous analytical tests
Laboratory procedures
Ionization, electrolysis, and electricity

The validity of the physical-science examination
was established "by examining the profile of correla-
tions test scores on this examination with scores of
the same groups of individuals on other measures.
Experts in the field were also employed to assist in
the study of its validity." The coefficient of
reliability, "computed by the Kuder-Richardson Formula No. 20, [was] .9 for the entire examination."

Mental ability (IQ) and chronological age were
selected as the basis of maintaining comparability
between the experimental and control groups. This
was done by the Johnson-Neyman method of analysis

in which it was possible to have groups equivalent
on the bases of two independent variates.

The final statistical comparisons were based
on the mean scores made by the equated groups on
the physical-science examination prepared by Peterson.
These comparisons were made for 96 pupils in the
experimental group who took the integrated course of
physical science in the University of Minnesota High
School and 267 pupils in the control groups who had
taken 1 or 2 years of other physical science courses
in large high schools in cities in Wisconsin, Minnesota, and a state not designated by the investigator. Of the 267 pupils in the control groups, 66
had "just completed a course in physics and had had
no chemistry;" 116 had just completed a course in
chemistry and had not had physics;" 35 had "just
completed a course in physics and [had already] had
chemistry;" 32 had "just completed chemistry and had
already had physics;" and 18 had "just completed
Senior Science and had had neither chemistry nor
physics."[84]

---

[84]Shailer Peterson, The Comparison of the Achievement of Students in the Traditional High School Physics
and Chemistry Courses Each of One Year's Duration With
the Achievement of Students in the Integrated Course in
Physics and Chemistry Over a One Year Period, op. cit.,
pp. 110 and 166-168.

Among the conclusions drawn by Peterson[85] was
the following:

> Under controlled conditions in which
> intelligence quotient and chronological age
> were statistically equated, the physical
> science mean scores of students who had had
> one year of the Fusion of Physics and Chem-
> istry were significantly higher than that of
> students who had had either 1. one year of
> traditional Physics, 2. one year of tradi-
> tional Chemistry, 3. one year of Senior Sci-
> ence, or 4. one year of traditional Physics
> plus one year of traditional Chemistry.

The fourth and final comparison made above was
further clarified by Johnson,[86] who directed the investigation by Peterson, and by reference to Peterson's[87]
dissertation. It was revealed by Johnson and by the
dissertation that the mean scores, on the physical-
science examination, of pupils who had had the one-
year integrated course were significantly higher than
those of pupils who had had 1 year of traditional
chemistry followed by 1 year of traditional physics.

---

[85] Shailer Peterson, "The Evaluation of a One-Year
Course, the Fusion of Physics and Chemistry, With Other
Physical Science Courses," op. cit., p. 263.

[86] Palmer O. Johnson, "The Scientific Study of
Problems in Science Education," Science Education,
XXIX (October, 1945), 178.

[87] Shailer Peterson, The Comparison of the Achievement of Students in the Traditional High School Physics
and Chemistry Courses Each of One Year's Duration With
the Achievement of Students in the Integrated Course in
Physics and Chemistry Over a One Year Period, op. cit.,
pp. 194, 197-9, and 202.

Furthermore, the mean scores of those who had had the integrated course were also higher than those of pupils who had had 1 year of traditional physics followed by 1 year of traditional chemistry, except for those pupils "older than seventeen years of age and with IQ's greater than 100."

It was also found that "in the fusion class, while there was no significant difference between the IQ's of students from the different grade groups, the 9th and 10th graders did better than the 11th graders and the 11th graders did better than the 12th graders on the physical science examination. Moreover, the 9th and 10th graders performed significantly better than the 12th graders."[88]

Insofar as the results of Peterson's investigation are valid and reliable, it may be concluded that pupils desiring to obtain a greater knowledge of physical science in the senior high school would better take a one-year integrated course of physical science in which subject matter from the fields of physics and chemistry is fused, than only 1 year of chemistry or physics, or even 1 year of chemistry followed by 1 year of physics. Furthermore, the

---

[88] Shailer Peterson, "The Evaluation of a One-Year Course, the Fusion of Physics and Chemistry, With Other Physical Science Courses," op. cit., pp. 263-264.

one-year integrated course of physical science would
be more profitable for pupils in the senior high school
than 1 year of physics followed by 1 year of chemistry,
except for those pupils "older than seventeen years of
age and with IQ's greater than 100."

A research investigation less extensive than the
one completed by Peterson was conducted by Rosenlof
and Wise[89] in an attempt to compare the one-year integrated course of physical science with separate one-
year courses in physics and chemistry. However, for
reasons beyond their control, 2 of 3 pre-tests were
not given at the beginning of the experiment as was
planned. In order to proceed with the investigation
as planned, they calculated theoretical scores that
pupils should have made at the beginning of the experiment on the 2 pre-tests. This procedure makes their
conclusions of questionable value, and therefore,
their techniques and results are not here more fully
reported. They did, nevertheless, conclude that
"Physical science is probably more effective than is
either chemistry or physics in teaching scientific
facts and information to pupils of equal native
ability."

---

[89] Rosenlof and Wise, op. cit., pp. 351-354.

The achievements on the same objective tests of
pupils taking a two-year integrated course of physical science at the Phillips Exeter Academy (Exeter,
New Hampshire) were compared for 7 years with those
of pupils taking separate one-year courses of both
physics and chemistry in the same school. The relative
achievements of the groups compared were reported by
Hogg[90] as follows:

> Toward the end of the second year the
> student in the combined [two-year] course
> [of physical science] takes the same final
> objective tests as those in the one-year
> course. ... Statistics show that the class
> median is higher in the case of [those
> groups taking the two-year course of inte-
> grated] "physical sciences" than in the
> separate studies, [one year of chemistry
> and one year of physics]. ... The same
> tendency is shown year after year with
> the regularity of clockwork.
>
> Probably the most startling comparison,
> however, is that of age. Since the inte-
> grated course simplifies the approach, it
> offers little difficulty even to boys of
> grade 10. ... In other words, the bulk of the
> students in "physical sciences" complete the
> second year of the course while still in the
> 11th grade, whereas the majority of the stu-
> dents in the separate courses are in the
> 12th grade. And, in spite of the handicap
> of one year in age, the "two-year" student
> [who took the integrated course] is superior,
> [on the basis of the same final objective
> tests, to the student who took one year of
> chemistry and one year of physics.]

[90]Hogg, op. cit., p. 132.

Heidel[91] conducted an investigation in the Chaska (Minnesota) High School during the year 1940-41 "to measure and compare the purported outcomes of instruction of a generalized high school senior science course stressing practical applications and consumer education and a conventional high school physics course....."

He gave to those pupils participating in the investigation Forms A and B of the Terman Group Test of Mental Ability and Form 0 of the Cooperative Physics Test at the beginning of the school year and again at the end of the year. The 1941 Minnesota State Board Physics Examination and a test of physics applications were also given at the end of the year. "In order to adjust ... inequalities [between the respective groups] and to provide valid bases of comparison, the methods of variance and covariance were used."

One conclusion drawn by Heidel[92] was:

> The generalized high school senior science course proved no less effective than the conventional high school physics course in the teaching of general scientific facts and principles [of physics] and applications of those principles to pupils when inequalities of mental ability and previous achievement were taken into account.

---

[91]Heidel, loc. cit.

[92]Ibid., p. 89.

The physics course was, however, superior to the senior science course "in developing in pupils understandings of specific physics materials."

Opinions of College Registrars

In an investigation of the acceptability of a physical-science course as a college entrance unit, Carleton[93] submitted 1 question to the admissions officers of 95 colleges and universities, including 83 schools which graduates of the Summit (New Jersey) High School had entered from 1941 through 1945 and "twelve additional schools to complete the coverage of geographical regions and various types of schools." The question submitted to the admissions officers was:

> Will your college or university grant entrance credit for the successful completion of the Summit High School course in Physical Science (as outlined in the enclosed Course of Study)* when presented

---

[93]Robert H. Carleton, "The Acceptability of Physical Science as a College-Entrance Unit," Science Education, XXX (April, 1946), 127.

*In a letter dated June 12, 1947 from Robert H. Carleton, Newark College of Engineering, to Vaden W. Miles, Boston University, Mr. Carleton stated that "The organization and content of the Course of Study for the Summit High School course in Physical Science is in basic accord with the organization and content of the physical-science textbook, Modern-Life Science, by Robert H. Carleton and Harry H. Williams, Chicago: J. B. Lippincott Company, 1942."

by the applicants seeking admission to
the non-scientific or non-technical curricula of your institution? This with
the provision, of course, that the ap-
plicant meets other academic and personal
requirements and carries the recommendation
of the high school principal that he is
capable of college-grade work.

The replies received by Carleton[94] to the above

question were summarized thus:

> Seventy-eight [or 100 percent of the]
> replicants gave approval, to some degree,
> to the proposal submitted to them; that is,
> the 78 colleges replying to the query will
> give entrance credit for the course in
> Physical Science. A small number of these
> colleges stated that credit would be granted,
> but with certain reservations, while a much
> larger number sent replies expressing the ap-
> proval and enthusiastic endorsement of their
> admissions officers and science department
> heads for the proposition submitted.

He[95] also concluded from the replies to the question

that "colleges are inclined to be more liberal in the

nature and variety of secondary-school courses which

they will accept as entrance units than many secondary-

school teachers, counselors, and administrators give

them credit for, [but] physical science as a recognized

course comparable in standing to chemistry and physics,

or even biology, still has some distance to go to assure

full respectability...."

---

[94]Ibid., p. 128.

[95]Ibid., pp. 130-1.

Important Reports

In <u>General</u> <u>Education</u> <u>in</u> <u>a</u> <u>Free</u> <u>Society</u>,[96] published in 1945, a Harvard University Committee composed
of members of the Faculty of Arts and Sciences and the
Faculty of Education recommended the following with
respect to the offerings in the physical sciences by
secondary schools for pupils preparing to enter college:

> [For] those students preparing to
> enter college but who have no direct in-
> terest in the sciences ... [a] course in
> physics and chemistry might be advised.
> Better still for such students would be a
> systematic presentation of concepts and
> principles of the physical sciences, such
> as is now being experimented with in a
> number of schools. This type of [physical-
> science] course draws illustrative materials,
> as they are appropriate to its central themes,
> from the fields of physics, chemistry, geol-
> ogy, and astronomy. [The primary aims of
> such a physical-science course] should be
> those of general education, not the develop-
> ment of the skills and technical knowledge
> of the potential physicist and chemist.
>
> Those who plan advanced work in science
> and mathematics in college should [take] a
> year of chemistry or physics or both. An inte-
> grated course in physical sciences might be of
> particular value to such students. A course
> like this can profitably extend into a second
> year. When properly designed such a two-year
> sequence should make a greater contribution to
> the student's general education and his preparation
> for future study than separate one-year courses
> in physics and chemistry.

---

[96]<u>General</u> <u>Education</u> <u>in</u> <u>a</u> <u>Free</u> <u>Society</u>, op. cit.,
pp. 159-160.

The first approbation by an authoritative national committee in the field of science education of the phases of the Harvard Report dealing with instruction in the physical sciences in the senior high school appeared, as follows, in Science Education in American Schools:[97]

> One may differ with the specific recommendations of the Harvard Report for the content and organization of the physical-science course and still recognize that this report promises to add considerable impetus to the physical-science movement. An important implication of this report is that the generalized physical-science course can be just as valuable for the college-bound students with nonscience interests as for those high-school students for whom secondary education is terminal.

The Forty-sixth Yearbook Committee[98] took cognizance of another timely report when it stated:

> The implications of the Educational Policies Commission report[99] [published in 1944] definitely favor a generalized-science type of course, rather than chemistry or physics, for the high-school student whose major abilities and interests are outside the realm of science.

[97]Science Education in American Schools, Forty-sixth Yearbook of the National Society for the Study of Education, Part I, p. 191. Chicago: The University of Chicago Press, 1947.

[98]Ibid.

[99]Educational Policies Commission, Education for All American Youth. Washington: National Education Association, 1944.

In 1946, the Cooperative Committee on Science
Teaching of the American Association for the Advancement of Science[100] gave its approval to the "fused"
physical-science course in the following statement:

> The high school science program which
> the Committee has in mind is one in which
> all students would take ... a year of
> physical science. The year of physical
> science might be physics, or chemistry,
> or a "fused" physical science course.

Furthermore, the British Association for the Advancement of Science pronounced even more forcefully than
did the Cooperative Committee for integrated courses
of physical science by saying, according to Carlson,[101]
that "chemistry and physics should be taken together
as part of 'physical science' ...."

Insofar as the official position of the United
States Office of Education with respect to the integrated course of physical science can be assumed to
be that of its present [1947] specialist in science
for secondary schools, it may be said that such a
course has the approval of that office. The

[100]American Association for the Advancement of
Science, The Cooperative Committee on Science Teaching, "Preparation of High School Science and Mathematics Teachers," School Science and Mathematics,
XLVI (February, 1946), 110.

[101]A. J. Carlson, "Footnotes on the Science
Core in Liberal Education," School Science and
Mathematics, XLVI (February, 1946), 122.

following appears in the writing of that specialist,
Johnson:[102]

> One of [the] new generalized courses
> may be an attempt to integrate the physical
> sciences much as the biological sciences are
> now integrated.
>
> Following ... general science, there
> should be semi-specialization ... in two
> broad areas; the biological sciences and
> the physical sciences. The latter should
> include some earth science and astronomy.
> Following [the] two broad courses there
> should be one or more specialized courses
> ... for the twelfth year and post graduate
> levels ... After the semi-specialization
> in biology and general physical science,
> students may elect for one or more terms
> courses which give them more thorough prep-
> aration in one or more circumscribed areas.
>
> According to this plan, all schools
> would offer a twelve year science program,
> composed of six years of elementary sci-
> ence, three years of general science, one
> year [of] biological science, one year [of]
> general physical science, and one or more
> terms of some rather specialized science.

The year 1947 is an important milestone in the
development of science programs in American schools,
for the enthusiastic endorsement of the physical-
science movement by the Forty-sixth Yearbook Committee in Science Education in American Schools[103]
practically assures that the introduction and

---

[102]Philip G. Johnson, "A Science Program for
All Students," Science Education, XXIV (October,
1940), 285-286.

[103]Science Education in American Schools, op. cit.

development of "fused" courses of physical sciences
will proceed at an accelerated rate. The enlightened
guidance proffered by the Committee with respect to
such courses merits careful consideration.

A student of the physical-science movement may
glean from the Yearbook such statements as the following which are indicative of the sound philosophy
of this important Committee whose pronouncements have
great potential influence on science education in
American schools.

> [Among the] important new movements
> in science education [which appear to] have
> far-reaching effects [is] the introduction
> of fused science courses at the upper
> secondary level.[104]

> In the senior high school, integrated
> courses such as general biology and phys-
> ical science may be offered along with or
> in place of specialized courses such as
> physics and chemistry. All courses at this
> level should be organized to provide both
> general and propaedeutic education.[105]

> [Therefore], if ... physical science is
> to realize its full potentialities, it must
> be made to serve both as a "college-prepara-
> tory" and as a terminal course.[106]

---

[104]Ibid., p. 1.

[105]Ibid., p. 42.

[106]Ibid., p. 46.

The devising of satisfactory courses in physical science is, [therefore], one of the greatest challenges in the field of secondary-school science. Their development is especially important for the smaller schools in which the equipment and scheduling of separate courses in physics and chemistry is often a serious problem.[107]

Many "fused" courses of physical science have been introduced into the senior high school during the last decade. Moreover, the number of such courses seems certain to increase. It is quite as logical to develop such a course at the present time as it was to begin the development of general biology about thirty-five years ago. The formulation of a satisfactory course in physical science has been retarded by a variety of different approaches to the problem, reflecting nebulousness and confusion of ideas with respect to the nature and functions of such a course.[108]

Further guidance is offered by the Committee with respect to the nature and function of the physical-science course. The Committee[109] is extremely helpful in offering "the following considerations [which] are deemed to be fundamental to a satisfactory solution of the problem of providing a satisfactory course in physical science:"

The content [of a physical-science course] should be planned so as to develop concepts and principles important not only

---

107[Ibid.](Ibid.)

108Ibid., p. 45.

109Ibid., pp. 45-46.

in physics and chemistry but also in other
branches of physical science, namely, geology, astronomy, and meteorology. For example,
an understanding of the principle of gravita-
tion may appropriately be developed by pre-
senting applications dealing with falling
bodies, decantation and precipitation, air
currents, erosion, tides, and movements of
heavenly bodies.

Practical considerations dictate that
the course should be planned for one year
and not for two. There is, of course, more
than enough material of unquestioned worth
to justify a two-year course [in fused physical science], but ... relatively few [pupils],
and these chiefly the ones corresponding to
those who now elect both physics and chemistry, would be able [to find time in their
crowded programs] to take the entire two
years! work. Consequently, the numbers of
pupils who would secure special training in
physical science would be even smaller than
where the one-year course is offered, because a large proportion of those who might
elect a year of physics or of chemistry
would be unlikely to elect one-half of a
two-year physical-science course.

The values of a course of physical
science are likely to be largely sacri-
ficed if attempts are made to simplify
it too greatly. ... Some pioneers in the
physical science movement sought to assemble ... material which would be easy
enough for the ready comprehension of any
pupils. These efforts in some cases re-
sulted in courses that were practically
on the level of effortless entertainment.
... The worth of many of these early physical-science courses was further lessened
by the omission of laboratory work.

The Committee[110] believes that a physical-science

course "can be evolved which can achieve its desired

---

[110]Ibid., p. 46.

objectives through a much less technical and mathematical approach and with many more contacts with
the daily lives of boys and girls than do the conventional present-day courses in physics and chemistry."

Also expressed by the Committee[111] is the opinion

> ... that the physical-science course
> in one form or another will ... far surpass
> the position it held among the high-school
> science offerings of 1940. Reasons for
> this belief include, first, recognition of
> the superior possibilities of a composite
> physical-science [course] over the separate
> traditional chemistry and physics courses
> in contributing to the aims of general edu-
> cation, and second, the disposition of col-
> leges to recognize the physical-science
> course as a bona-fide college-entrance unit
> for the nonscience major.

Scientific Principles as a Basis for Organizing Materials of Instruction in Science

Fifteen years ago the Thirty-first Yearbook Committee[112] of the National Society for the Study of
Education departed from the traditional field-covering
approach to curriculum construction in science and
proposed "that the curriculum in science for a program of general education be organized about large

---

[111] Ibid., p. 191.

[112] A Program for Teaching Science, p. 44. Thirty-
first Yearbook of the National Society for the Study
of Education, Part I. Bloomington, Illinois: Public
School Publishing Company, 1932.

objectives." It further advocated that "the objectives
... be stated as the [scientific] principles and generalizations that are functional for the individual,
in that they enable him to interpret the experiences
of living."[113] The Committee further stated that
"the principles and generalizations that ramify most
widely into human affairs may be stated as objectives
of science education."[114]

The Committee defined principles or generalizations as "abstractions formed from the connections of
related situations and responses" and maintained that
"the understanding of principles and generalizations
comes from the association of ideas that are developed from experiences."[115] The Committee stated further
that "A functional understanding of a principle has
been obtained if the learner has acquired ability to
associate with the principle ideas from his subsequent
experience that are related to it and if he is able
to apply the principle to practical situations."[116]

In concluding its recommendations concerning
the objectives and the organization of instruction
in science, the Committee recognized "the objectives

[113]Ibid., p. 43.

[114]Ibid., p. 43.

[115]Ibid., p. 42.

[116]Ibid., p. 42.

of science teaching to be the functional understanding of the major generalizations [or principles] of science and the development of associated scientific attitudes."[117] Furthermore, it recommended "using the laboratory for the purpose of developing better understanding and interpretations of the principles of science ...."[118]

In the same year (1932) that the Thirty-first Yearbook Committee proposed principles as one of the major goals of instruction in science, a survey of instruction in science, made as a part of a National Survey of Secondary Education, revealed, among other innovating practices, "a shift ... from the organization of courses in terms of topics and subtopics to organization around certain ideas or concepts [such as] generalizations or principles of science ...."[119]

In 1938, the Thayer Commission on Secondary School Curriculum of the Progressive Education Association[120] recommended that the materials for inclusion

[117]Ibid., p. 57.

[118]Ibid., p. 270.

[119]Wilbur L. Beauchamp, Instruction in Science, p. 62. U.S. Office of Education, Bulletin, 1932, No. 17, National Survey of Secondary Education, Monograph No. 22. Washington: Government Printing Office, 1933.

[120]Progressive Education Association, Commission on Secondary School Curriculum, op. cit., pp. 55, 61, and 27.

in science courses be organized in such a manner that
the educational experiences result in "understandings"
of "generalizations" [or principles] which are related
to one or more of the basic aspects or areas of living:
(1) personal living; (2) immediate personal-social
relationships; (3) social-civic relationships; and
(4) economic relationships. The Commission emphasized
that "a [scientific] principle becomes an understanding for an individual only when and as it throws new
light for him on a group of relationships not previously sensed and so brings about a reorganization
of his behavior."

Noll,[121] in agreement with other leaders in the
field of science education, clearly saw principles
of science as a basis for organizing materials of
instruction in science in a manner which would cut
across subject-matter boundaries of closely related
fields when he said:

> ... the trend toward integration is
> evident in the organization of science
> instruction around principles that are
> significant in life today. ... Whether
> the materials are organized around the
> "big ideas" [or principles] of science
> as suggested by the [Thirty-first Year-
> book] Committee of the National Society

---

[121]Victor H. Noll, "What About Integration in
Science?," School Science and Mathematics, XLI
(March, 1941), 243.

for the Study of Education or whether
around areas of life needs and human
relationships as suggested by the ...
Progressive Education Association, the
net result is a strong impetus in the
direction of integration in science and
the overlooking of subject-matter boundaries.

The Harvard Committee would also organize mate-

rials of instruction in a physical-science course

around principles.

The Forty-sixth Yearbook Committee[122] considers

"the functional understanding of [scientific] prin-

ciples ... to be an important objective of science

teaching." It believes, moreover, that "[principles]

provide focal points for the organization of instruc-

tional material," and that "[principles] constitute

the generalizations toward the formulation of which

most work in science is directed."

According to this Committee, the type of course

of physical science that will best fulfill the needs

of general education, in its broadest sense, is one

which provides "integrations of the various facts,

concepts, and principles drawn from all the fields

of physical science for the purpose of helping young

people gain competency in solving their problems of

---

[122]Science Education in American Schools, op.
cit., p. 31.

of adjustment in the world of today."[123]

Research on Principles as Goals
of Instruction in Science

The reports of the Thayer Commission of the Progressive Education Association, of the Harvard Committee, and of the Forty-sixth Yearbook Committee gave added impetus to an interest in principles as goals of instruction in science already engendered by the Thirty-first Yearbook, in particular, and by the research on principles directed by four of the members of the committees which prepared the Yearbooks. According to Martin,[124]

> There are three independent centers of research at which the work toward the clarification of the concept of a scientific principle and toward the refinement of principles has chiefly been carried out, namely:
> 1. The University of Chicago where the research was under the direction of Elliot R. Downing.
> 2. Columbia University where the research was under the direction of S. Ralph Powers and Gerald S. Craig and,
> 3. The University of Michigan where the research was under the direction of Francis D. Curtis.

---

[123]Ibid., p. 192.

[124]William Edgar Martin, A Determination of the Principles of the Biological Sciences of Importance for General Education, p. 15. Unpublished Doctor's dissertation, University of Michigan, 1944.

In 1945, Martin[125,126] reported a chronological survey of research studies on principles as objectives of instruction in science, including a description of his own study and 29 other studies. Similar studies of considerable merit not reported by Martin were those by Ivens,[127] Edwards,[128] James,[129] Edmiston,[130] and Reek.[131] These 5 studies were, moreover, not used as a contributing study in any of the 30 studies reported

_____

[125]Ibid., pp. 8-58.

[126]W. Edgar Martin, "A Chronological Survey of Research Studies on Principles as Objectives of Instruction in Science," Science Education, XXIX (February, 1945), 45-52.

[127]H. J. Ivens, The Determination and Evaluation of Some Scientific Principles as Found in Six Widely Used Textbooks of Physics. Unpublished Master's thesis, University of Michigan, 1933.

[128]Elmo W. Edwards, The Selection of Principles Suitable as Goals of Instruction in High School Physics. Unpublished Master's thesis, Colorado State College of Education, 1935.

[129]Edward W. James, The Principles of Chemistry for Secondary Science Instruction. Unpublished Master's thesis, Colorado State College of Education, 1935.

[130]Arnold J. Edmiston, An Evaluation of the Relative Importance of Certain Principles as Goals of Instruction in High School Physics. Unpublished Master's thesis, University of Nebraska, 1942.

[131]Doris Lucille Reek, A Study of the Principles of Science Found in Four Series of Textbooks of Elementary Science. Unpublished Master's thesis, University of Michigan, 1943.

by Martin. The numbers of research studies on principles as objectives of instruction in science now
total 44. Included in the 44 studies are the earlier
unreported ones by Ivens, Edwards, James, Edmiston, Ree K,
and the ones completed by Fleish[132] and Keeslar[133]
in 1945, by Jones,[134] Blanchet,[135] McGrath,[136]
and Bergman[137] in 1946, and by Leonelli,[138]

[132]Sylvia Fleish, The Formulation of the Science
Principles That Should Become the Objectives of General Science Teaching in the Junior High School. Unpublished Master's thesis, Boston University, 1945.

[133]Oreon Pierre Keeslar, Contributions of Instructional Films to the Teaching of High School
Science. Unpublished Doctor's dissertation, University of Michigan, 1945.

[134]Ruth V. Jones, A Study of the Principles of
Science Found in Ninth-Grade Textbooks of General
Science. Unpublished Master's thesis, University of
Michigan, 1946.

[135]Waldo Emerson Blanchet, A Basis for the
Selection of Course Content for Survey Courses in
the Natural Sciences. Unpublished Doctor's dissertation, University of Michigan, 1946.

[136]Guy Dean McGrath, An Investigation of the
Relative Significance and Use of Principles and
Generalizations of Chemistry in General Education.
Unpublished Doctor's thesis, University of Colorado, 1946.

[137]George J. Bergman, "A Determination of the
Principles of Entomology of Significance in General
Education. I," Science Education, XXXI (February,
1947), 23-32; II, Science Education, XXXI (April,
1947), 144-157.

[138]Renato E. Leonelli, Principles of Physical
and Biological Science Found in Eight Textbooks of
General Science for Grade Eight. Unpublished Master's
thesis, Boston University, 1947.

Eastman,[139] and Lurensky[140] in 1947.

Of the 44 research studies reported on principles as goals of instruction in science, only 2, one by Wise[141] and the other by Blanchet,[142] have implications for the present investigation. In 1941, Wise sought to determine the principles of physical science which are most important for general education. This involved the development of a comprehensive list of different principles of physical science, each stated succinctly and technically accurate in wording.

A composite list of principles of chemistry, geology, and physics (including astronomy and meteorology) was compiled by Wise from separate lists developed in studies by Arnold, Hartmann and Stephens,

---

[139]Durward Wells Eastman, A Study of Important Principles of Physical Science Developed in Grades Seven Through Twelve of a Town in Massachusetts With Applications of Those Principles in Seven Local Industries. Unpublished Master's thesis, Boston University, 1947.

[140]Maurice Leon Lurensky, A Determination of the Applications of the Principles of Biology Found in Four Textbooks of Biology for the Senior High School. Unpublished Master's thesis, Boston University, 1947.

[141]Harold E. Wise, A Determination of the Relative Importance of Principles of Physical Science For General Education. Unpublished Doctor's dissertation, University of Michigan, 1941.

[142]Blanchet, op. cit.

Pruitt, and Robertson. A jury of 3 qualified persons
then eliminated dulpications from the composite list
and analyzed each remaining principle for adherence
to the following 4 criteria:

To be a principle, a statement

(1) Must be a comprehensive generalization describing some fundamental
process, constant mode of behavior,
or property relating to natural
phenomena.
(2) Must be true without exception
within limitations specifically
stated.
(3) Must be capable of illustration.
(4) Must not be a definition.

Principles which in the opinion of the jury
satisfied the criteria, or were reworded by the jury
to meet the criteria better, were retained in a tentative list while those which could not be satisfactorily restated to meet the criteria were eliminated.

The tentative list of principles resulting from
the application of these techniques and criteria contained 252 principles consisting of 165 in physics,
68 in chemistry, and 19 in geology.

This list of 252 principles was then submitted
to a specialist in physics who also checked each
principle for adherence to the same 4 criteria. No
principles were eliminated by him; his suggestions,

however, were incorporated into the statements of
the respective principles. Subsequently, a subject-
matter specialist in each of the 3 fields of science
represented, chemistry, physics, and geology, further
checked the principles in his particular field for
accuracy of statement (criterion 2) and the principles
were then reworded in accordance with written recommendations made by these specialists.

In a second phase of the study, the determination
of the relative importance of principles as measured
by the scope of their applicability in the solution
of frequently encountered problems, criteria for the
selection of applications from textbooks were formulated and 11 textbooks were analyzed for applications
in accordance with the criteria. The numbers of textbooks so analyzed for applications were, for the high-
school level: physics, 2; chemistry, 2; survey textbooks of physical science, 2; and general science, 2;
for the junior-college level: survey textbooks of
physical science, 3.

The applications so selected were assigned to
principles they represented and the investigator's
judgment as to the identity of applications and their
assignment to the proper principles was checked by
4 competent, experienced teachers of science.

Twenty principles were formulated and added to
the tentative list of 252 principles as a result of
the appearance of applications which could not be
assigned to those principles already formulated.
These 20 principles were subjected to the same criteria and to the same checking procedure as that employed
in obtaining the list to which they were added. No
further attempt was made in succeeding phases of the
study to add to the list of 272 principles.

Wise's study concluded with a list of 264 principles of physical science arranged in descending
order of their relative importance for general education, grades I-XIV, inclusive. The relative importance
of these principles was determined by a synthesis of
the results of 12 curricular studies in the field of
science education.

The importance and usefulness of Wise's complete
list of 272 principles of physical science is manifest
in the fact that it was subsequently employed by
Blanchet[143] in a "determination of the principles of
science most suitable as goals [of instruction] for
survey courses in the natural sciences at the junior-
college level."

_____

143 Ibid., pp. 35-39.

Blanchet, 4 other specialists in the teaching of science, and 4 subject-matter specialists, who were experienced teachers of physical-science survey courses or introductory courses [of science] in their respective fields of specialization, evaluated independently on a scale of 1 to 5 each principle in Wise's complete list of 272 principles of physical science. The judgments were made on the basis of the value of a functional understanding of the principle as an outcome of survey courses in the physical sciences at the junior-college level. Two criteria employed by the evaluators limited the survey courses under consideration to those whose purpose is general education.

After a mean of the values assigned to each principle by the 9 evaluators was calculated, the 272 principles were ranked in descending order of their mean values. In effect, the 272 principles of physical science were ranked in the descending order of their relative values as goals of instruction for survey courses of physical science at the junior-college level.

Summary

The physical-science course is a relatively recent innovation in the science curricula of senior high schools. The following summary of the high-school physical-science course, and of related research seems reasonable:

1. There was as early as 1914 an advocacy of an integrated course of physical-science involving important principles of the various physical sciences.

2. According to available evidence, the first physical-science course in which at least two of the physical sciences were integrated to any great degree was offered in a senior high school in 1931-32.

3. According to available evidence, the first two-year sequence of an integrated course of physical science in a senior high school was established in 1934-35.

4. A number of different types of physical-science courses, chiefly one year in length, rapidly appeared in the curricula of high schools during the latter part of the decade 1930-40.

5. The onset of World War II in 1941 stopped the introduction and slowed the development of physical-science courses in high schools. In all probability, this temporary delay of the promising physical-science movement was due to the demand for pre-induction courses.

6. Fused or integrated one-year and two-year courses of physical science, including laboratory work, are replacing separate courses of physics and chemistry for many pupils preparing for college and for many more pupils in the non-college group. It is thus indicated that the fused or integrated course of physical science has both terminal and propaedeutic values.

7. Those pupils planning to specialize in the sciences or engineering sometimes take in high school, in addition to a one-year physical-science course, a year of either advanced physics or advanced chemistry, or one semester of each.

8. Integrated courses of physical science usually include subject matter from the fields of physics (including astronomy and meteorology), chemistry, and geology.

9. The available research evidence is interpreted as indicating that pupils who take an integrated course of physical science, restricted to physics and chemistry and of at least one year in length, learn somewhat more of the subject matter of physics and chemistry than do those who take separate courses in one or both of these subjects.

10. A less rigorous treatment of the fundamentals of science and greater emphasis on consumer problems than is common in conventional courses of chemistry and physics are accepted practices in physical-science courses for the non-college group of pupils.

11. At least two important national committees now advocate the offering of integrated courses of physical science in senior high schools.

12. Physical-science courses are now approved and are accepted as an entrance unit by representative colleges and universities.

13. It is widely agreed that the development of a functional understanding of the important principles of science is one of the major objectives of science teaching, and that such principles are well-suited for use as a basis for organizing materials of instruction in science. It is, moreover, strongly recommended that physical-science courses be so organized.

14. The Forty-sixth Yearbook, Science Education in American Schools, seems destined to add even greater impetus than did earlier reports to the movement to use principles of physical science as focal points for the organization of instructional materials in physical-science courses.

15. Wise has determined on a research basis a list of 272 principles of physical science of which 264 are arranged in descending order of their relative importance for general education, grades, I-XIV, inclusive. His list of 272 principles of physical science is the most comprehensive one available for the physical sciences to have been determined on a research basis.

16. Blanchet has applied acceptable research techniques in ranking Wise's list of 272 principles of physical science in the descending order of their relative values as goals of instruction for survey courses of physical science at the junior-college level.

The Need for Further Investigation

Wise's complete list of 272 principles of physical science, and also his list of 264 principles of physical science arranged in descending order of their relative importance for general education, grades I-XIV, inclusive, provide bases for course construction in harmony with best modern practices and professional opinions.

Even though 44 research studies on principles as objectives of instruction in science have been reported, none has attempted to determine the scientific principles which should serve as goals of instruction in an integrated course of physical science for the senior high school. Furthermore, there have been no attempts to determine the experiments which are most likely to be contributory to the development of an understanding of designated, important principles of physical science. There is, therefore, a need for the present investigation.

Statement of the Problem

The purpose of this investigation is (1) to determine the relative importance of the principles of physical science which are desirable for inclusion in an integrated course of physical science for senior high school; and (2) to determine the relative values of the experiments which are desirable for inclusion in such a course, and whether each of those experiments would more appropriately be done as a laboratory experiment or as a demonstration.

CHAPTER II

THE SELECTION OF PRINCIPLES FOR A COURSE OF PHYSICAL SCIENCE

Statement of the Problem

The purpose of this part of the investigation was to determine the relative importance of the principles of physical science which are desirable for inclusion in an integrated course of physical science for senior high school.

Definitions of Terms

The following definitions of terms were used in this part of the investigation:

A [scientific] "principle" is defined in terms of four criteria:[1]
A. To be a principle a statement must be a comprehensive generalization describing some fundamental process, constant mode of behavior, or property relating to natural phenomena.

---

[1]Harold E. Wise, A Determination of the Relative Importance of Principles of Physical Science for General Education, p. 18. Unpublished Doctor's dissertation, University of Michigan, 1941.

B. It must be true without exception within limitations specifically stated.
C. It must be capable of illustration.
D. It must not be a definition.

The term "physical science" includes only the fields of physics (including astronomy and meteorology), chemistry, and geology.

An "integrated course of physical science" is one in which subject matter from the fields of physics (including astronomy and meteorology), chemistry, and geology is unified, and which is contributory to the development of an understanding of principles of physical science.

The term "senior high school" means grades 10, 11, and 12 of the secondary-school system.

Techniques Employed

It was necessary to secure first a list of principles of physical science to be evaluated on the basis of the desirability of each for inclusion in the desired course. Wise's list of 272 principles was assumed to constitute a satisfactory one for this purpose.

Keeslar[2] presents substantial evidence from 5 research studies by Frutchey,[3] Olson and Wilkinson,[4] Anderson,[5] Nesbitt,[6,7] and Tyler[8] which indicates that individual evaluations by a jury of as few as 3 individuals are both reliable and valid.

_____

[2]Oreon Pierre Keeslar, Contribution of Instructional Films to the Teaching of High School Science, pp. 104-115. Unpublished Doctor's dissertation, University of Michigan, 1945.

[3]Fred P. Frutchey, "Measuring the Ability to Apply Chemical Principles," Educational Research Bulletin (Ohio State University), XII (December 13, 1933), 255-260.

[4]Willard C. Olson and Muriel M. Wilkinson, "The Measurement of Child Behavior in Terms of Its Social Stimulus Value," Journal of Experimental Education, I (1932), 92-95.

[5]Harold H. Anderson, "Domination and Integration in the Social Behavior of Young Children in an Experimental Play Situation," Genetic Psychology Monographs, XIX (August, 1937), 343-408.

[6]Margaret Nesbitt, Adult-Child Relationships: Student and Child Relationships in the Nursery School. Unpublished Doctor's dissertation, University of Michigan, 1942.

[7]Margaret Nesbitt, "Student and Child Relationships in the Nursery School," Child Development, XIV (September, 1943), 143-166.

[8]Ralph W. Tyler, "Ability to Use Scientific Method," Educational Research Bulletin (Ohio State University), XI (January 6, 1932), 1-9.

> ... providing (1) that the judges be
> well-trained and experienced; i.e., experts
> in their fields of specialization; and (2)
> that the criteria in terms of which the
> judgments are to be made be clearly and
> concisely stated for the purpose.[9]

It was assumed, therefore, that 5 would constitute an

acceptable number of evaluators of the principles.

Four specialists in the teaching of science, in

addition to the investigator, agreed to evaluate the

principles. All 5 specialists were well qualified

in terms of their teaching experience and their

subject-matter training.

A copy of Wise's list of 272 principles of phys-

ical science was submitted to each of the 5 evaluators

with the following explanations and instructions:

> I need the help of several "experts," --
> specialists in the teaching of science, who
> are well qualified in terms of teaching ex-
> perience and subject-matter training to
> assist me in the determination of those prin-
> ciples which are desirable for inclusion in
> an integrated course of physical science for
> senior high school. May I have your assist-
> ance?

> Attached to this letter is a list of
> 272 principles of physical science. A subject-
> matter specialist in each of the fields of
> physics, chemistry, and geology has approved
> the principles related to his respective
> field, for accuracy of statement. No effort
> has been made, however, to state these prin-
> ciples in a vocabulary suitable for use at
> the high-school level.

---

[9]Keeslar, op. cit., p. 115

The criteria which delimit the purpose
of the physical-science course and which
therefore are to serve as bases for the
judgments to be made by you are:

The integrated course of physical
science for senior high school

(1) is planned to serve not only
as a college-preparatory course
but also as a terminal course
for those capable of profiting
by such a course; and

(2) is intended to accomplish for
physical science the same
purposes that are now served
by a high-school course in
general biology.

The principles are to be marked according to the following directions:

"Please write E, D, or U at the
left of each principle to indicate,
respectively, whether you consider
it to be

(1) essential (E) for inclusion
in an integrated course of
physical science for senior
high school,

(2) merely desirable (D) if time
permits its inclusion, or

(3) undesirable (U) in such a
course because it is too
abstract or too difficult."

For the purposes of this evaluation, you
are asked to adopt the following definitions
of terms:

1. The term "physical science" includes
only the fields of physics (including astronomy and meteorology),
chemistry, and geology.

2. An "integrated course of physical
science" is one in which subject
matter from the fields of physics
(including astronomy and meteorology), chemistry, and geology is
unified, and which is contributory
to the development of an understanding of principles of physical science.

3. The term "senior high school" means
grades 10, 11, and 12 of the secondary-school system.

After the list of principles was marked independently by the 5 evaluators and returned, each principle
was then assigned a numerical value. This was the sum
of the individual evaluations of that principle by the
5 judges on a scale in which each designation as
"essential" was arbitrarily assigned the value of +3;
each, as "desirable," was given the value of +2; and
that of "undesirable," -2. For example, "All liquids
are compressible but only to a slight degree" was
judged essential (+3) by 3 evaluators, desirable (+2)
by 1, and undesirable (-2) by 1. The algebraic sum
of (+3 x 3) + (+2 x 1) + (-2 x 1) is 9. The numerical
value assigned to this principle was, therefore, 9.

TABLE I presents, in descending order of relative
importance, the principles deemed by the judges to be
desirable for inclusion in the proposed course.[*]

---

[*]Those deemed undesirable for inclusion are
presented in Appendix A, page 208.

TABLE I

PRINCIPLES DESIRABLE FOR INCLUSION IN AN INTEGRATED
COURSE OF PHYSICAL SCIENCE FOR SENIOR HIGH SCHOOL,
IN DESCENDING ORDER OF THEIR RELATIVE IMPORTANCE

Principles	Relative Importance
1. Energy can never be created or destroyed (except in nuclear physics); it can be changed from one form to another only with exact equivalence.	15*
2. A gas always tends to expand throughout the whole space available.	15
3. When there is a gain in mechanical advantage by using a simple machine, there is a loss in speed and vice versa.	15
4. In the lever the force times its distance from the fulcrum equals the weight times its distance from the fulcrum.	15
5. The work obtained from a simple machine is always equal to the work put into it less the work expended in overcoming friction.	15
6. Sound is produced by vibrating matter and is transmitted by matter.	15
7. Solids are liquefied and liquids are vaporized by heat; the amount of heat used in this process, for a given mass and a given substance, is specific and equals that given off in the reverse process.	15
8. Most bodies expand on heating and contract on cooling; the amount of change depending upon the change in temperature.	15
9. Heat is liberated when a gas is compressed, and is absorbed when a gas expands.	15

*The numerical values are the algebraic sums of the individual evaluations of the five judges on the scale for essential (+3), desirable (+2), and undesirable (-2).

TABLE I (CONTINUED)

Principles	Relative Importance
10. The atmospheric pressure decreases as the altitude increases.	15
11. The higher the temperature of the air, the greater is the amount of moisture required to saturate it.	15
12. Bodies of land heat up and cool off more rapidly than bodies of water.	15
13. The principal cause of wind and weather changes is the unequal heating of different portions of the earth's surface by the sun; thus all winds are convection currents caused by unequal heating of different portions of the earth's atmosphere, and they blow from places of higher atmospheric pressure to places of lower atmospheric pressure.	15
14. If a beam of light falls upon an irregular surface, the rays of light are scattered in all directions.	15
15. Dark, rough or unpolished surfaces absorb or radiate energy more effectively than light, smooth or polished surfaces. ..	15
16. The colors of objects depend upon the wave lengths of the light rays they transmit, absorb or reflect.	15
17. Light travels in straight lines in a medium of uniform optical density.	15
18. Waves travel in straight lines while passing through a homogeneous or uniform medium.	15
19. When light is reflected, the angle of incidence is equal to the angle of reflection.	15
20. Like electrical charges repel and unlike electrical charges attract.	15

TABLE I (CONTINUED)

Principles	Relative Importance
21. A magnet always has at least two poles and is surrounded by a field of force.	15
22. Like magnetic poles always repel each other and unlike magnetic poles always attract each other.	15
23. Pieces of iron, steel, cobalt or nickel may become magnetized by induction when placed within a magnetic field.	15
24. An electric current may be produced in three ways: by rubbing or friction, chemical action, and using a magnetic field.	15
25. An electric current will flow in the external circuit when two metals of unlike chemical activity are acted upon by a conducting solution, the more active metal being charged negatively.	15
26. An electromotive force is induced in a circuit whenever there is a change in the number of the lines of magnetic force passing through the circuit.	15
27. Elements are made up of small particles of matter called atoms which are alike in the same element (except for occasional differences in atomic weight; i.e., isotopes) but different in different elements.	15
28. All substances are made up of small particles called molecules which are alike in the same substance (except for variations in molecular weight due to isotopes) but different in different substances.	15
29. All matter is composed of single elements or combinations of several elements.	15
30. Every pure sample of any substance, whether simple or compound, under the same conditions will show the same physical properties and the same chemical behavior.	15

TABLE I (CONTINUED)

Principles   Relative
                                                Importance

31. The materials forming one or more
substances, without ceasing to exist,
may be changed into one or more new and
measurably different substances.   15

32. Oxidation always involves the removal
or sharing of electrons from the element
oxidized while the reduction always adds or
shares with the element reduced.   15

33. Oxidation and reduction occur
simultaneously and are quantitatively equal.   15

34. The exchange of the negative and
positive ions of acids and bases results in
the formation of water and a salt.   15

35. Electrolytes dissolved in water exist
partially or completely as electrically
charged particles called ions.   15

36. All matter is made up of protons,
neutrons, and electrons.   15

37. The electrons within an atom form
shells about the nucleus, each of which
contains a definite number of electrons. ..   15

38. When elevations or depressions are
created upon the surface of the earth, the
elevations are usually attacked by the
agents of erosion, and the materials are
carried to the depressions.   15

39. Streams, generally, are lowering the
surface land in some places and building it
up in other places.   15

40. Rocks may be formed by the compacting
and cementing of sediments.   15

41. A fluid has a tendency to move from a
region of higher pressure to one of lower
pressure; the greater the difference, the
faster the movement.   14

TABLE I (CONTINUED)

Principles	Relative Importance

42. Any two bodies attract one another with a force which is directly proportional to the attracting masses and inversely proportional to the square of the distance between their centers of mass. 14

43. Movements of all bodies in the solar system are due to gravitational attraction and inertia. 14

44. The pressure in a fluid in the open is equal to the weight of the fluid above a unit area including the point at which the pressure is taken; it therefore varies with the depth and average density of the fluid. 14

45. Bodies in rotation tend to fly out in a straight line which is tangent to the arc of rotation. 14

46. A body immersed or floating in a fluid is buoyed up by a force equal to the weight of the fluid displaced. 14

47. The pressure at a point in any fluid is the same in all directions. 14

48. Heat is conducted by the transfer of kinetic energy from molecule to molecule. . 14

49. When two bodies of different temperature are in contact, there is a continuous transference of heat energy from the body of higher temperature to the one of lower temperature, the rate of which is directly proportional to the difference of temperature. 14

50. The lower the temperature of a body, the less the amount of energy it radiates; the higher the temperature, the greater is the amount of energy radiated. 14

TABLE I (<u>CONTINUED</u>)

Principles   Relative
Importance

51. Heat is transferred by convection in
currents of gases or liquids, the rate of
transfer decreasing with an increase in
the viscosity of the circulating fluid. ...   14

52. Every pure liquid has its own specific
boiling and freezing point.   14

53. The higher the pitch of a note, the
more rapid the vibrations of the producing
body and <u>vice versa</u>.   14

54. Musical tones are produced when a
vibrating body sends out regular vibrations
to the ear while only noises are produced
when the vibrating body sends out irregular
vibrations to the ear.   14

55. Energy is often transmitted in the
form of waves.   14

56. When waves strike an object, they may
be absorbed, transmitted, or reflected. ...   14

57. When light rays are absorbed, some of
the light energy is transformed into heat
energy.   14

58. The darker the color of a surface, the
better it absorbs light.   14

59. The intensity of illumination decreases as the square of the distance from a
point source.   14

60. Radiant energy travels in waves along
straight lines; its intensity at any distance
from a point source is inversely proportional to the square of the distance from
the source.   14

61. When light rays pass obliquely from
a rare to a more dense medium, they are
bent or refracted toward the normal and when
they pass obliquely from a dense to a rarer
medium, they are bent away from the normal.   14

TABLE I (CONTINUED)

Principles	Relative Importance
62. An image appears to be as far back of a plane mirror as the object is in front of the mirror and is reversed.	14
63. Parallel light rays may be converged or focused by convex lenses or concave mirrors; diverged by concave lenses or convex mirrors.	14
64. Protons and neutrons only are found in the nucleus of an atom.	14
65. In an uncharged body there are as many protons as electrons and the charges neutralize each other while a deficiency of electrons produces a plus charge on a body and an excess of electrons produces a negative charge.	14
66. An electrical charge in motion produces a magnetic field about the conductor, its direction being tangential to any circle drawn about the conductor in a plane perpendicular to it.	14
67. All materials offer some resistance to the flow of electric current, and that part of the electrical energy used in overcoming this resistance is transformed into heat energy.	14
68. The resistance of a metallic conductor depends on the kind of material from which the conductor is made, varies directly with the length, inversely with the cross-sectional area, and increases as the temperature increases.	14
69. The electrical current flowing in a conductor is directly proportional to the potential difference and inversely proportional to the resistance.	14
70. Electrical power is directly proportional to the product of the potential difference and the current.	14

TABLE I (CONTINUED)

Principles   Relative
                                                      Importance

71. When a current-carrying wire is placed
in a magnetic field, there is a force acting
on the wire tending to push it at right
angles to the direction of the lines of force
between the magnetic poles, providing the
wire is not parallel to the field.   14

72. The atoms of all radioactive elements
are constantly disintegrating by giving off
various rays (alpha, beta and gamma) and
forming helium and other elements.   14

73. The solubility of solutes is affected by
heat, pressure, and the nature of the solute
and solvent.   14

74. The valence of an atom is determined by
the number of electrons it gains, loses or
shares in chemical reactions.   14

75. Most atoms have the property of losing,
gaining or sharing a number of out shell
electrons.   14

76. The energy shown by atoms in completing
their outer shell by adding, losing or
sharing electrons determines their chemical
activity.   14

77. The properties of the elements show
periodic variations with their atomic
numbers.   14

78. Each combustible substance has a
kindling temperature which varies with its
condition but may be greater or less than
the kindling temperature of some other
substance.   14

79. Matter may be transformed into radiant
energy and radiant energy into matter; in
either case, the mass is unchanged.   14

80. The total mass of a quantity of matter
is not altered by any chemical or physical
changes occurring among the materials
composing it. (except in nuclear physics)....   14

TABLE I (<u>CONTINUED</u>)

Principles   Relative
                                                    Importance

81. The rates of many reactions are affected
by the presence of substances which do not
enter into the completed chemical reaction. .   14

82. Acids and bases in water solution
ionize to give hydrogen and hydroxyl ions,
respectively, from their constituent elements.   14

83. The ingredients of a solution are homogeneously distributed through each other.   14

84. When different amounts of one element
are found in combination with a fixed weight
of another element (in a series of compounds)
the different weights of the first element
are related to each other by ratios which may
be expressed by small whole numbers.   14

85. The earth's surface may be elevated or
lowered by interior forces.   14

86. Strata of rocks occur in the earth's
crust in the order in which they were deposited, except in the case of overthrust
faults.   14

87. The energy which a body possesses on
account of its position or form is called
potential energy and is measured by the work
that was done in order to bring it into the
specified condition.   13

88. When the resultant of all the forces
acting on a body is zero, the body will stay
at rest if at rest, or it will keep in
uniform motion in a straight line if it is
in motion.   13

89. When one body exerts a force on a
second body, the second body exerts an equal
and opposite force on the first.   13

90. When pressure is applied to any area of
a fluid (liquid or gas) in a closed container,
it is transmitted in exactly the same intensity
to every area of the container in contact
with the fluid.   13

TABLE I (CONTINUED)   83

Principles

91. The average speed of molecules
increases with the temperature and pressure.   13

92. Condensation will occur when a vapor
is at its saturation point if centers of
condensation are available and if heat is
withdrawn.   13

93. A change in state of a substance from
gas to liquid, liquid to solid, or vice
versa, or from solid to gas or vice versa,
is usually accompanied by a change in
volume.   13

94. The presence of a non-volatile substance will cause the resulting solution to
boil at a higher temperature and to freeze
at a lower temperature than pure water.   13

95. The volume of an ideal gas varies
inversely with the pressure upon it, providing the temperature remains constant. ...   13

96. Whenever an opaque object intercepts
radiant energy traveling in a particular
direction, a shadow is cast behind the
object.   13

97. The dispersion of white light into a
spectrum by a prism is caused by unequal
refraction of the different wave lengths
of light.   13

98. Positively charged ions of metals may
be deposited on the cathode, as atoms, when
a direct current is sent through an
electrolyte.   13

99. In a transformer the ratio between
voltages is the same as that between the
number of turns.   13

100. Energy in kilowatt hours is equal to
the product of amperes, volts, and time
(in hours) divided by one thousand.   13

101. The mass of an atom is concentrated
almost entirely in the nucleus.   13

TABLE I (CONTINUED)

Principles

102. Atoms of all elements are made up of
protons, neutrons, and electrons, and
differences between atoms of different
elements are due to the number of protons
and neutrons in the nucleus and to the
configuration of electrons surrounding
the nucleus. 13

103. Earthquakes are produced by the
sudden slipping of earth materials along
faults. 13

104. In the inclined plane, weight times
height equals acting force times length,
providing friction is neglected and the
force is parallel to the plane. 12

105. When two forces act upon the same
object, the resultant is the diagonal of
a parallelogram whose sides represent the
direction and magnitude of the two forces.
A single force represented by the diagonal
may be resolved into two forces represented
by the sides of the parallelogram. 12

106. At any point on the earth's surface,
all bodies fall with a constant acceleration
which is independent of the mass or size of
the body if air resistance be neglected. . 12

107. Sliding friction is dependent upon
the nature and condition of the rubbing
surfaces, proportional to the force pressing the surfaces together and independent
of area of contact. 12

108. The loudness of a sound depends
upon the energy of the sound waves and, if
propagated in all directions, decreases
inversely as the square of the distance
from the source. 12

109. If the same pressure is maintained,
the volume of a gas is varied directly
as the absolute temperature. 12

TABLE I (<u>CONTINUED</u>)   85

Principles

Relative
Importance

110. If the volume of a confined body of
gas is kept constant, the pressure is
proportional to the absolute temperature. .   12

111. The boiling point of any solution
becomes lower as the pressure is decreased
and higher as the pressure is increased. ..   12

112. The atmosphere of the earth tends to
prevent the heat of the earth's surface
from escaping and the earth begins to cool
only when the amount of heat lost during
the night exceeds that gained during the
day.   12

113. The more nearly vertical the rays of
radiant energy the greater the number that
will fall upon a given horizontal area, and
the greater is the amount of energy that
will be received by that area.   12

114. The dimensions of an image produced
by a lens or a mirror are to the dimensions
of the object as their respective distances
from the lens or mirror are to each other..   12

115. The force of attraction or repulsion
between two magnetic poles varies directly
as the product of the pole strengths and
inversely as the square of the distance
between the poles.   12

116. The magnitude of an induced electromotive force is proportional to the rate
at which the number of lines of magnetic
force change and to the number of turns
of wire in the coil.   12

117. Charges on a conductor tend to stay
on the outside surface and to be greatest
on the sharp edges and points.   12

118. Metals may be arranged in an activity
series according to their tendency to pass
into ionic form by losing electrons.   12

TABLE I (CONTINUED)

Principles	Relative Importance
119. The solubility of a gas in an inert solvent varies directly with the pressure to which the gas is subjected.	12
120. Falls or rapids tend to develop in a stream bed where the stream flows over a hard stratum to a soft one.	12
121. Rocks may be folded to form mountains.	12
122. Rocks may be metamorphosed, or changed by heat, pressure and flexion.	12
123. When forces act in the same direction, the resultant is their algebraic sum.	11
124. The speed gained by a body with a constant acceleration is equal to the product of the acceleration and the time.	11
125. The acceleration of a body is proportional to the resultant force acting on that body and is in the direction of that force.	11
126. The velocity of a wave is equal to the product of its frequency and wave length.	11
127. When energy is transmitted in waves, the medium which transmits the wave motion does not move along with the wave, but the energy does.	11
128. Salts of strong acids and strong bases undergo negligible hydrolysis, while salts of inactive acids and inactive bases undergo more marked hydrolysis.	11
129. The activity of an acid or base is proportional to the degree of ionization of the compound when in solution.	11
130. Streams, potentially, have a regular cycle; youth, maturity, and old age.	11
131. The total change in length of a metal bar is equal to its coefficient of linear expansion times the original length times the change of temperature in degrees Centigrade.	10

TABLE I (CONTINUED)

Principles

132. Sound waves or other energy impulses
may set up vibrations in a body the amplitude
of which is increased if the impulses are
exactly timed to correspond to any one of
the natural periods of vibration of the body.   10

133. The speed of sound increases with an
increase in temperature of the medium
conducting it.   10

134. A number of substances will emit
electrons and become positively charged when
illuminated by light.   10

135. When a stream of high-speed electrons
strikes a body, the atoms of that body emit
x-rays.   10

136. Parent material for the development
of soils is formed through the physical
disintegration and chemical decomposition of
rock particles and organic matter.   10

137. The energy which a body possesses on
account of its motion is called kinetic energy
and is proportional to its mass and the
square of its velocity.   9

138. All liquids are compressible but only
to a slight degree.   9

139. The atmospheric pressure decreases with
increasing water vapor content, other things
being equal.   9

140. The rate of evaporation of a liquid
varies with temperature, area of exposed
surface, nature of the liquid itself, and
saturation and circulation of the gas in
contact with the liquid.   9

141. Any homogeneous body of liquid free to
take its own position, will seek a position
in which all exposed surfaces lie on the
same horizontal plane.   9

142. Diffusible substances tend to scatter
from the point of greatest concentration
until all points are at equal concentration.   9

TABLE I (CONTINUED)

Principles	Relative Importance

S 143. The quality of a musical tone is determined by the pitch and intensity of the different simple tones or harmonics into which it may be resolved. 9

E 144. In a series circuit, the current is the same in all parts, the resistance of the whole is the sum of the resistance of the parts, and the voltage loss of the whole is the sum of the voltage losses of the parts. 9

E 145. In a parallel circuit, the total current is the sum of the separate currents, the voltage loss is the same for each branch, and the total resistance is less than the resistance of any one branch. 9

E 146. Some elements have more than one atomic weight due to differences in the neutron content of their nuclei. 9

147. Metals comprise a group of elements (other than hydrogen) whose atoms have a tendency to lose electrons readily and whose compounds when dissolved in polar solvents are capable of forming positive ions. 9

Geo 148. The natural movements of air, water and solids on the earth are due chiefly to gravity plus rotation of the earth. 9

Geo 149. The rate of erosion is inversely proportional to the resistance of rocks to decomposition and disintegration. 9

A 150. The distance a body travels, starting from rest with a constant acceleration, is one-half the acceleration times the square of the time. 8

f 151. As the velocity of flow through a constricted area increases, the pressure diminishes, and vice versa. 8

TABLE I (CONTINUED)

Principles	Relative Importance

152. When a gas expands, heat energy is converted into mechanical energy. 8

153. The amount of heat which a constant mass of a liquid or solid acquires when its temperature rises a given amount is identical with the amount it gives off when its temperature falls by that amount. 8

154. The charges on a conductor may be separated through the influence of a neighboring charge. 8

155. The products of reacting substances may react with each other to form the original substances. 8

156. Equal volumes of all gases under similar conditions of temperature and pressure contain very nearly the same number of molecules. 8

157. Rocks may be formed by the cooling and solidifying of molten material. 8

158. The amount of momentum possessed by an object is proportional to its mass and to its velocity. 7

159. The free surface of a liquid contracts to the smallest possible area due to surface tension. 7

160. Sound waves are reflected in a direction such that the angle of incidence is equal to the angle of reflection. 7

161. When parallel light strikes a concave spherical mirror the rays, after reflection, pass directly through the principal focus only if the area of the mirror is small compared to its radius of curvature. 7

TABLE I (<u>CONTINUED</u>) 90

Principles | Relative Importance

162. An induced current always has such a direction that its magnetic field tends to oppose whatever change produced the current; whenever a change is made in an electrical system there is brought into existence something which opposes that change. 7

163. Whenever a high frequency oscillating current produces in the field around it oscillating electric and magnetic fields, energy in the form of an electromagnetic wave is transmitted through space. 7

164. Electrons are emitted from any sufficiently hot body. 7

165. The speed of chemical reaction is increased by increasing the concentration of any of the reactants; and is decreased by decreasing the concentration of any of the reactants. 7

166. Non-metals comprise a group of elements whose atoms tend to gain or share electrons and whose compounds, when dissolved in polar solvents, are capable of forming negative ions. 7

167. Every chemical element when heated to incandescence in a gaseous state has a characteristic glow and a characteristic spectrum which can be used to identify very small quantities of the element and which is related to the molecular and atomic structure of the gas. 7

168. All chemical reactions which start with the same quantities of original substances liberate the same amounts of energy in reaching a given final state, irrespective of the process by which the final state is reached. 7

169. A few elements are inert or chemically inactive because their atoms are so constructed as to be complete in themselves; i.e., their outer electron rings have no tendency to gain or lose electrons. 7

TABLE I (CONTINUED) 91

Principles   Relative
                                              Importance

170. Igneous rock may be formed from extruded
magma and materials intruded into other rocks.   7

171. The frequency of the vibration of a
stretched string is inversely proportional to
its length, diameter, and square root of its
density, and directly proportional to the
square root of the stretching force.   6

172. All rays passing through the center of
curvature of a mirror are reflected upon
themselves.   6

173. Forces within the earth may cause breaks
to appear in the earth's crust.   6

174. Under the high pressures which occur
in the earth's interior, materials that
usually are solid have the capacity to flow
slowly and thus bring about equalization of
pressure differences on the surface.   6

175. Glacial conditions are as a rule
approached by increasing latitudes or
altitudes.   6

176. Gases may be converted into liquids
and liquids into solids by reducing the
speed of their molecules or removing the
faster molecules.   5

177. Electrons will always flow from one
point to another along a conductor if this
transfer releases energy.   5

178. No chemical change occurs without an
accompanying energy change.   5

179. Non-metals may be arranged in an activity
series according to their tendency to pass
into ionic form by gaining electrons.   5

180. The amount of heat developed in doing
work against friction is proportional to the
amount of work thus expended.   4

TABLE I (<u>CONTINUED</u>)

Principles   Relative
                                             Importance

181. In the northern hemisphere great
volumes of air revolve in a counterclockwise direction, and in the southern
hemisphere, they revolve in a clockwise
direction.   4

182. Luminous vapors and gases emit only
certain kinds of light producing bright-
line spectra.   4

183. Magnets depend for their properties
upon the arrangement of the metallic ions
of which they are made.   4

184. An electric current will be produced
in a closed circuit including two strips
of different metals if one of the
junctions is heated or cooled.   4

185. Elements may be changed into other
elements by changing the number of protons
in the nucleus.   4

186. Since the earth rotates from west to
east, the exact time (Arlington time) at
which the sun is nearest overhead, grows
continually later as one travels westward
around the earth's surface.   4

187. In every sample of any compound
substance formed, the proportion by weight
of the constituent elements is always the
same as long as the isotopic compositions
of each element is constant.   4

188. Carbon atoms form a number of "type
groups" of compounds which are determined
by the elements present and by the
structural combinations of the atoms
within the molecules.   4

189. Freezing point depression and boiling
point elevation are proportional to the
concentration of the solution.   3

190. Harmonious musical intervals correspond to very simple frequency ratios.   3

TABLE I (CONTINUED)

Principles   Relative
                                             Importance

191. Two sound waves of the same or nearly
the same frequency will destructively
interfere with each other when the conden-
sations of the one coincide with the
rarefactions of the other provided that
the directions of propagations are the same.   3

192. When a sounding body is moving toward
or away from an observer the apparent pitch
will be higher or lower, respectively, than
the true pitch of the sound emitted.   3

193. The amount of heat produced by an
electric current is proportional to the
resistance, the square of the current and
the time of flow.   3

194. Atoms have great sub-atomic energy. ..   3

195. Atoms or molecules may lose electrons
when struck by high speed electrons or ions.   3

196. Suspended particles of colloids have
a continuous, erratic movement due to
colloidal, molecular, or ion impacts.   3

197. The height to which a liquid rises in
a capillary tube is directly proportional to
the surface tension of the liquid and
inversely proportional to the density of
the liquid and to the radius of the tube. ..   2

198. The distortion of an elastic body is
proportional to the force applied provided
the elastic limit is not exceeded.   2

199. A spinning body offers resistance to
any force which changes the direction of the
axis about which the body rotates.   2

200. The rate of osmosis is directly
proportional to the difference in concentration on opposite sides of the membrane.   2

TABLE I (<u>CONTINUED</u>) 94

Principles   Relative
                Importance

201. The pressure of a saturated vapor is constant at a given temperature, and increases with an increase of temperature. ... 2

202. Substances which expand upon solidifying have their melting points lowered by pressure; those which contract upon solidifying have their melting points raised by pressure. 2

203. In a plane mirror a line running from any point on the object to the image of that point is perpendicular to the mirror. 2

204. Incandescent solids and liquids emit all wave lengths of light and give a continuous spectrum. 2

205. Gases conduct electric currents only when ionized. 2

206. Condenser capacitance varies directly with the area of the plates, and inversely as the thickness of the insulation between them. 2

207. Alternating current charges a condenser twice during each cycle inducing opposite charges on the two plates with the result that a current appears to flow through the condenser. 2

208. Electromagnetic waves may produce electrical oscillation in a condenser circuit which is so adjusted as to oscillate naturally with the same frequency as that of the incoming waves. 2

209. Atoms may be broken down by bombarding the nucleus with highspeed particles such as protons, alpha particles, or neutrons. 2

210. Radioactive emission involves nuclear changes. 2

211. At a definite temperature and pressure, the relative combining volumes of gases and of gaseous products may be expressed approximately in small whole numbers. 2

TABLE I (CONCLUDED)

Principles	Relative Importance
212. Orderly arrangement of molecules, atoms, or ions in crystals give crystals regular form.	2
213. The properties of alloys are dependent upon the relative amount of their components, the extent of their compound formation, and upon the crystalline structure of the mixture. ...	2
214. Glacial abrasion occurs in proportion to the weight of the ice and the velocity of its movement.	2

Findings

1. Two hundred fourteen of 272 principles were given positive values by the 5 evaluators to indicate their desirability for inclusion in an integrated course of physical science for senior high school. Forty of these principles received an aggregate value of 15 (deemed essential by all 5 judges); 46, a value of 14 (deemed essential by 4, and desirable by 1); and 17, a value of 13 (deemed essential by 3, and desirable by 2).

2. Of the 103 principles which received 13, 14, or 15 as their aggregate values, 72, or 69.9 percent, are principles of physics; 25, or 24.2 percent, are principles of chemistry; and 6, or 5.8 percent, are principles of geology.

3. Of the 40 principles which were deemed essentia
by all judges, and hence received 15 as an aggregate
value, 26, or 65.0 percent, are principles of physics;
11, or 27.5 percent, are principles of chemistry; and 3,
or 7.5 percent, are principles of geology.

CHAPTER III

THE SELECTION AND EVALUATION OF LABORATORY AND DEMONSTRATION EXPERIMENTS

Statement of the Problem

The purpose of this part of the investigation was to determine the relative values of the experiments which are desirable for inclusion in an integrated course of physical science for senior high school, and whether each of those experiments would more appropriately be done as a laboratory experiment or as a demonstration.

Definitions of Terms

The following definitions of terms not previously defined were used in this part of this investigation:

The term "experiment" means any kind of activity in connection with which apparatus or materials are manipulated or field trips are made in an attempt to solve a problem in the field of science.

97

A "laboratory experiment" is one which is
pupil-performed for observation by only the
performer or performers.

A "demonstration experiment" is one which
is performed by the teacher and/or one or more
pupils, and is for observation by all members
of the class.

Techniques Employed

The solution of the main problem as stated above
involved, first, the completion of two minor problems,
namely:

1. To assemble experiments appropriate for
   use at the senior-high-school level.

2. To assign these experiments to the
   various principles of physical science.

Method of Assembling Experiments

Textbooks and laboratory manuals, along with
masters' theses and doctors' dissertations, were considered to be readily available sources of experiments.

The following list of 30 publishing houses, which
were deemed by the investigator as most likely to publish textbooks and laboratory manuals of science for
use in senior high schools, was selected from the

approximately four-hundred in The Publisher's Trade List Annual, 1945:[1]

Allyn and Bacon
American Book Company
American Technical Society
D. Appleton-Century Company, Inc.
The Blakiston Company
Bruce Publishing Company
College Entrance Book Company
Ginn and Company
Harcourt, Brace and Company
D. C. Heath and Company
Henry Holt and Company, Inc.
Houghton Mifflin Company
Laurel Book Company
J. B. Lippincott Company
Lyons and Carnahan
The Macmillan Company
McGraw-Hill Book Company, Inc.
Mentzer, Bush and Company
Oxford Book Company
Prentice-Hall, Inc.
Rand McNally and Company
Benj. H. Sanborn and Company
Scott, Foresman and Company
Charles Scribner's Sons
Silver Burdett Company
D. Van Nostrand Company, Inc.
Webster Publishing Company
John Wiley and Sons, Inc.
The John C. Winston Company
World Book Company

Two sales representives of large publishing houses, each of whom had sold science textbooks to secondary schools for more than twenty years, were asked to add to the list the names of other houses which publish textbooks or laboratory manuals of science for use

---

[1]The Publisher's Trade List Annual, 1945. New York: R. R. Bowker Co., 1945.

in senior high schools. They added no publishers to
the list.

The latest catalogues in which books of high-
school science were listed, were secured from these
publishers. A list of all textbooks and laboratory
manuals of physical science for use in high schools
was compiled from these catalogues. The latest edi-
tions or revisions of these were then ordered from
the companies. Forty-five textbooks and 44 laboratory manuals were received.

Criteria for the Selection of Textbooks and Laboratory Manuals for Analysis

The textbooks and laboratory manuals were examined
by the investigator, and those which satisfied the following four criteria were retained for further consideration as possible sources to be analyzed for experiments:

1. The publication must be intended for use
   in the senior high school as stated in
   the preface of the publication, or in
   the publisher's catalogue.

2. The publication must be intended for use
   as a textbook or a laboratory manual in
   one or more courses of physical science
   offered in senior high schools and commonly called physics; chemistry; physical science; earth science, physiography, or physical geography; consumer
   science; senior science; or aeronautics.

3. The publication must be the latest edition or revision available from the publisher in November, 1945.

4. The publication must have a copyright date during the decade 1936-1945, or have had at least 5 reprintings during that decade.

Forty-three textbooks and 43 laboratory manuals satisfied the four criteria. From these textbooks and manuals, the following groups were chosen for analysis as sources of experiments:

1. The 5 textbooks of physics and the 5 of chemistry, selected after a page-by-page analysis of all 29 such books, as the ones which would provide a greater number of different experiments than would any other similar number.

2. All 14 textbooks of the physical sciences, in addition to those intended for use in separate courses of physics and chemistry.

3. All 43 laboratory manuals, including from 1 to 20 for each of the physical sciences.

The 5 physics textbooks were:

Bower, Ernest O., and Robinson, Edward P. Dynamic Physics. New York: Rand McNally and Company, 1942. Pp. x+798.

Burns, Elmer E., Verwiebe, Frank L., and Hazel, Herbert C. Physics a Basic Science. New York: D. Van Nostrand Company, Inc., 1943. Pp. xii+637.

Clark, John A., Gorton, Frederick Russell, and Sears, Francis W. Physics of Today. Boston: Houghton Mifflin Company, 1943. Pp. vi+664.

Dull, Charles E. Modern Physics, Revised. New York: Henry Holt and Company, 1943. Pp. x+598.

Williard, Lester R. Experiences in Physics.
Boston: Ginn and Company, 1939. Pp. x+640.

The 5 chemistry textbooks were:

Ahrens, Maurice R., Bush, Norris, F., and Easley,
Ray K. Living Chemistry. Boston: Ginn and
Company, 1945. Pp. vi+528.

Elack, Newton Henry, and Conant, James Bryant.
New Practical Chemistry, Revised. New York:
The Macmillan Company, 1942. Pp. x+644.

Dull, Charles E. Modern Chemistry. New York:
Henry Holt and Company, 1942. Pp. xi+604.

Jaffe, Bernard. New World of Chemistry. New
York: Silver Burdett Company, 1942. Pp. xi+
679.

McPherson, William, Henderson, William Edwards,
and Fowler, George Winegar. Chemistry at
Work. Boston: Ginn and Company, 1942.
Pp. x+636.

The 14 other textbooks were in the fields of

Aeronautics

Aviation Education Research Group, Teachers
College, University of Nebraska. Elements
of Pre-flight Aeronautics for High Schools.

Aviation Education Research Group, Teachers
College, Columbia University. Science of
Pre-flight Aeronautics, Revised. New York:
The Macmillan Company, 1944. Pp. xxi+702.

Pope, Francis, and Otis, Arthur S. Elements
of Aeronautics, Revised. New York: World
Book Company, 1941. Pp. x+642.

Pope, Francis, and Otis, Arthur S. The Airplane Power Plant. New York: World Book
Company, 1944. Pp. iii+173.

Consumer Science

Bush, George L., Ptacek, Theodore W., and
Kovats, John, Jr. Senior Science. New
York: American Book Company, 1937.
Pp. vii+822.

Hausrath, Alfred H., Jr., and Harms, John H.
Consumer Science. New York: The Macmillan
Company, 1939. Pp. xii+671.

Earth Science

Dryer, Charles Redway. High School Geography:
Physical, Economic, and Regional. New York:
American Book Company, 1940. Pp. 9+526.

Finch, Vernor C., Trewartha, Glenn T., and
Shearer, M. H. The Earth and Its Re-
sources. New York: McGraw-Hill Book
Company, Inc., 1941. Pp. x+580.

Fletcher, Gustav L. Earth Science, Revised.
Boston: D. C. Heath and Company, 1943.
Pp. vi+548.

Tarr, Ralph S., and von Engeln, O. D.
New Physical Geography, Revised. New
York: The Macmillan Company, 1944.
Pp. xi+608.

Physical Science

Carleton, Robert H. and Williams, Harry H.
Modern-Life Science. Chicago: J. B. Lippincott Company, 1942. Pp. x+625.

Eby, George S., Waugh, Charles L., Welch,
Herbert E., and Buckingham, Burdette H.
The Physical Sciences. Boston: Ginn and
Company, 1943. Pp. vi+483.

Eckels, Charles F., Shaver, Chalmer B., and
Howard, Bailey W. Our Physical World.
Chicago: Benjamin H. Sanborn and Company,
1938. Pp. xi+785.

Nettels, Charles H., Devine, Paul F., Nourse,
Walter L., and Herriott, M. E. Physical
Science. Boston: D. C. Heath and Company,
1942. Pp. xxiv+442.

The 20 physics laboratory manuals were:

Black, Newton Henry. Laboratory Experiments in Elementary Physics. New York: The Macmillan Company, 1938. Pp. xiii+248.

Bower, Ernest O., and Robinson, Edward P. Laboratory Manual Dynamic Physics. New York: Rand McNally and Company, 1943. Pp. vi+284.

Brooks, William O. Directed Activities in Physics. New York: Oxford Book Company, 1939. Pp. vii+264.

Buell, Mahlon H., and Schuler, Frederick W. Physics Workbook, Revised. Chicago: J. B. Lippincott Company, 1944. Pp. vi+374.

Burns, Elmer E., Verwiebe, Frank L., and Hazel, Herbert C. Workbook with Laboratory Exercises for Use with Physics. New York: D. Van Nostrand Company, Inc., 1945. Pp. iv+390.

Clark, John A., Gorton, Frederick Russell, and Sears, Francis W. Laboratory Manual in Physics. Boston: Houghton Mifflin Company, 1943. Pp. vi+134.

Clark, John A., Gorton, Frederick Russell, and Sears, Francis W. Workbook in Physics. Boston: Houghton Mifflin Company, 1944. Pp. vii+274.

Cushing, Burton L. A Laboratory Guide and Workbook. Boston: Ginn and Company, 1937. Pp. vi+239.

Cushing, Burton L. Directed Studies in Physics. Boston: Ginn and Company, 1941. Pp. vi+272.

Davis, Ira C., and Holley, Clifford. Physics Guide and Lab Activities. Chicago: Lyons and Carnahan, 1944. Pp. vii+310.

Dull, Charles E. Laboratory Exercises in Physics, Revised. New York: Henry Holt and Company, 1940. Pp. vii+208.

Dull, Charles E. Physics Workbook, Revised. New York: Henry Holt and Company, Inc., 1940. Pp. ix+274.

Fletcher, Gustav L., and Lehman, Sidney.
Laboratory Manual for Unified Physics.
New York: McGraw-Hill Book Company,
Inc., 1938. Pp. xiii+204.

Fuller, Robert W., Brownlee, Raymond B.,
and Baker, D. Lee. New Laboratory
Experiments in Physics. Boston: Allyn
and Bacon, 1945. Pp. xii+295.

Gail, Harry R. Physics Workbook and Laboratory Guide. Boston: Ginn and Company,
1944. Pp. v+382.

Henderson, W. D. Physics Guide and Laboratory
Exercises. Chicago: Lyons and Carnahan,
1945. Pp. xxii+255.

Tuleen, Lawrence F. and Porter, George S.
Prepare Yourself! Chicago: Scott, Foresman
and Company, 1943. Pp. vi+298.

Turner, Hallie F. Your Experiment Guide in
Physics. New York: College Entrance Book
Company, Inc., 1940. Pp. viii+142.

Turner, Hallie F. Discovery Problems in Physics.
New York: College Entrance Book Company,
Inc., 1944. Pp. vi+344.

White, Ernest H. and Wilson, John C. Directed
Experiments in Physics. New York: College
Entrance Book Company, Inc., 1942. Pp.
viii+116.

The 17 chemistry laboratory manuals were:

Ahrens, Maurice R., Bush, Norris F., and Easley,
Ray K. Laboratory Problems for Living Chem-
istry. Boston: Ginn and Company, 1942.
Pp. vii+239.

Ames, Maurice U., and Jaffee, Bernard. Laboratory and Workbook Units in Chemistry. New
York: Silver Burdett Company, 1940. Pp
xx+267.

Baisch, Carl W., Gladieux, Rolland J., and Goodrich, Russell V. Directed Activities in Chemistry. New York: Oxford Book Company, 1939. Pp. xiv+296.

Biddle, Harry C., Bush, George L. and Connor, William L. Laboratory Manual for Dynamic Chemistry. New York: Rand McNally and Company, 1936. Pp. x+250.

Black, Newton Henry. New Laboratory Experiments in Practical Chemistry. New York: The Macmillan Company, 1936. Pp. ix+181.

Brauer, Oscar L. Exploring the Wonders of Chemistry, A Workbook and Laboratory Guide. New York: American Book Company, 1938. Pp. ix+224.

Brownlee, Raymond B., Fuller, Robert W., Hancock, William J., Sohon, Michael D., and Whitsit, Jesse E. New Laboratory Experiments in Chemistry. Boston: Allyn and Bacon, 1943. Pp. xi+353.

Carpenter, Floyd F., and Carleton, Robert H. Comprehensive Units in Chemistry. Chicago: J. B. Lippincott Company, 1942. Pp. xvi+416.

Dull, Charles E. Laboratory Exercises in Chemistry, Revised. New York: Henry Holt and Company, Inc., 1943. Pp. ix+203.

Eckert, Theodore E., Lyons, Harley K., and Strevell, Wallace H. Discovery Problems In Chemistry. New York: College Entrance Book Company, Inc., 1942. Pp. viii+344.

Horton, Ralph E. Laboratory Manual in Chemistry. Boston: D. C. Heath and Company, 1937. Pp. xi+96.

Jones, Byron J., Mathias, Louis J., and Weiser, Raymond S. Workbook and Laboratory Manual in Chemistry. New York: College Entrance Book Company, Inc., 1937. Pp. viii+290.

Kruh, Frank O., Carleton, Robert H., and Carpenter, Floyd F. Experiments in Modern-Life Chemistry. Chicago: J. B. Lippincott Company, 1937. Pp. viii+224.

McGill, Martin V., and Bradbury, G. M. New
Chemistry Guide and Laboratory Exercises.
Chicago: Lyons and Carnahan, 1944.
Pp. xxi+367.

McPherson, William, and Henderson, William
Edwards. Laboratory Units in Chemistry,
Boston: Ginn and Company, 1942. Pp. xii+
330.

Tuleen, Lawrence F., Muehl, Willard L., and
Porter, George S. Test It Yourself!
Chemistry Experiments with Consumer Appli-
cations. Chicago: Scott, Foresman and
Company, 1941. Pp. xii+294.

Wilson, Sherman R. Activity Notebook in
Chemistry and Physics for Consumers.
New York: Henry Holt and Company, Inc.,
1941. Pp. x+102.

The other laboratory manuals were in the fields of

Aeronautics

Civil Aeronautics Administration and American
Council on Education. Demonstrations and
Laboratory Experiences in the Science of
Aeronautics. New York: McGraw-Hill Book
Company, Inc., 1945. Pp. viii+153.

Consumer Science

Hausrath, Alfred H. Jr. and Harms, John H.
Let's Investigate! An Experimental Approach
to Consumer Science. New York: The
Macmillan Company, 1942. Pp. iv+154.

Earth Science

Fletcher, Gustav L. Laboratory Exercises in
Physiography. Boston: D. C. Heath and
Company, 1939. Pp. x+162.

Shearer, M. H. Laboratory Exercises in Physical
Geography. New York: McGraw-Hill Book
Company, Inc., 1941. Pp. viii+139.

Tarr, Ralph S. and von Engeln, O. D. A Laboratory Manual for Physical and Commercial Geography, Revised. New York: The Macmillan Company, 1941. Pp. x+230.

Physical Science

Eby, George S., Waugh, Charles L., and Welch, Herbert E. Laboratory Guide for the Physical Sciences. Boston: Ginn and Company, 1943. Pp. vii+160.

Method of Locating Possible Sources of Experiments Other Than Textbooks and Laboratory Manuals

The following reference sources were searched for possible sources of lists of physical-science experiments, exclusive of textbooks and laboratory manuals:

Bibliography of Research Studies in Education, 1926-1939, inclusive.

Doctoral Dissertations Accepted by American Universities, 1933-1945, inclusive.

The Education Index, 1929-1945, inclusive.

Readers' Guide to Periodical Literature, 1900-1945, inclusive.

Education Abstracts, 1936-1943, including the continuation of such service in The Phi Delta Kappan.

Cumulative Book Index, 1928-1945, inclusive, including the United States Catalogue of books in print January 1, 1928.

The following 6 sources of experiments were secured as a result of the searching of the reference sources:

Brown, H. Emmett. The Development of a Course
in the Physical Sciences for the Senior High
School of the Lincoln School of Teachers
College. New York: Bureau of Publications,
Teachers College, Columbia University, 1939,
Pp. ix+205.

Hitchcock, Richard C. Demonstration Experiments for Courses in Physics for General
Education. Unpublished Doctor's dissertation, New York University, 1939. Pp. 513.

Hyde, Jay. Vitalizing High School Physics.
Unpublished Master's thesis, University of
Arizona, 1939. Pp. iv+90.

Joseph, Alexander. A Source Book of Extra-
curricular Activities in Physical Science
for Senior High Schools. Unpublished
Doctor's dissertation, New York University,
1941. Pp. ii+229.

Ward, William T. Practical Laboratory Exercises
in Elementary Chemistry. Unpublished Master's
thesis, University of Alabama, 1938. Pp.
iii+130.

Wiser, James Eldred. Demonstrations in Colloid
Chemistry for High-School Students. Un-
published Master's thesis, George Peabody
College for Teachers, 1940. Pp. viii+158.

From all these possible sources of experiments the
final selections included 73, namely, twenty-four textbooks, 1 non-textbook, 43 laboratory manuals, 3 masters'
theses, and 2 doctors' dissertations.

Methods of Collecting, of Grouping,
and of Refining the Statements of
the Purposes of the Experiments

All statements of the purposes of experiments,
which were followed by directions for their performance,

were collected from these sources. Each of the 73
sources was carefully read page by page, and the
purpose of each experiment so located was written
as a question on a separate three-by-five white card.
The source of the experiment was also designated on
the card by author, title, and page. Whenever the
statement of the purpose of an experiment seemed un-
satisfactory for subsequent presentation to evaluators,
it was revised into question form.

In all, approximately twenty three hundred experiments were secured from these sources. As a means of
detecting and eliminating duplications the experiments
were assigned to different categories. Those for
physics were: mechanics, heat, sound, light, electricity, modern physics, astronomy, and meteorology. Those
for chemistry included acids, bases, salts, oxygen,
hydrogen, nitrogen, sulfur, and metals. All geology
experiments were grouped together and not assigned
to categories.

When the duplicate experiments had been eliminated, it was found that closely related experiments
could be combined by restating the purpose. For example, the following multiple purpose represents a
consolidation of five experiments previously carded
separately from different sources:

111

Can heat energy be produced by compression (using a bicycle pump)? By friction (rubbing hands)? By electricity (connecting two terminals of a dry cell with a small copper wire)? By a chemical change (pouring sulfuric acid on sugar)? By light (passing light through glass to a piece of metal painted black)?

As a means of facilitating the subsequent assignment of experiments to principles, every experiment which was found only in a physics source was written on a yellow card; every one found only in a chemistry source was written on a salmon card. All other experiments were written on blue cards. In all cases in which the experiments had been derived from sources other than physics and chemistry and/or from more than one source (as chemistry and physics or chemistry and geology), the source or sources were recorded on the card.

The number of blue cards was deemed insufficient to justify a special analysis of the experiments thus recorded on them.

Index of Reliability of the Analysis to Secure the Experiments

A possible source of variability, inherent in the technique employed, existed in the selection of experiments from textbooks. It was reasonable to assume that there was negligible, or no, variability in the selection of experiments from the laboratory manuals, theses, and dissertations, because the experiments in them were clearly indicated. The experiments in the textbooks, however, were not so clearly indicated. Only those in the textbooks, therefore, were used in computing an "index of reliability" of the analysis of the sources in order to secure the experiments.

The "index of reliability" of the analysis to secure the experiments was arbitrarily defined as the quotient obtained by dividing the total number of experiments common to the two lists secured from the two analyses of the same source materials by the total number of different experiments obtained from the two analyses.

One-hundred pages selected at random from 2 textbooks, 1 of physics and 1 of chemistry, were reanalyzed six months after the first analysis of them. It seems reasonable to assume that any practice effect would be negligible after six months. No materials of this nature, moreover, were analyzed during these six months. The definition and the technique here used were modified from those used by Wise.[2]

TABLE II presents the "index of reliability" of the analysis to secure the experiments.

_____

[2]Harold E. Wise, A Determination of the Relative Importance of Principles of Physical Science for General Education, pp. 69-70. Unpublished Doctor's dissertation, University of Michigan, 1941.

TABLE II

INDEX OF RELIABILITY OF THE ANALYSIS TO SECURE THE EXPERIMENTS

Number of Pages Selected at Random From Textbooks	A Number of Experiments Common to the Two Lists	B Number of Experiments Found in First Analysis That Were Not Found in Second	C Number of Experiments Found in Second Analysis That Were Not Found in First	D Total Number of Different Experiments Obtained (A + B + C)	E Index of Reliability of the Analysis A/D
100	58	1	1	60	0.97

Validity of the Analysis
to Secure the Experiments

Fifty experiments, representing together those
found in the different types of the sources analyzed,
were selected at random. The purpose of each of the
50 and the source, or sources, from which each was
taken or derived were written on individual white
cards. The purpose was written in the form of a
question. A specialist in the teaching of science
then read for each experiment the purpose written on
the card,and also the directions for its performance
as they appeared in the original source, or sources.
He indicated for each on a check list that the question as stated on the card was or was not, in his
opinion, a correct statement of the purpose of the
experiment.

Fifty experiments were considered in this manner.
The specialist and the investigator were in agreement
on all 50. It, therefore, seemed reasonable to assume
that the validity of the analysis to secure the experiments was sufficiently high.

Method of Assigning Experiments to Principles

The second minor problem was to assign the assembled experiments to the various principles of physical
science. These experiments were assigned by the investigator, wherever possible, to the 214 principles

which had previously been given positive values by
all the judges, thus indicating their appropriateness
for inclusion in an integrated course of physical
science for senior high school. The criterion on the
basis of which each assignment was made was that the
performance of the experiment must be contributory to
the development of an understanding of the principle.

When an experiment was assigned to more than one
principle, duplicates of the original card for that
experiment were made and so assigned. The number of
each principle to which an experiment was assigned
was written across the top of each such card. The
number in the upper right corner of each card always
designated the principle to which that card and its
experiment was assigned.

Twenty-five hundred different assignments of
experiments to principles were thus made. Some experiments were assigned to as many as 16 principles.
Each of 163 experiments which the investigator was
unable to allocate to at least one principle ~~are~~ *is* found
in Appendix D, page 421.

Index of Reliability of the Assignments of the Experiments to the Principles

It seemed likely that there might be some variability in the assignments of the experiments to the

principles if the assignments were made again, especially at a considerably later time. It was, therefore,
deemed necessary to determine an "index of reliability"
for these assignments.

The "index of reliability" was arbitrarily defined as the quotient obtained by dividing the total
number of assignments common to the two lists resulting from twice assigning the same group of experiments
to the same principles, by the total number of different
assignments made in assigning the experiments twice.

An assistant made two white cards for each of 50
different experiments which he selected at random from
the twenty-five hundred assignments of experiments to
the 214 principles. He wrote on one of these cards
the purpose of an experiment, and, at the top, the
individual numbers of all principles to which that experiment had been assigned by the investigator; and on
the other only the purpose. After 9 months, during
which time the cards were not seen by the investigator,
the latter reassigned to the same 214 principles the
50 experiments on the cards which did not also have on
them the numbers of the principles to which they had
previously been assigned. The individual numbers of
the different principles to which an experiment was
assigned this second time were written across the
bottom of the card, so that the cards of each pair

would not subsequently be confused. The data on the two sets of cards showing the separate allocations for each of the 50 experiments were assembled into two lists for use in computing the index of reliability. During the last 6 months of the 9 between the 2 assignments, the investigator had had no practice in assigning, or in evaluating the assignment of, experiments to principles.

The determination of the validity of the assignments of the experiments to the principles is considered on page 125.

TABLE III presents the "index of reliability" of the assignments of the experiments to the principles.

TABLE III

INDEX OF RELIABILITY OF THE ASSIGNMENTS OF THE EXPERIMENTS TO THE PRINCIPLES

	A	B	C	D	E
	Number of Assignments Common to the Two Lists	Number of Assignments Made First Time That Were Not Made Second Time	Number of Assignments Made Second Time That Were Not Made First Time	Total Number of Different Assignments Made (A + B + C)	Index of Reliability of the Assignments of the Experiments A/D
Number of Experiments Selected at Random					
50	134	2	8	144	0.93

Evaluation of the Experiments

It was assumed that the degree to which the performance of the different experiments might reasonably be expected to be contributory to the development of an understanding of a principle, is an acceptable basis for determining the relative values of those experiments for inclusion in the course. It was further assumed that the use of the judgments of specialists in the teaching of science to determine the relative values of the experiments, and to determine the appropriateness of an experiment for performance as a laboratory experiment or as a demonstration, is defensible.

The jury technique was employed for the evaluations. It was assumed that 4 would constitute an acceptable number of evaluators of the experiments. Three specialists in the teaching of science, in addition to the investigator, agreed to evaluate the experiments. All 4 specialists were well qualified in terms of their teaching experience and their subject-matter training.

A copy of the investigator's list of 214 principles, together with the experiments assigned to each of them, was submitted to each evaluator with the following explanations and instructions:

I need the help of several "experts," --
specialists in the teaching of science, to
assist me in the evaluation of experiments
for inclusion in an integrated course of
physical science for senior high school.
May I have your assistance?

Submitted with this letter are 214
principles of physical science which were
deemed by 5 specialists in the teaching of
science to have some positive value for
inclusion in such a course. A subject-
matter specialist in each of the fields of
physics, chemistry, and geology has approved the principles in his respective field,
for accuracy of statement. No attempt has
been made to express the principles in a
vocabulary suitable for use at the high-
school level.

You will find assigned to most of the
214 principles one or more experiments
which were included in textbooks and laboratory manuals intended for use in courses
of physical science offered in senior-high
schools. These courses have commonly been
called physics, chemistry, physical science,
earth science or physiography or physical
geography, consumer science, senior science,
or aeronautics. A few of the experiments
came from unpublished Masters' theses and
Doctors' dissertations which contained
lists of experiments for use in the physical sciences at the senior-high-school
level. An experiment was assigned to a
principle whenever, in the opinion of the
investigator, the performance of the experiment might reasonably be expected to
be contributory to the development of an
understanding of the principle.

The following letters and figures are
to the right of each experiment:
N D L 1 2 3 4 5. Will you kindly mark each
experiment according to the following
directions:

"Please encircle the appropriate symbol to the right of each experiment to indicate, respectively, whether you consider that the performance of the experiment

> N -- would <u>not</u> be contributory to the development of an understanding of the principle to which it is assigned;

> D -- would be contributory and would more appropriately be done as a <u>demonstration</u> experiment than as a laboratory experiment; or

> L -- would be contributory and would more appropriately be done as a <u>laboratory</u> experiment than as a demonstration experiment.

"If you consider the experiment to be equally appropriate for demonstration and laboratory purposes please encircle both the D and the L.

"The experiment should be marked as being more appropriately done as a demonstration (D) than as a laboratory experiment, if

> 1. The experiment involves an element of danger when performed unskilfully.

> 2. The experiment involves very difficult and detailed manipulation.

> 3. The experiment requires too much time for its successful performance by pupils in terms of the values they might reasonably be expected to gain from doing the experiment.

4. The experiment involves very
   expensive apparatus and equipment.

5. The experiment is designed to
   acquaint the pupils with the
   apparatus and with acceptable
   techniques of experimentation.

"Also, please encircle the appropriate symbol to the right of each experiment to indicate, respectively,
whether you consider that the experiment

1 -- Is not at all suited for in-
     clusion in an integrated course
     of physical science for senior
     high school; and for the develop-
     ment of an understanding of the
     principle;
2 -- Is poorly suited;
3 -- Is neither well nor poorly
     suited;
4 -- Is well suited; or
5 -- Is ideally suited for inclusion
     in such a course and for the
     development of an understanding
     of the principle.

The criteria which delimit the purpose of
the physical-science course and which therefore
are to serve as bases for the judgments to be
made by you on the scale of 1-5 are:

The integrated course of physical
science for senior high school

(1) is planned to serve not only
    as a college-preparatory course
    but also as a terminal course
    for those capable of profiting
    by such a course; and

(2) is intended to accomplish for
    physical science the same
    purposes that are now served
    by a high-school course in
    general biology.

Additional criteria which are also to
serve as bases for the judgments to be made
by you on the scale of 1-5 are:

The experiment

(1) must be simple enough for ready
comprehension; and

(2) must be practicable within the
time which is commonly available.

"If you do not encircle the N or the 1,
please encircle the D or the L, or both the
D and the L, and then a 2, 3, 4, or 5."

The following are examples of the different
types of marking which may be made in accordance
with the directions given:

Principle

No chemical change occurs without
an accompanying energy change.

Experiments

1. Does the cylinder of a
bicycle pump become hotter
or cooler as air is pumped
into a tire? ....Ⓝ D L 1 2 3 4 5

      The N was encircled because only phys-
ical changes occur during the performance
of the experiment; therefore, the experiment would not be contributory to the development of an understanding of the
chemical principle to which it was assigned.

2. Will gasoline vapor in a
tightly stoppered bottle
explode violently when mixed with air and ignited by
an electric spark?.........N D L Ⓛ 2 3 4 5

      The 1 was encircled because the experi-
ment was considered to be not at all suited
for inclusion in an integrated course of
physical science for senior high school.

3. Does burning thermite
produce much heat? .... N (D) L 1 2 3 (4) 5

The D was encircled because the experiment, which would be contributory to the
development of an understanding of the principle to which it was assigned, involves an
element of danger when performed unskilfully.
It would, therefore, more appropriately be
done as a demonstration than as a laboratory
experiment. The 4 was then encircled because the experiment was deemed to be well
suited for inclusion in the course, and for
the development of an understanding of the
principle.

4. Does magnesium ribbon burn
with an intense white flame?N D (L) 1 2 3 4 (5)

The L was encircled because the experiment was considered more appropriately done
as a laboratory experiment than as a demonstration. The 5 was then encircled because
the experiment was considered to be ideally
suited for inclusion in the course, and for
the development of an understanding of the
principle.

5. Does oxygen support combustion; that is, does wood
or sulfur burning in air
continue to burn in oxygen? N (D)(L) 1 2 3 4 (5)

Both the D and the L were encircled because the experiment was considered to be
equally appropriate for demonstration and
laboratory purposes. The 5 was then encircled because the experiment was considered to be ideally suited for inclusion in
the course, and for the development of an
understanding of the principle.

For the purposes of this evaluation, you are aske
to adopt the following definitions of terms:

1. The term "physical science" includes only
the fields of physics (including astronomy
and meteorology), chemistry, and geology.

2. An "integrated course of physical science"
is one in which subject matter from the
fields of physics (including astronomy
and meteorology), chemistry, and geology
is unified, and which is contributory to
the development of an understanding of
principles of physical science.

3. The term "senior high school" means grades 10, 11, and 12 of the secondary-school system.

After the list of experiments had been marked by the 4 evaluators and returned, the data were tabulated. Every experiment which had been marked by at least 2 of the 4 evaluators as being unsuited to the proposed course was placed in a separate list. Every experiment which had been marked by one or more of the evaluators as not being contributory to the development of an understanding of the principle to which the investigator had assigned it was moved to the same list. Duplications in this list were eliminated. The resulting final list contained, after the eliminations, 655 experiments which were deemed undesirable for inclusion in the course. These are presented in Appendix C, page 376.

Validity of the Assignments of the Experiments to the Principles

Since only 5 of the investigator's 2500 assignments of experiments to principles had been disapproved by one or more judges on the grounds that they did not contribute to an understanding of the principle to which they had been assigned, it seems justifiable to assume that the validity of the method by which these assignments had been made was sufficiently high.

TABLE IV presents the evaluations obtained.

TABLE IV

THE RELATIVE VALUES AND RANKS OF LABORATORY AND
DEMONSTRATION EXPERIMENTS ALLOCATED TO THE
PRINCIPLES OF PHYSICAL SCIENCE DESIRABLE
FOR INCLUSION IN AN INTEGRATED COURSE OF
PHYSICAL SCIENCE FOR SENIOR HIGH SCHOOL

Experiments Allocated to Principles	Value	Rank	
Principles Deemed Essential by All Evaluators			
1. Energy can never be created or destroyed; it can be changed from one form to another only with exact equivalence.			
Experiments			
Can heat energy be produced by compression (using a bicycle pump)? By friction (rubbing hands)? By electricity (connecting two terminals of a dry cell with a small copper wire)? By a chemical change (pouring sulfuric acid on sugar)? By light (passing light through glass to a piece of metal painted black)?........	20*	1.5	L*
What kinds of energy changes occur when a storage battery, an electric fan, an electric heater, and an electric lamp are connected to a source of current?...	20	1.5	D
How does a cutaway model of a reciprocating steam engine operate "to convert heat energy into mechanical energy?"..............................	18	3	D

*The numerical values assigned to the experiments are the algebraic sums of the individual evaluations of the four judges on the scale of 1-5.

**The symbol L or D following a rank indicates, respectively, that the experiment was considered by the four evaluators as being more appropriately performed as a laboratory experiment or as a demonstration. X indicates equal appropriateness for either method.

TABLE IV (CONTINUED)   127

Experiments Allocated to Principles	Value	Rank	
How does a toy steam turbine convert heat energy into mechanical energy?.....	17	4	D
Does fuse wire or a narrow piece of tin foil connecting the two wires at one end of an extension cord melt when the other end is connected to an 110-volt A.C. circuit?.........................	16	5	D

2. A gas always tends to expand throughout the whole space available.

Experiments

If a gas jet is barely open, can the odor of gas soon be detected at a considerable distance from the jet?........	18	1.5	D
If a bottle of ammonia water is opened in a room, can the odor soon be detected at a considerable distance from the bottle?............................	18	1.5	D
Does hydrogen diffuse readily from an upper bottle of hydrogen to a lower bottle of air placed mouth to mouth?....	16	3	D

3. When there is a gain in mechanical advantage by using a simple machine, there is a loss in speed and vice versa.

Experiments

What is the actual mechanical advantage of a single fixed pulley? A single movable pulley? A system of pulleys using various combinations of fixed and movable pulleys? What relation exists between the actual mechanical advantage and the number of strands supporting the load? Is effort gained at the expense of speed or vice versa?........................	19	1	X
What is the actual and theoretical mechanical advantage and the efficiency of a commercial block and tackle? Is effort gained at the expense of speed or vice versa?........................	18	2.5	D

TABLE IV (CONTINUED)   128

Experiments Allocated to Principles	Value	Rank
What is the actual and theoretical mechanical advantage and the efficiency of a wheel and axle? Does the effort times the effort arm equal the resistance times the resistance arm? How does the ratio of the resistance to the effort compare with the ratio of the radius of the wheel to the radius of the axle? Is effort gained at the expense of speed or vice versa when the force is applied to the wheel? To the axle as in a belt system?.................	18	2.5 D
What is the actual and theoretical mechanical advantage and the efficiency of a commercial jackscrew? Is effort gained at the expense of speed or vice versa?.................................	17	4.5 D
Is the mechanical advantage of a first-, second-, and third-class lever, respectively, less than one, one, or more than one?.........................	17	4.5 D

4. In the lever the force times its distance from the fulcrum equals the weight times its distance from the fulcrum.

Experiments

	Value	Rank
In a balanced weighted uniform lever (first class) is the sum of the products of each effort and its distance from the fulcrum equal to the sum of the products of each resistance and its distance from the fulcrum, that is, when a uniform lever is in equilibrium, how does the sum of the clockwise moments compare with the sum of the counterclockwise moments?	20	1 L
If a uniform lever balanced at its midpoint is rebalanced with two unequal weights on opposite sides of the point of support (fulcrum), what is the relation between the weights applied to the lever and their distances from the fulcrum? If one of the weights is called the effort and the other the resistance, what is the mechanical advantage of the lever?..........................	19	2 L

TABLE IV (CONTINUED)

129

Experiments Allocated to Principles	Value	Rank	
What are the two necessary and sufficient conditions which must always exist in order to have parallel forces in the same plane in equilibrum? If a horizontal uniform meter stick with one or more weights attached is supported near each end by a spring balance, how do the total upward forces compare with the total downward forces? How does the sum of the clockwise moments compare with the sum of the counterclockwise moments about any point of reference on the stick or in space at either end of it?..............	16	3	D

5. The work obtained from a simple machine is always equal to the work put into it less the work expended in overcoming friction.

Experiments

	Value	Rank	
In a system of pulleys, how does the work done on the resistance compare with the work done by the effort?............	18	1	L
What is the actual and theoretical mechanical advantage and the efficiency of an inclined plane at a given angle of inclination? What effect does changing the angle of inclination have upon these? How does the work done in rolling a loaded car up an inclined plane compare with that done in lifting it through the same vertical distance?.....................	17	2	L

6. Sound is produced by vibrating matter and is transmitted by matter.

Experiments
When sound is produced, must something be vibrating? What is observed when the tines of a tuning fork are struck and touched to the surface of water? Touched

TABLE IV (CONTINUED)   130

Experiments Allocated to Principles	Value	Rank
lightly to an ear or finger? Brought near a suspended pith ball? What is observed when the free end of a yard stick clamped to a desk is pulled and let go? When a tight string on a musical instrument is plucked? When fingers are held on the throat while the alphabet is pronounced?	20	1 L
How is a soap film (ear drum) over the smaller end of a megaphone affected when the tone a-a-a-h is sounded in the larger end (outer ear)?......................	17	2 D

7. Solids are liquefied and liquids are vaporized by heat; the amount of heat used in this process, for a given mass and a given substance, is specific and equals that given off in the reverse process.

Experiments

	Value	Rank
What is the heat of fusion of ice; that is, how many calories of heat are needed to change one gram of ice at zero degrees Centigrade to water at the same temperature as determined by the "method of mixtures?"..........................	20	1 L
What is the heat of condensation of steam (or heat of vaporization of water); that is, how many calories of heat are given out by one gram of steam when it condenses to water at the same temperature as determined by the "method of mixtures?"............................	18	2.5 L
If a thermometer is placed in a test tube of water in a mixture of cracked ice and salt, does the temperature (thermometer reading) rise, fall, or remain the same until ice begins to form? While ice is being formed? After all water has changed to ice? If the mixture of ice and salt is removed and the thermometer is read while the ice is melting, is the melting point of ice the same temperature as the freezing point of water?......................	18	2.5 X

TABLE IV (<u>CONTINUED</u>)   131

Experiments Allocated to Principles	Value	Rank
How is ice made in a commercial plant (a field trip)?..........................	16	5.5 D
Can a liquid be separated from a solution by distillation and condensation? If common salt is dissolved in water can the water be obtained from the solution by heating the solution in a flask and condensing the vapors with a Liebig condenser or by passing the vapors into a test tube set in ice?..................	16	5.5 D
When water is at its boiling temperature, does adding more heat increase its temperature?...........................	16	5.5 L
After absorbent cotton wound on the bulb of a thermometer is removed from liquid ether, does the temperature (thermometer reading) rise, fall, or remain the same?......................	16	5.5 D

8. Most bodies expand on heating and contract on cooling, the amount of change depending upon the change in temperature.

Experiments

	Value	Rank
Does a solid body expand or contract, when it is heated? When it is cooled? Will a ball which barely passes through a ring at room temperature also pass through after the ball is heated? After the ring is heated? After the ring is cooled?................................	20	1 D
Does a solid body expand or contract when it is heated? When it is cooled? If a weight suspended at the end of a vertical iron wire barely clears a base when swung as a pendulum, does the weight still clear the base after a Bunsen flame is moved up and down the wire several times? After the wire cools?................................	19	4 D

TABLE IV (<u>CONTINUED</u>)   132

Experiments Allocated to Principles	Value	Rank	
Does a body of liquid expand or contract when it is heated? When it is cooled? If colored water fills a flask and is part way up in a glass tube inserted in the stopper to the flask, does the level of water in the tube rise or fall as the flask is heated? As the flask is cooled?......................	19	4	D
If water projects upward into a narrow glass tube from a glass bulb set in cracked ice, does the water have the least volume at zero, three, or twenty degrees Centigrade?....................	19	4	D
Does a body of air expand or contract when it is heated? If the open end of a deflated balloon is placed over the only outlet to a flask of air, does the balloon become inflated when the flask of air is heated?.....................	19	4	D
If a Charles' law tube (air enclosed in the closed end of an open tube of uniform bore by a globule of mercury) is placed in cracked ice and then in steam, what is the relation between the volume and the absolute temperature of the enclosed gas under constant (atmospheric) pressure?.................	19	4	D
Does a solid body expand or contract when it is heated? When it is cooled? If a nail is stuck through a pointer made of cardboard and a metal rod with one end fastened securely has its other end across the nail which is free to be rolled, does the pointer move through an arc to indicate that the rod expands (or contracts) when heated along its length with a Bunsen flame? When cooled?................................	17	9	D
Does a body of air expand or contract when it is heated? When it is cooled? If an inflated balloon is adjusted between two rings on a stand so that the balloon just touches the rings, does the balloon expand or contract when hot water is poured over it? When cold water is poured over it?	17	9	D

TABLE IV (CONTINUED)

Experiments Allocated to Principles	Value	Rank	
Does a body of air expand or contract when it is heated? If two balloons inflated with air are the same size, does one held over an electric hot plate increase or decrease more in size than one not held over the plate?.....................	17	9	D
Does the air in a flask expand or contract when heated? When cooled? If an inverted flask of air with a glass tube through the stopper dips into water, does the water inside the tube move down to indicate expansion of the air or up to indicate contraction of the air when a warm hand is held on the flask? When a cloth wet with cold water is placed on the flask?.....................	17	9	D
Does a body of air expand or contract when it is heated? When it is cooled? Is there more or less than a flaskful of air after an inverted flask, fitted with a delivery tube which extends through a vessel of water into an inverted drinking glass entirely full of water is heated with a Bunsen flame? After the air in the flask is cooled?...................	17	9	D
Does a straight compound bar of brass and iron become convex on the brass side or the iron side when heated; that is, do two different metals expand at different rates when heated?.....................	16	12.5	D
After molten paraffin in a beaker has solidified, is the center of the top surface of the paraffin raised, level, or depressed; that is, does paraffin contract or expand on solidification?.......	16	12.5	D

9. Heat is liberated when a gas is compressed, and is absorbed when a gas expands.

Experiments

Does the cylinder of a bicycle pump become hotter or cooler as air is pumped into a tire or inner tube?..............	20	1.5	X

TABLE IV (CONTINUED)

134

Experiments Allocated to Principles	Value	Rank	
After the valve in an inflated inner tube is opened, does the tube feel warmer or cooler?.....................................	20	1.5	X
How is ice made in a commercial plant (a field trip)?.....................................	16	1.5	D
10. The atmospheric pressure decreases as the altitude increases.			
Experiment			
Does the barometer reading (atmospheric pressure) increase, decrease, or remain the same when it is taken from the first floor or basement to the third floor of a building?.....................	19	1	D
11. The higher the temperature of the air, the greater is the amount of moisture required to saturate it.			
Experiments			
What is the relative humidity of the air in the classroom as determined by the use of tables for the thermometer readings taken from a sling psychrometer or a stationary wet and dry-bulb thermometer?...........................	20	1	D
What is the dew point for the air in the classroom; that is, at what average temperature does moisture first appear on and disappear from the outside of a drinking glass (or polished metal cup) after ice (and later warm water) is added to water in the cup?...........	17	2	L
Does fog produced in a flask (lowland) disappear quickly if exposed to radiant energy (sunlight or a Bunsen flame)?.....................................	16	3	D

TABLE IV (CONTINUED)   135

Experiments Allocated to Principles	Value	Rank
12. Bodies of land heat up and cool off more rapidly than bodies of water.		
Experiments If a test tube half full with dry dirt and another half full with water are placed in a test tube rack after remaining in boiling water for five minutes, which tube remains warm much longer than the other; that is, which will cool off first after the sun sets, the land or the water along a shore?....	20	1.5 L
Does water or earth absorb heat more readily? If the same volumes of water and earth are heated for five minutes over similar Bunsen flames, does the water or the earth feel warmer to the hands?.....................................	20	1.5 L
13. The principal cause of wind and weather changes is the unequal heating of different portions of the earth's surface by the sun; thus all winds are convection currents caused by unequal heating of different portions of the earth's atmosphere, and they blow from places of higher atmospheric pressure to places of lower atmospheric pressure.		
14. If a beam of light falls upon an irregular surface, the rays of light are scattered in all directions.		
15. Dark, rough or unpolished surfaces absorb or radiate energy more effectively than light, smooth or polished surfaces.		

TABLE IV (CONTINUED)   136

Experiments Allocated to Principles	Value	Rank	
Experiments			
If two thermometer bulbs, one wrapped in black cloth and the other in white cloth, are held in bright white light, which thermometer registers the greater rise in temperature?............	19	1	L
Does a black dull surface lose (radiate) heat more quickly than a light smooth surface, or _vice versa_? If equal amounts of boiling water fill a light smooth tin can and a similar black dull can, is the fall in the temperature greater for a thermometer in the black dull can than for one in the light smooth can, or _vice versa_?..............	18	2	D
Is radiant energy (heat and light) absorbed more rapidly by a dark surface or by a similar surface of lighter color? Does snow (or finely cracked ice) melt more rapidly under a piece of black metal (or cloth) exposed to sunlight (or a Bunsen flame) than under a similar piece of metal (or cloth) of lighter color, or _vice versa_?..........	16	3.5	D
Is radiant energy (heat and light) absorbed more rapidly by a dark dull surface or a light smooth surface? If a Bunsen flame is placed equidistant between two closed tin cans, one with a black dull surface and the other with a light smooth surface and both containing equal amounts of water at the same low temperature, does the thermometer in the black dull can or the one in the light smooth can show the greater increase in temperature?...........................	16	3.5	D
16. The colors of objects depend upon the wave lengths of the light rays they transmit, absorb or reflect.			

TABLE IV (CONTINUED)   137

Experiments Allocated to Principles	Value	Rank	
Experiments On what does the color of an opaque object depend? What color does white, red, and blue cloth, respectively, appear to be when held separately in white, red, and blue light?............	18	2	X
On what does the color of transparent objects depend? Does a piece of transparent red glass (also green) transmit or absorb to a high degree white light? Red light? Green light?	18	2	X
If red, blue, and green pieces of transparent glass are held separately between the eye and sunlight, what color is transmitted by each piece of glass? If blue and green glass is held in front of the red glass, what color is transmitted?..................	18	2	L
17. Light travels in straight lines in a medium of uniform optical density.			
Experiment Does light travel in straight lines through air? If a ball is placed against a cardboard in front of a small bright source of light, is the shortest line drawn from the edge of the shadow to the source of light curved or straight?..............................	17	1	L
18. Waves travel in straight lines while passing through a homogeneous or uniform medium.			
19. When light is reflected, the angle of incidence is equal to the angle of reflection.			
Experiment How does the angle of incidence compare with the angle of reflection using a plane mirror, pins and a ruler?	20	1	L

TABLE IV (CONTINUED)   138

Experiments Allocated to Principles	Value	Rank
20. Like electrical charges repel and unlike electrical charges attract.		
Experiments		
Is a positively charged pith ball or piece of cork (slightly moistened or painted with aluminum and suspended on silk) attracted or repelled on approach of a glass rod stroked with silk? Of a hard rubber rod stroked with fur?.......	20	2.5 D
Can different kinds of electric charges be produced by rubbing silk on glass and fur (or woolen cloth) on hard rubber (or sealing wax); that is, if the leaves of an electroscope stand apart when the knob of the electroscope is touched with glass rubbed with silk, do they collapse when the knob is touched with hard rubber rubbed with fur?.......	20	2.5 D
Do two pith balls with the same kind of charge move farther apart or toward each other when a rod with a similar charge (also with a different kind of charge) is placed between them?.........	20	2.5 D
Is a charged rod free to move horizontally attracted or repelled on approach of a rod with the same kind of charge? With the opposite kind of charge?...................................	20	2.5 D
Can pith dolls (or balls) be made to "dance" between two parallel metal plates connected to a static machine?..........	19	5. D
Does a hard-rubber comb pick up small pieces of paper before and after the comb is pulled rapidly through dry hair?...................................	18	6.5 D
Does a piece of paper "stick" to a wall before and after the paper is rubbed vigorously with the side of a pencil?...................................	18	6.5 X

TABLE IV (CONTINUED)

Experiments Allocated to Principles	Value	Rank	
Do two inflated rubber balloons suspended almost side-by-side attract or repel each other when they are given the same kind of charge by rubbing them with flannel? When they are given different kinds of charges by rubbing one balloon with flannel and the other one with sulfur?......................	17	8.5	D
Can an electroscope carrying a known charge be used to detect the kind of charge on another body?.............	17	8.5	D
Do the paper strands of an electric plume stand apart when connected to one terminal of a static machine or do the threads of a tassel of embroidery silk stand apart before and after being stroked with rubber?.................	16	12	D
Can an electroscope be charged negatively if a charged glass rod is held near the knob, the knob is touched with a finger, and the finger is removed before the rod is removed?.............	16	12	D
Can the top plate of an electrophorus be charged by induction; that is, if the lower plate of an electrophorus is rubbed with fur, the top plate is set on the lower plate and grounded with a finger, and the finger and then the top plate are removed, can a spark be drawn from the top plate by placing a finger near it or are the leaves of an electroscope moved apart when the plate is touched to the knob?.................	16	12	D
If a suspended uncharged pith ball is grounded with the finger while a charged rubber rod is under, but not touching the ball, is the pith ball more or less strongly attracted by the rod than before touching the ball with the finger? Does a charged glass rod attract or repel the pith ball; that is, when a negatively charged object is used to charge a body by induction, what charge results in the body?.................	16	12	D

TABLE IV (CONTINUED)

Experiments Allocated to Principles	Value	Rank	
Does a large tack (lightning rod) set on top of a low tin can (house) between two parallel metal plates (cloud and earth) connected to a static machine prevent an electric discharge from the upper plate directly to the can?	16	12	D

21. A magnet always has at least two poles and is surrounded by a field of force.

Experiments

	Value	Rank	
Is a steel knitting needle magnetized (given polarity) by stroking it in one direction with one end of a bar magnet?..................................	20	2	L
Which parts of a bar (or U-shaped magnet) have the greatest concentration of magnetic lines of force and therefore pick up the greatest number of nails?...	20	2	L
What is the shape of the magnetic field surrounding an isolated bar (or U-shaped) magnet, as determined by shaking iron filings across a cardboard over a horizontal magnet and tapping the cardboard?......................	20	2	L
What is the shape of the magnetic field surrounding an isolated bar (or U-shaped) magnet, as determined by shaking iron filings across blueprint paper over a horizontal magnet and exposing the paper to light in a partly darkened room?...............................	17	4	D

22. Like magnetic poles always repel each other and unlike magnetic poles always attract each other.

Experiments

	Value	Rank	
If a pole of a bar magnet is brought near a pole of a second magnet which is free to move horizontally, does the same kind (and opposite kinds) of magnetic poles attract or repel each other?......	20	1	X

TABLE IV (CONTINUED)

141

Experiments Allocated to Principles	Value	Rank
Are iron filings on the ends of two separate bar (or U-shaped) magnets attracted or repelled as the same kind (and opposite kinds) of magnetic poles is brought near each other?..............	19	2.5 D
If the north pole of a horizontal bar magnet beneath a pan of water is placed under a north pole of a Mayer's floating magnet (a magnetized needle thrust vertically through a cork), what path is taken by the floating magnet?...	19	2.5 X
What is the inclination (angle between the horizontal and the direction in which a compass needle, free to move vertically, actually points) at this locality?.................................	18	4 D
How is a simple electric motor constructed and made to run?..............	17	5 L
Can a rod of soft iron be magnetized if held pointed toward the south-magnetic pole (down from the north-geographic pole) and tapped repeatedly on the end? Can the polarity of a soft iron rod be reversed by similar tapping when its south pole is pointed toward the south-magnetic pole? Does a magnetized rod of soft iron lose nearly all of its magnetism when held in an east-west line and tapped repeatedly?	16	6.5 D
If a flat stationary coil of wire is placed parallel to a similar lightweight coil suspended from a high point and free to move, is the suspended coil attracted or repelled by the stationary coil when direct current in the latter is started? Stopped? Is the direction of the current induced in the movable coil always such as to produce a polarity for the movable coil which will oppose the building up and dying out of the magnetic field of the stationary coil; that is, whenever a change is made in an electromagnetic system is there always brought into existence something which opposes that change (Lenz's law)?....................	16	6.5 D

TABLE IV (CONTINUED)

Experiments Allocated to Principles	Value	Rank	
23. Pieces of iron, steel, cobalt or nickel may become magnetized by induction when placed within a magnetic field.			
Experiments			
Can iron or steel be made a magnet by induction; that is, by merely bringing it near a magnet? Does the point of a large nail hold smaller nails before and after one pole of a strong bar magnet is brought near the head of the large nail? After the bar magnet is withdrawn?............	20	1.5	L
Is the polarity of the ends of a nail held near one end of a bar magnet reversed when the magnet is reversed?.....	20	1.5	L
Can a piece of magnetic material (iron rod) be magnetized by passing an electric current through a coil of insulated wire around the material?.......	19	3	X
Which of the following materials are strongly attracted by a magnet: glass, wood, paper, iron, copper, zinc, aluminum?................................	17	5	L
Which of the following materials do magnetic lines of force pass through; that is, does a magnet attract iron filings through thin sheets of rubber, glass, paper, wood, copper, lead, zinc, aluminum or iron?......................	17	5	L
Can a rod of soft iron be magnetized if held pointed toward the south-magnetic pole (down from the north-geographic pole) and tapped repeatedly on the end? Can the polarity of a soft iron rod be reversed by similar tapping when its south pole is pointed toward the south-magnetic pole? Does a magnetized rod of soft iron lose nearly all of its magnetism when held in an east-west line and tapped repeatedly?.............	17	5	D

TABLE IV (CONTINUED)   143

Experiments Allocated to Principles	Value	Rank	
24. An electric current may be produced in three ways: by rubbing or friction, chemical action, and using a magnetic field.			
Experiments			
Is an electric current produced in a closed circuit when two dissimilar elements are immersed in an electrolyte? Does a galvanometer register current when connected to an iron nail and a copper wire sticking in a lemon? To a penny and a dime separated by a piece of blotting paper which has been dipped in salt water?..........................	20	2	X
Is current induced in a copper wire moved rapidly down or up between the poles of a U-shaped magnet?............	20	2	L
Is an electromotive force (e.m.f.) induced in a coil of wire (as indicated by a current through a galvanometer in series with the coil) when a magnet is thrust into or rapidly withdrawn from the coil, that is, when magnetic lines of force (flux) cut a wire in a closed circuit?...........................	20	2	L
Does a small electric bell ring when its two terminals are connected to the zinc (amalgamated) and copper (or carbon) electrodes, respectively, of a Voltaic cell containing dilute sulfuric acid as the electrolyte? Does the bell ring when the two electrodes are the same element?.....................	19	4.5	L
If a armature of a St. Louis-type motor-generator is connected in series with a galvanometer, how is the current output affected by slow and rapid rotation of the armature?..............	19	4.5	L

TABLE IV (CONTINUED)

Experiments Allocated to Principles	Value	Rank
25. An electric current will flow in the external circuit when two metals of unlike chemical activity are acted upon by a conducting solution, the more active metal being charged negatively.		
Experiments Is an electric current produced in a closed circuit when two dissimilar elements are immersed in an electrolyte? Does a galvanometer register current when connected to an iron nail and a copper wire sticking in a lemon? To a penny and a dime separated by a piece of blotting paper which has been dipped in salt water?.................................	20	1.5 L
Does a small electric bell ring when its two terminals are connected to the zinc (amalgamated) and copper (or carbon) electrodes, respectively, of a Voltaic cell containing dilute sulfuric acid as the electrolyte? Does the bell ring when the two electrodes are the same element?...............................	20	1.5 L
Which of the following combinations of electrodes in a Voltaic cell with sulfuric acid as the electrolyte produces the greatest voltage; copper-zinc, copper-carbon, aluminum-zinc, aluminum-lead, copper-lead?.............	18	3 L
26. An electromotive force is induced in a circuit whenever there is a change in the number of the lines of magnetic force passing through the circuit.		
Experiments Is an electromotive force (e.m.f.) induced in a coil of wire (as indicated by a current through a galvanometer in series with the coil) when a magnet is thrust into or rapidly withdrawn from the coil, that is, when magnetic lines of force (flux) cut a wire in a closed circuit?.................................	20	2 L

TABLE IV (UNDERLINE: CONTINUED)

Experiments Allocated to Principles	Value	Rank	
Is current induced in a closed copper wire moved rapidly down or up between the poles of a U-shaped magnet?...	20	2	L
If a flat rectangular coil of insulated wire (no. 26), in series with a galvanometer (zero center), is rotated quickly past a straight line between the poles of a U-shaped magnet, is the galvanometer needle deflected? If the coil, rotated in the same direction, quickly passes between the poles again, is the needle deflected in the same or in the opposite direction (electric generator)?	20	2	D
When two coils of wire on separate closed circuits are placed side by side or one within the other, does current flow in one coil (the secondary) when current is started, stopped, varied or steady in the other coil (the primary), that is, when the number of magnetic lines of force (flux) passing through the secondary coil is changed or steady?	19	4.5	L
Is the amount of an induced electromotive force (as indicated by the deflection of a galvanometer) increased on increasing the strength of a varying magnetic field by using two magnets instead of one or by sending more current through the primary of two coils? On increasing the rate at which the magnetic lines of force (flux) cut a coil of wire by increasing the speed of motion of a magnet with respect to a closed coil, or vice versa, or by "making" and "breaking" a primary circuit? On increasing the number of turns of wire in a single coil or in the secondary of an induction coil or transformer?..........	19	4.5	X
If the armature of a St. Louis-type motor-generator is connected in series with a galvanometer, how is the current output affected by slow and rapid rotation of the armature?..............	16	6	X

TABLE IV (CONTINUED)

146

Experiments Allocated to Principles	Value	Rank
27. Elements are made up of small particles of matter called atoms which are alike in the same element (except for occasional differences in atomic weight; i.e., isotopes) but different in different elements.		
28. All substances are made up of small particles called molecules which are alike in the same substance (except for variations in molecular weight due to isotopes) but different in different substances.		
29. All matter is composed of single elements or combinations of several elements. Experiment Can hydrogen and oxygen be obtained by passing direct current through an acid solution of water in a Hoffman or similar apparatus? What gas bubbles "rise" from the anode? Cathode? What is the ratio of the volume of the gas collected at the cathode to that collected at the anode, that is, what is the composition of water by volume?.............................	17	1 D
30. Every pure sample of any substance, whether simple or compound, under the same conditions will show the same physical properties and the same chemical behavior. Experiments What are the distinguishing properties of the minerals which make up the common rocks, namely, the color, hardness, luster, cleavage and acid test for quartz, orthoclase, feldspar, biotite mica, hornblende, calcite, and kaolin, respectively?	18	1.5 L

TABLE IV (<u>CONTINUED</u>)

147

Experiments Allocated to Principles	Value	Rank
What are some distinguishing properties of some of the ores of common metals and some non-metallic minerals which are commercially important, namely, the color, luster, streak, crystal form, specific weight (specific gravity), hardness, attraction by magnet, and taste for hematite, magnetite, chalcopyrite, galena, sphalerite, halite (rock salt), gypsum, chrysolite (asbestos), sulfur, pyrite (fool's gold), and graphite, respectively?..................	18	1.5 L
How are some typical physical changes different from some typical chemical changes? Do the substances retain their original identifying properties or are new substances with different identifying properties formed when heat is applied to glass, wood, bright copper, and magnesium? When sulfuric acid is poured on sugar? When dry salt and salt solution are tasted? When a piece of blackboard chalk is broken and powdered? When iron nails are placed in nitric acid? When a magnet is passed over a mixture of iron filings and powdered sulfur before heating? After heating? When solutions of silver nitrate and sodium chloride are mixed? When a piece of Wood's metal is placed in boiling water?.................	17	3 L

31. The materials forming one or more substances, without ceasing to exist, may be changed into one or more new and measurably different substances.

Experiments
  Can oxygen be prepared by heating potassium chlorate with a catalyst, manganese dioxide, or by heating red mercuric oxide or by dripping water on sodium peroxide?......................

	Value	Rank
	19	1.5 L

TABLE IV (CONTINUED)

Experiments Allocated to Principles	Value	Rank	
Can hydrogen be prepared by displacement from an acid (sulfuric or hydrochloric) by a metal ("mossy"zinc)?......	19	1.5	L
Can a chemical change be produced by synthesis (heating iron and sulfur)? By decomposition (heating mercuric oxide)? By single replacement (hydrochloric acid on "mossy"zinc)? Double replacement (solutions of silver nitrate and sodium chloride)? By oxidation and reduction (heating sodium nitrate with lead)?.....	17	3	L
32. Oxidation always involves the removal or sharing of electrons from the element oxidized while the reduction always adds or shares with the element reduced.[1]			
33. Oxidation and reduction occur simultaneously and are quantitatively equal.[1]			
Experiments			
Do the oxidizing and reducing agents need to be in actual contact with the reacting substances or are oxidation and reduction caused only by a transfer of electrons?.............................	19	1	

[1]Since each experiment which contributes to an understanding of Principle number 32 would also contribute to an understanding of Principle number 33, and vice versa, the experiments which are here listed under Principle 33 are considered to be listed also under Principle 32, and the evaluation given each experiment is considered to apply equally to both principles.

TABLE IV (<u>CONTINUED</u>)   149

Experiments Allocated to Principles	Value	Rank	
Can hydrogen be prepared by displacement from an acid (sulfuric or hydrochloric) by a metal ("mossy" zinc)?	16	2	L
34. The exchange of the negative and positive ions of acids and bases results in the formation of water and a salt.			
Experiments Will the color of a solution of sodium hydroxide with phenolphthalein disappear when the proper amount of dilute hydrochloric acid is added?......	17	1	D
Can a solution of baking soda be neutralized with vinegar?.............	16	2	L
35. Electrolytes dissolved in water exist partially or completely as electrically charged particles called ions.			
Experiment Which of the following are good electrolytes (cause an electric lamp in series to glow brightly), poor electrolytes, and non-electrolytes, respectively: distilled water, tap water, dry sodium chloride; separate solutions of sodium chloride, hydrochloric acid, sulfuric acid, ammonium hydroxide, glycerine, sugar, alcohol; carbon tetrachloride?............................	18	1	D
36. All matter is made up of protons, neutrons, and electrons.			
37. The electrons within an atom form shells about the nucleus, each of which contains a definite number of electrons.			

TABLE IV (CONTINUED)

Experiments Allocated to Principles	Value	Rank	
38. When elevations or depressions are created upon the surface of the earth, the elevations are usually attacked by the agents of erosion, and the materials are carried to the depressions.			
Experiment What is the character of an area shown on a given contour map? Do contour lines bend toward or away from the source of a river?...............................	16	1	L
39. Streams, generally, are lowering the surface land in some places and building it up in other places.			
Experiments What are some changes in surface relief brought about by river deposition and floods (The Salton Sea Quadrangle)?	19	1	L
Are there alluvial fans at the base of cliffs, or railway or highway cuts?..	16	3.5	D
What are some of the characteristics found in a given area (or on a topographic map) which indicate an early stage of stream erosion?......................	16	3.5	X
What are some of the characteristics found in a given area (on a topographic map) which indicate a region of mature drainage?	16	3.5	X
What are some of the characteristics found in a given area (or on a topographic map) which indicate an old river?	16	3.5	X
40. Rocks may be formed by the compacting and cementing of sediments.			
Experiment How are sedimentary rocks (comglomerate, sandstone, shale, limestome, gypsum, and halite or rock salt) alike and different with respect to general appearance, crystalline and granular structure, hardness, taste, and the acid test?......	16	1	L

TABLE IV (CONTINUED)   151

Experiments Allocated to Principles	Value	Rank
Principles Having a Total Assigned Value of Fourteen*		

41. A fluid has a tendency to move from a region of higher pressure to one of lower pressure; the greater the difference, the faster the movement.

Experiments
    What conditions are necessary in order that water may be siphoned from one vessel to another? Must the short arm and the long arm of a siphon always be entirely full of water? Must the outlet and the intake always be under water? Does the water always flow through the siphon toward the vessel which has its water level at the greater or at the smaller height above sea level? — 18, 1, L

    What happens to a rubber membrane over a wide opening in a bell jar or aspirator bottle as air is taken out of the jar or bottle? — 17, 3, D

    How can water be made to run faster through one siphon than through another siphon? How is the rate of flow of a siphon affected by the kind of liquid? The internal diameter of the tube? The difference in height (pressure, not weight) between the upper water level and the lower water level or end open to air? — 17, 3, L

    As the piston of a model glass lift pump moves upward, is water moved higher than its immediate source? — 17, 3, D

    What is the effect on a "closed" can as air is alternately removed from and returned to the can? — 16, 9.5, D

*The numerical values assigned to the principles are the sums of the individual evaluations of the five judges on the scale for essential (+3), desirable (+2), and undesirable (-2). These principles are therefore judged essential by all evaluators except one who considered them to be desirable for inclusion in the integrated course if time permitted.

TABLE IV (CONTINUED)   152

Experiments Allocated to Principles	Value	Rank
What happens to a varnish or oil can which is closed tightly after a small amount of water in it has been boiled for some time?.....................	16	9.5 D
If air is exhausted from a bottle fitted with a stopcock, what happens when the tube is held below the surface of water and the stopcock is opened?....	16	9.5 D
What happens to a hard boiled egg (shell removed) or an inflated balloon placed in the neck of a dry milk bottle in which tissue paper is burning?.......	16	9.5 D
What happens when the rubber bulb of a medicine dropper or a squirt gun is pressed and released with the opposite end under water?.....................	16	9.5 D
Does the mercury in a barometer tube inside a bell jar rise or fall as the bell jar is evacuated? As air is allowed to enter the bell jar again?.........	16	9.5 D
If bottles A and B under a bell jar are connected by a U-tube reaching near the bottom of each bottle and bottle A is nearly full with a colored liquid and tightly stoppered, what happens as air is pumped out of the bell jar? As air again enters the bell jar?..............	16	9.5 D
Does the air in a flask expand or contract when heated? When cooled? If an inverted flask of air with a glass tube through the stopper dips into water, does the water inside the tube move down to indicate expansion of the air or up to indicate contraction of the air when a warm hand is held on the flask? When a cloth wet with cold water is placed on the flask?..............................	16	9.5 D
If an ink bottle filled with hot colored water and equipped with a two-hole stopper containing two large glass tubes, one of which extends upward and the other extends downward, is submerged in a battery jar filled with cold water, does the cold water force the hot colored water out of the bottle?.............	16	9.5 D

TABLE IV (CONTINUED)   153

Experiments Allocated to Principles	Value	Rank
Is a stream of material ejected from the nozzle of an inverted fire extinguisher of the soda-acid type with considerable pressure?.....................	16	9.5 D
42. Any two bodies attract one another with a force which is directly proportional to the attracting masses and inversely proportional to the square of the distance between their centers of mass.		
43. Movements of all bodies in the solar system are due to gravitational attraction and inertia.		
Experiment How do comets curve around the sun when they come near it and why do they make such paths? If a ball bearing (one-half inch in diameter) rolls down a grooved inclined plane which may have its lower end directed toward or away from the end of the core of an electromagnet (current from a storage battery) on a level with and near the bottom of the grooved plane, what is the path of the "comet" (ball) when not near the sun (Current is off.)? With the current on, can the trough be aimed closer and closer to the magnet so that the "comet" (ball) will go around the "sun" (magnet) and come back almost in the same direction from which it came?...............	18	1 D
44. The pressure in a fluid in the open is equal to the weight of the fluid above a unit area including the point at which the pressure is taken; it therefore varies with the depth and average density of the fluid.		
Experiments If water (and salt water or gasoline) is raised and lowered in a set of Pascal's vases of different shapes but with similar bases attached above a metal diaphragm		

Experiments Allocated to Principles	Value	Rank	
connected to a pressure gauge, what relation exists between the pressure and the depth of the water above the diaphragm? The pressure and the density of the liquid for a given depth? If water is at the same level in the vases of different shapes, is the pressure dependent on or independent of the shape of the vessel?......................	19	1	D
If a mercury manometer is placed in a glass tube alongside a meter stick with a movable reservoir to raise and lower the liquid in the tube, what is the relation between the pressure exerted by the liquid (on the mercury in the short arm of the manometer as measured by the difference in height between the two mercury levels in the manometer) and the depth of submersion (of the mercury in the short arm)? What is the relation between the pressure exerted by a liquid upon a submerged object (the surface of mercury in the short arm) and the density of the liquid (water and gasoline or salt water)?.....	17	2	D
If a light lever, with one end hinged on a pivot and the other free to move over a scale, rests on a cork placed on a rubber dam stretched tightly over a thistle tube which is connected to a glass cylinder alongside the vertical scale (simple pressure gauge), what is the relation between the pressure recorded on the scale and the depth of water in the cylinder above the level of the dam? If the large cylinder is replaced with a small tube filled to the same depth, is the pressure more, less, or the same; that is, is the pressure exerted by a liquid on the bottom of a vessel independent of or dependent on the shape of the container? The depth of the liquid?......................	16	3.5	D

TABLE IV (CONTINUED)

Experiments Allocated to Principles	Value	Rank
Is the pressure upward, downward, and sidewise the same or different at a given level in a liquid as judged by a mercury manometer connected to the long arm of a J-tube which has connected to its short arm a movable thistle tube with a rubber dam, the center of which can be kept at a given level below the surface of water when pointed upward, downward, or sidewise? How does the pressure on a submerged surface change with the depth as judged by moving the center of the dam vertically? With the density as judged by placing the center of the dam at the same depth below the surface of fresh water and salt water or gasoline?.......	16	3.5 D

45. Bodies in rotation tend to fly out in a straight line which is tangent to the arc of rotation.

Experiments
 If a piece of metal is held against a rotating grinding wheel in what direction from the points of contact do the sparks seem to fly?............................

| | 18 | 1.5 D |

 What facts about centrifugal force can be felt or observed as a blackboard eraser is whirled at the end of a weak string?................................ 18 1.5 D
 Can a small pail of water held at arm's length be swung up and over the head without spilling the water?........ 16 3.5 D
 As the speed of a rotating governor increases and decreases what happens to the balls?................................ 16 3.5 D

46. A body immersed or floating in a fluid is buoyed up by a force equal to the weight of the fluid displaced.

TABLE IV (CONTINUED)

Experiments allocated to Principles	Value	Rank	
Experiments			
How does the buoyant force (apparent loss in weight) on a floating body (and on one that sinks) compare with the weight of liquid displaced by it as determined by using spring or beam balances, or an overflow can?.............	20	1	L
Does a body sink in a fluid, remain submerged neither rising nor sinking, or float if the weight of the fluid it displaces is less than, equal to, and more than the weight of the body?...........	17	3	L
Does a wooden block sink deeper in a liquid heavier than water or in one lighter than water?....................	17	3	D
Does a hydrometer float higher in a fully charged or in a discharged cell of an automobile battery?.................	17	3	D
Does a brick (or rock) submerged in water while hanging on a spring balance seem to weigh the same as, less than, or more than it does in air?..............	16	7.5	L
What is the lifting power of a balloon filled with hydrogen and tied to a pan of a platform balance?.............	16	7.5	D
Can a tin can (boat) carry a greater weight of nails (cargo) without sinking when it is in fresh water or salt water, that is, what is the relation between the density of a liquid and its lifting force (buoyancy)?....................	16	7.5	X
What fractional part of the volume of a floating body (wood coated with paraffin) will sink in a liquid as determined by using an overflow can?......	16	7.5	X
What is the relation between the density of a body and the fractional part of its volume which is submerged when it floats in water?......................	16	7.5	D
Does more of a cube of ice remain above the surface of water when the cube is in fresh or in salt water?...........	16	7.5	L

TABLE IV (CONTINUED)

Experiments Allocated to Principles	Value	Rank
47. The pressure at a point in any fluid is the same in all directions.		
Experiments Is the pressure upward, downward, and sidewise the same or different at a given level in a liquid as judged by a mercury manometer connected to the long arm of a J-tube which has connected to its short arm a movable thistle tube with a rubber dam the center of which can be kept at a given level below the surface of water when pointed upward, downward, or sidewise? How does the pressure on a submerged surface change with the depth as judged by moving the center of the dam vertically? With the density as judged by placing the center of the dam at the same depth below the surface of fresh water and salt water or gasoline?..........................	20	1 D
Is the pressure upward, downward, and sidewise the same or different at a given level in a liquid as judged by the levels of the mercury in a J-tube when the open end of the short arm is extended upward under water in a glass jar, then an inverted U-tube is connected to the short arm but the open end is retained at the same level, and finally a horizontal tube with its open end at the same level is connected to the short arm?.......................	17	2 D

TABLE IV (<u>CONTINUED</u>)

158

Experiments Allocated to Principles	Value	Rank
48. Heat is conducted by the transfer of kinetic energy from molecule to molecule.[1]		
49. When two bodies of different temperature are in contact, there is a continuous transference of heat energy from the body of higher temperature to the one of lower temperature, the rate of which is directly proportional to the difference of temperature.[1]		
<u>Experiments</u> If one end of a copper wire about a foot long is held in a flame, do the fingers holding the other end become warm quickly? Is metal a good conductor of heat?.........................	20	1 L
If three similar rods (or wires) of copper, iron, and aluminum are clamped so that one end of each may be equally heated in the same flame, in which order does the falling of B-B shot, stuck to the other end of each rod by paraffin, occur or do all shot drop at the same time?...	19	2.5 D
Does heat energy travel by conduction with equal speed through different metals (similar strips of copper, iron, and aluminum) to light heads of matches equally spaced along the strips?	19	2.5 D

[1]Since each experiment which contributes to an understanding of Principle number 48 would also contribute to an understanding of Principle number 49, and <u>vice versa</u>, the experiments which are here listed under Principle 49 are considered to be listed also under Principle 48, and the evaluation given each experiment is considered to apply equally to both principles.

TABLE IV (CONTINUED)

Experiments Allocated to Principles	Value	Rank	
If similar rods of copper, aluminum, brass and iron, covered with paraffin, have one end inserted into hot water, in what order does the paraffin melt from the rods?......................	18	5	D
If an inner box containing a thermometer and an electric lamp is separated from an outer box by a narrow dead-air space, does the greatest rise in temperature occur in the inner box when the space between the walls is air, asbestos wool, glass wool, or air with a sheet of aluminum on each side?.............	18	5	D
If a copper wire in one hand and an iron wire of the same length and size in the other hand are both held in the same Bunsen flame at the same time, which wire is dropped first?.................	18	5	L

50. The lower the temperature of a body, the less the amount of energy it radiates; the higher the temperature, the greater is the amount of energy radiated.

Experiment

If one cup of water at sixty and another at seventy degrees Fahrenheit are placed in a refrigerator whose temperature is less than fifty degrees, which cup cools faster?................	16	1	L

51. Heat is transferred by convection in currents of gases or liquids, the rate of transfer decreasing with an increase in the viscosity of the circulating fluid.

TABLE IV (CONTINUED)   160

Experiments Allocated to Principles	Value	Rank	

Experiments
If a lighted candle is placed under
one of two lamp chimneys over openings
in the top of a closed box, what happens
to smoke produced at the opening to the
other chimney?........................ 20 1 D

Is a better circulation of air
(smoke) secured through a shoe box
(bedroom) when a flap (window) is opened
at the bottom, at the top, or at both
bottom and top?........................ 18 2 D

Are convection currents set-up in a
model of a hot-water heating system? If
a glass tube, rectangular in shape, has
an outlet from a lower corner deep into
a flask (boiler) which is closed except
for a high funnel filled with water
(overflow tank), ~~through filled with
water (overflow tank),~~ through what path
does wet sawdust in the flask circulate
as heat is applied to the flask?........ 17 3.5 D

What is the path of circulation in a
model of a hot-water heating system? If
a lower flask and an upper flask (inverted
aspirator) filled with water have large
glass tubing extending from their respective stoppers deep into the other flask,
in what path does ink placed in the upper
flask circulate when water in the lower
flask is heated?........................ 17 3.5 D

If a divider extends down a lamp
chimney to the edge of the flame of a
candle in a pan of water, what happens
to smoke produced at the top of the
chimney on the side of the divider
opposite the candle?.................... 16 6 D

If a Bunsen flame is applied below a
crystal of potassium permanganate (or
sawdust) at one edge of a beaker of
water, does the color (or sawdust)
circulate in an uniform direction?...... 16 6 D

TABLE IV (CONTINUED)   161

Experiments Allocated to Principles	Value	Rank
If an ink bottle filled with hot colored water and equipped with a two-hole stopper containing two large glass tubes, one of which extends upward and the other extends downward, is submerged in a battery jar filled with cold water, does the cold water force the hot colored water out of the bottle?	16	6 D
52. Every pure liquid has its own specific boiling and freezing point.		
Experiments What is the temperature of boiling water? Of the steam above boiling water?	17	1.5 L
Can fractional distillation and condensation be used to separate two miscible liquids (alcohol and water) which have different boiling points?....	17	1.5 D
53. The higher the pitch of a note, the more rapid the vibrations of the producing body and vice versa.		
Experiments What relation exists between the pitch produced by holding a card against the teeth of a rotating wheel and the speed of the wheel?.............	18	1.5 D
Is a higher or a lower pitch produced by a siren disk when a jet of air is directed at circles with increased numbers of holes?......................	18	1.5 D
54. Musical tones are produced when a vibrating body sends out regular vibrations to the ear while only noises are produced when the vibrating body sends out irregular vibrations to the ear.		

TABLE IV (CONTINUED)   162

Experiments Allocated to Principles	Value	Rank	
Experiment If air from a jet passes through the regularly spaced holes on a rotating siren disk, is the sound produced a musical note or noise? Is music or noise produced when the irregularly spaced holes are used?......................	20	1	D
55. Energy is often transmitted in the form of waves.			
Experiments If small pieces of cork float on the surface of water in a pan and the water is tapped with the finger, in what direction do the water waves move? In what direction do the corks move? By what means is the energy of the finger tapping the water transmitted?.............	16	1.5	D
If one end of a horizontal rope ten feet long is fastened to a firm support, can the free end be moved up and down at a speed which will make the rope vibrate as standing waves in two or more segments with points of minimum motion (nodes) and maximum motion (antinodes)?	16	1.5	D
56. When waves strike an object, they may be absorbed, transmitted, or reflected.			
Experiment If red, blue, and green pieces of transparent glass are held separately between the eye and sunlight, what color is transmitted by each piece of glass? If blue and green glass is held in front of the red glass, what color is transmitted?......................	16	1	X

TABLE IV (CONTINUED)   163

Experiments Allocated to Principles	Value	Rank
57. When light rays are absorbed, some of the light energy is transformed into heat energy.		
Experiments		
If two thermometer bulbs, one wrapped in black cloth and the other in white cloth, are held in bright white light, which thermometer registers the greater rise in temperature?............	19	1 X
Is radiant energy (heat and light) absorbed more rapidly by a dark surface or by a similar surface of lighter color? Does snow (or finely cracked ice) melt more rapidly under a piece of black metal (or cloth) exposed to sunlight (or a Bunsen flame) than under a similar piece of metal (or cloth) of lighter color, or vice versa?.................	18	2 X
If a white-tipped match held at the focal point of light rays does not ignite, will it ignite after being darkened with a soft pencil lead?.......	17	3 X
Is radiant energy (heat and light) absorbed more rapidly by a dark dull surface or a light smooth surface? If a Bunsen flame is placed equidistant between two closed tin cans, one with a black dull surface and the other with a light smooth surface and both containing equal amounts of water at the same low temperature, does the thermometer in the black dull can or the one in the light smooth can show the greater increase in temperature?...........................	16	4 X
58. The darker the color of a surface, the better it absorbs light.		
Experiment		
If paper of different colors is folded and held over an electric lamp above a light meter, which color increases the reading of the light meter most and should be used on the inside of shades for reading lamps?..............	17	1 D

TABLE IV (CONTINUED)

Experiments Allocated to Principles	Value	Rank	
59. The intensity of illumination decreases as the square of the distance from a point source. Experiment If a light (foot-candle) meter is read when one, two, three, and four feet below a bright electric lamp, how does the intensity of illumination on the light meter vary with its distance from the source?............................	20	1	X
60. Radiant energy travels in waves along straight lines, its intensity at any distance from a point source is inversely proportional to the square of the distance from the source.			
61. When light rays pass obliquely from a rare to a more dense medium, they are bent or refracted toward the normal and when they pass obliquely from a dense to a rarer medium, they are bent away from the normal. Experiments Does an object under water appear to be at a greater depth or nearer the surface than it actually is when viewed at an angle to the surface? If only one edge of a coin in a cup can barely be seen over the edge of a cup, what does the coin appear to do as water is poured into the cup without moving the head?...	19	2	L
Does a ruler or spoon observed from above appear to be straight, bent, or broken when it is stood straight up in a glass of water with part in air? When it is placed at an angle to the surface?	19	2	L

TABLE IV (CONTINUED)

Experiments Allocated to Principles	Value	Rank	
If a narrow beam of strong light passes downward at a forty-five degree angle through a hole in a piece of metal hanging over the edge of a glass tank partly filled with water made cloudy with soap solution, does the beam continue straight, bend toward, or bend away from the normal on passing from the less dense to the more dense medium (air to water) and <u>vice versa</u>?.................	19	2	X
If, as one looks down into a tall glass cylinder filled with water, a finger is placed where the bottom appears to be, is the water deeper than it seems?	16	4.5	L
If a triangular glass prism is held with its base parallel to the ceiling of the room as a person looks through the prism at a window, does the window seem to be above, below, or straight in front of the prism?...........................	16	4.5	L

62. An image appears to be as far back of a plane mirror as the object is in front of the mirror and is reversed.

<u>Experiments</u>

When a person faces his image in a plane mirror, is the right hand of his image on his left or right? Does his image seem to be as far back of the mirror as he is in front of it regardless of whether he steps toward or away from the mirror?.....................	18	1	L
If a lighted candle is placed in front of a plane mirror and a second candle is placed at the apparent position of the image, how do the distances of each of the two candles from the mirror seem to compare?........	17	2	L
Does the second hand of a watch rotate clockwise or counterclockwise when viewed normally? When viewed in a mirror?................................	16	4	L

Experiments Allocated to Principles	Value	Rank	
If initials are written in order and in reverse on separate lines perpendicular to a vertical mirror, what is observed?..............................	16	4	L
If an arrow or triangle (object) is drawn obliquely to a plane mirror, how does the image compare with the object in respect to size? Shape? Position? Distance from the mirror? Is a line from any point on the object to the image of that point perpendicular to the mirror?.............................	16	4	L

63. Parallel light rays may be converged or focused by convex lenses or concave mirrors; diverged by concave lenses or convex mirrors.

Experiments

	Value	Rank	
Does a double convex lens focus sunlight toward one spot? What is the focal length of a double convex lens using the sun? What is the appearance and location of the image of a landscape formed on a paper by a double convex lens?..........	18	1	L
How does ones image change in size as a concave shaving mirror (also a convex mirror) is moved slowly away from the face?...................................	16	2	L

64. Protons and neutrons only are found in the nucleus of an atom.

65. In an uncharged body there are as many protons as electrons and the charges neutralize each other while a deficiency of electrons produces a plus charge on a body and an excess of electrons produces a negative charge.

TABLE IV (<u>CONTINUED</u>)   167

Experiments Allocated to Principles	Value	Rank	
Experiments			
Does a hard-rubber comb pick up small pieces of paper before and after the comb is pulled rapidly through dry hair?...................................	20	2	D
Does a piece of paper "stick" to a wall before and after the paper is rubbed vigorously with the side of a pencil?................................	20	2	X
Can different kinds of electric charges be produced by rubbing silk on glass and fur (or woolen cloth) on hard rubber (or sealing wax); that is, if the leaves of an electroscope stand apart when the knob of the electroscope is touched with glass rubbed with silk, do they collapse when the knob is touched with hard rubber rubbed with fur?.......	20	2	X
Can the top plate of an electrophorus be charged by induction; that is, if the lower plate of an electrophorus is rubbed with fur, the top plate is set on the lower plate and grounded with a finger, and the finger and then the top plate are removed, can a spark be drawn from the top plate by placing a finger near it or are the leaves of an electroscope moved apart when the plate is touched to the knob?...................	18	4	D
If a hard rubber rod is turned within a flannel cap which is then removed by means of a silk cord, is the charge on the rod the same as that on the cap?	17	5.5	D
Can an electroscope be charged negatively if a charged glass rod is held near the knob, the knob is touched with a finger, and the finger is removed before the rod is removed?...............	17	5 5	D
Does an inflated rubber balloon "stick" to the under side of an uncharged book before and after being rubbed with flannel? To a wall before and after the balloon is rubbed against the wall?.................................	16	7	D

TABLE IV (<u>CONTINUED</u>) 168

Experiments Allocated to Principles	Value	Rank
66. An electrical charge in motion produces a magnetic field about the conductor, its direction being tangential to any circle drawn about the conductor in a plane perpendicular to it.		

Experiments

	Value	Rank	
What is the shape of a magnetic field around a wire carrying direct current; that is, do iron filings shaken on a cardboard perpendicular to a vertical wire through the cardboard arrange themselves in concentric circles around the wire carrying direct current when the board is tapped? Is the needle of a compass moved around a vertical wire carrying direct current always tangent to a circle perpendicular to the wire?	20	1	D
Does a wire carrying an electric current have a magnetic field around the wire; that is, is a compass needle below (or above) and parallel to a wire deflected when current from a dry cell passes through the wire? If deflection occurs, is the compass needle deflected in the opposite direction when the direction of the current through the wire is reversed?...........	18	2	X
If a straight vertical wire carrying a direct current is grasped with the right hand so that the thumb points in the direction the current flows, do the fingers encircle the wire in the direction of the magnetic lines of force and vice versa, that is, in the direction in which the north pole of a compass needle points when it is moved around the wire?.............................	17	3.5	L
If an electromagnet (or a helix) is grasped with the right hand so that the fingers encircle the magnet (or core) in the direction the current flows, does the extended thumb point to the north pole of the magnet (or helix)?....	17	3.5	L

TABLE IV (CONTINUED)   **169**

Experiments Allocated to Principles	Value	Rank	
If a flat rectangular coil of insulated wire (no. 26) is suspended by a thread with its edges between and in line with the north and south poles of a U-shaped magnet, is the coil deflected when current is passed through it (D'Arsonval galvanometer)? Does an increase of current through the coil cause greater deflection? Does reversing the direction of the current through the coil also reverse the direction of its deflection?.............................	16	5	D
67. All materials offer some resistance to the flow of electric current, and that part of the electrical energy used in overcoming this resistance is transformed into heat energy.			
Experiments			
If an iron wire and a copper wire of the same diameter and length are connected to an 110-volt A.C. circuit, do paper riders on the iron and copper wires burn when the wires are in series? In parallel?...................	19	1.5	D
Will the current from two dry cells melt (overload) a short piece of small (no. 30) copper wire? The same length of larger wire (no. 14) used for wiring homes?...............................	19	1.5	X
If a piece of iron wire is inserted in a circuit of copper wire of similar diameter, does the iron or copper wire become hot more readily when current passes through the circuit?.............	18	3.5	X
Does fuse wire or a narrow piece of tinfoil connecting the two wires at one end of an extension cord melt when the other end is connected to an 110-volt A.C. circuit?..........................	18	3.5	X

TABLE IV (CONTINUED)

Experiments Allocated to Principles	Value	Rank	
68. The resistance of a metallic conductor depends on the kind of material from which the conductor is made, varies directly with the length, inversely with the cross sectional area, and increases as the temperature increases.			
Experiments			
If current (from a storage battery or dry cells) passes for a very short time through equal lengths (100 cm) of the same kind of wire (copper) of different cross-sectional area (the diameter of B and S no. 18 is twice that of no. 21.), what is the relation between the resistance of wire (calculated by using voltmeter and ammeter readings in Ohm's Law) and its cross-sectional area?......................	20	1	X
If current (from a storage battery or dry cells) passes for a very short time through equal lengths (100 cm) of different kinds of wire (German silver and copper) of the same size, do these different materials of the same size and length have different resistances (calculated by using voltmeter and ammeter readings in Ohm's Law)?.........	19	2.5	X
If current (from a storage battery or dry cells) passes for a very short time through fifty and then 100 centimeters of the same kind of wire (no. 30 copper wire or the wire on a Wheatstone bridge), what is the relation between the resistance of the uniform wire (calculated by using voltmeter and ammeter readings in Ohm's Law) and its length?................................	19	2.5	X
Does an electric toaster use more current before or after it becomes hot, that is, does the resistance of a metallic conductor increase (less current) or decrease (more current) with a rise in temperature?.........................	16	4	D

TABLE IV (CONTINUED)

Experiments Allocated to Principles	Value	Rank
69. The electrical current flowing in a conductor is directly proportional to the potential difference and inversely proportional to the resistance.		
Experiments When direct current (from two dry cells) flows through a series circuit containing an ammeter and a known resistance (coils of wire of about one, three, or four ohms), is the voltage loss across the resistance always equal to the product of the resistance in ohms and the current in amperes? Is the current flowing in a series circuit, when resistances of different values are used, directly proportional to the voltages across the resistances and inversely proportional to the resistances themselves?......................................	20	1 X
When a steady current (from a storage battery) is flowing along a conductor (wire on a Wheatstone bridge), how does the voltage loss between two points vary with the resistance (length)? When the resistance (length of wire) remains the same, does the voltage loss across the resistance increase, decrease, or remain the same when the current is increased by varying a rheostat?........	16	2 X
70. Electrical power is directly proportional to the product of the potential difference and the current.		
Experiments What is the cost of operating a home electrical appliance for one hour as determined by using readings taken from a voltmeter connected in parallel across the terminals of the appliance and an ammeter in series with it?..............	20	1 L

TABLE IV (CONTINUED)   172

Experiments Allocated to Principles	Value	Rank
If an iron wire and a copper wire of the same diameter and length are connected to an 110-volt A.C. circuit, how does the power used by each wire compare when the two wires are connected in series? In parallel?..................................	16	2 L
71. When a current-carrying wire is placed in a magnetic field, there is a force acting on the wire tending to push it at right angles to the direction of the lines of force between the magnetic poles, providing the wire is not parallel to the field.		
Experiment		
Does a wire free to swing between the poles of a U-shaped magnet move when a current is passed through the wire (motor)?.................................	19	1 L
72. The atoms of all radioactive elements are constantly disintegrating by giving off various rays (alpha, beta and gamma) and forming helium and other elements.		
Experiment		
What does the microscope reveal about the escape of particles from the radioactive materials on the hands of a clock?..................................	19	1 L
73. The solubility of solutes is affected by heat, pressure, and the nature of the solute and solvent.		

TABLE IV (CONTINUED)   173

Experiments Allocated to Principles	Value	Rank	
Experiments			
Does the solubility of a solid increase, decrease, or remain the same as the temperature of the solvent is increased? Can more or less sugar be dissolved in a glass of hot water than in an equal volume of cold water? If a beaker of water saturated with sugar has undissolved sugar on the bottom, do the grains of sugar disappear as the contents of the beaker are heated to a higher temperature?....................	20	1.5	L
Are some solvents more effective than others under similar conditions, in dissolving a definite amount of a specific solid solute? Does iodine in crystal form dissolve more readily in water, alcohol, or carbon tetrachloride?.......	20	1.5	L
Are some solids more soluble than others in the same solvent under similar conditions? How many grams of potassium chlorate, sodium chloride, and potassium nitrate, respectively, can be dissolved in 100 cubic centimeters of water at sixty degrees Centigrade?................	19	4	L
Can a crystalline solid ("hypo" or sodium thiosulfate; sugar; common salt) be obtained from its saturated solution by lowering the temperature? By evaporation?.............................	19	4	L
Does the amount of gas which a liquid can hold decrease as the temperature rises? Do bubbles of gas appear on the inside of a glass of ice water in a warm room? Does gas escape more rapidly from a warm bottle of soda-pop or from an ice cold bottle of the same beverage? From heated household ammonia or from ammonia at room temperature?...................	19	4	D
Does the gas in a bottle of soda water or "pop" come out of the liquid when the pressure on the gas is decreased by removing the cap?............	18	6	D

TABLE IV (CONTINUED)

Experiments Allocated to Principles	Value	Rank
74. The valence of an atom is determined by the number of electrons it gains, loses or shares in chemical reactions.[1]		
75. Most atoms have the property of losing, gaining or sharing a number of out shell electrons.[1]		
Experiments Is the valence of iron increased by oxidation, that is, does potassium permanganate solution lose its color slowly as it oxidizes ferrous to ferric iron?....................................	16	2 D
Can an electric current (electrons) reduce brownish-yellow ferric chloride to colorless ferrous chloride? Oxidize ferrous to ferric chloride?.............	16	2 D
Are electrons liberated as a metal dissolves in a solvent? When the zinc terminal of a battery of six small Voltaic cells is connected to a lower metal disc on a leaf electroscope and the copper terminal is connected to an upper disc insulated from the lower one with shellac, does removing the connections and then the upper disc leave the electroscope negatively charged with electrons liberated at the zinc terminal as a result of chemical action?..........	16	2 D

[1]Since each experiment which contributes to an under standing of Principle number 74 would also contribute to an understanding of Principle number 75, and vice versa, the experiments which are here listed under Principle 75 are considered to be listed also under Principle 74, and the evaluation given each experiment is considered to apply equally to both principles.

TABLE IV (CONTINUED)   175

Experiments Allocated to Principles	Value	Rank
76. The energy shown by atoms in completing their outer shell by adding, losing or sharing electrons determines their chemical activity.		
Experiments Which metals (sodium, magnesium, aluminum, lead, copper) displace hydrogen from dilute hydrochloric or sulfuric acid? Does a metal displace hydrogen from the acid if the metal is above hydrogen in the "activity or replacement series for metals?" If the metal is below hydrogen in the series? Is the chemical reaction faster if the metal and hydrogen are farther apart or closer together in the series?..........	16	1.5 D
If strips of zinc and copper, respectively, are placed in separate sets of six solutions, namely, dilute hydrochloric acid, lead nitrate, silver nitrate, nitric acid, copper sulfate, and aluminum sulfate, what elements does zinc replace from the compounds in solution? Not replace? What elements does copper replace from the compounds in solution? Not replace? Do metals higher in the "activity or replacement series for metals" displace metals lower in the series from solutions of their compounds, or **vice versa**?	16	1.5 D
77. The properties of the elements show periodic variations with their atomic numbers.		
78. Each combustible substance has a kindling temperature which varies with its condition but may be greater or less than the kindling temperature of some other substance.		

Experiments Allocated to Principles	Value	Rank	
Experiments Do different substances take fire at different temperatures when other conditions are the same? In what order do sulfur, paper, wood, and yellow phosphorus take fire when placed at the edge of a circle on a flat iron plate with a Bunsen flame applied at the center of the circle?....................................	20	1	D
Do different substances take fire at different temperatures when other conditions are the same? In order for similar heated glass rods to ignite the vapors above the liquids in beakers containing carbon disulfide, alcohol, and gasoline, respectively, must the rods be held in the same Bunsen flame different lengths of time?.................................	16	2	D
79. Matter may be transformed into radiant energy and radiant energy into matter; in either case, the mass is unchanged.			
80. The total mass of a quantity of matter is not altered by any chemical or physical changes occurring among the materials composing it. (except in nuclear physics).			
Experiments If a test tube of silver nitrate solution set in a closed flask containing a clear solution of sodium chloride is weighed before and after the two solutions are mixed, does the weight of the flask and its contents increase, decrease, or remain the same? What evidence is there that a chemical change has taken place after the two solutions are mixed? Are similar results obtained when solutions of lead nitrate and potassium chromate are mixed?......................	20	1	X

TABLE IV (CONTINUED)

Experiments Allocated to Principles	Value	Rank
Does the weight of a new photoflash lamp increase, decrease, or remain the same after use?........................	19	2.5 D
Does the total weight of known weights of tacks and common salt increase, decrease, or remain the same after they are mixed?...............................	19	2.5 X

81. The rates of many reactions are affected by the presence of substances which do not enter into the completed chemical reaction.

Experiments

If three test tubes, one containing potassium chlorate alone, a second containing manganese dioxide alone, and a third containing a mixture of those same amounts of the two compounds, are heated under similar conditions, what effect does the presence of the manganese dioxide with the potassium chlorate have on the amount of oxygen obtained? On the speed and steadiness of the liberation of oxygen with constant heat? Does the manganese dioxide appear to be changed?	19	1 X
Does the addition of the catalyst manganese dioxide to hydrogen peroxide hasten its decomposition with the liberation of oxygen?..................	17	2 D

82. Acids and bases in water solution ionize to give hydrogen and hydroxyl ions, respectively, from their constituent elements.

83. The ingredients of a solution are homogeneously distributed through each other.

TABLE IV (CONTINUED)

Experiments Allocated to Principles	Value	Rank
Experiment If sugar is stirred in a tall glass of water until the sugar has all dissolved, does a pipette full taken from the top taste just as sweet as one from the middle of the glass or from the bottom?....................................	16	1 L
84. When different amounts of one element are found in combination with a fixed weight of another element (in a series of compounds) the different weights of the first element are related to each other by ratios which may be expressed by small whole numbers.		
85. The earth's surface may be elevated or lowered by interior forces.		
Experiment If three sets of six differently colored thick layers of cloth are placed side by side, where are faults, synclines and anticlines produced when the set on the left is raised from its bottom near the junction with the middle set? When both the middle set and the set on the right are raised simultaneously from their bottoms near their junction?......	16	1 D
86. Strata of rocks occur in the earth's crust in the order in which they were deposited, except in the case of overthrust faults.		

TABLE IV (CONTINUED)

Experiments Allocated to Principles	Value	Rank	
Principles Having a Total Assigned Value of Thirteen *			
87. The energy which a body possesses on account of its position or form is called potential energy and is measured by the work that was done in order to bring it into the specified condition.			
Experiments			
After a watch has been wound, what evidence is there that energy has been "stored" in the spring?...............	16	1.5	D
After an air gun is pumped and the trigger is pulled, what evidence is there that energy has been "stored" in the gun?	16	1.5	D
88. When the resultant of all the forces acting on a body is zero, the body will stay at rest if at rest, or it will keep in uniform motion in a straight line if it is in motion.			
Experiments			
What happens to a coin resting on a cardboard on top of an empty drinking glass when the cardboard is quickly pulled horizontally from over the glass?....	18	1.5	D
If a pound weight is placed on one end of a long horizontal strip of paper on a table and the other end is pulled slowly and then quickly from rest, what happens in each case?.................	18	1.5	D
If a coin resting on a card balanced on a fingertip is quickly snapped with the finger of the other hand, what happens?.............................	17	3.5	D

*The numerical values assigned to the principles are the algebraic sums of the individual evaluations of the five judges on the scale for essential (+3), desirable (+2), and undesirable (-2). These principles are therefore judged essential by 3 and merely desirable by 2 of the 5 evaluators for inclusion in the integrated course.

TABLE IV (CONTINUED)   **180**

Experiments Allocated to Principles	Value	Rank	
Does a round ball remain in position when a card between the ball and the mouth of a bottle is suddenly snapped in a horizontal direction?..................	17	3.5	D
Will a heavy weight suspended on a spring move very much when the spring is suddenly moved up or down (principle of the seismograph)?......................	16	6	D
If a horizontal pull is exerted on a spring balance attached to a flat object, does it take more, the same, or less force to start the object sliding than it does to keep it sliding?............	16	6	L
Is more force as measured by a spring balance required to start a weighted car moving than is needed to keep it moving?	16	6	L

89. When one body exerts a force on a second body, the second body exerts an equal and opposite force on the first.

Experiment
Is the reading on each of three spring balances connected end to end, the same or different when a steady pull is applied to the two balances on the ends?..............................   16   1   X

90. When pressure is applied to any area of a fluid (liquid or gas) in a closed container, it is transmitted in exactly the same intensity to every area of the container in contact with the fluid.

Experiments
If a cork inserted into a gallon glass jug completely filled with water is struck a sharp blow with the hand (or board or hammer), what happens?.....   18   1   D
If a small bottle nearly full of water is inverted in a glass jar partly filled with water, what happens to the small bottle (Cartesian diver or bottle imp) when pressure applied to the rubber dam across the top of the jar is alternately increased and decreased?....   17   2   D

TABLE IV (<u>CONTINUED</u>) 181

Experiments Allocated to Principles	Value	Rank
91. The average speed of molecules increases with the temperature and pressure.		
92. Condensation will occur when a vapor is at its saturation point if centers of condensation are available and if heat is withdrawn.		
<u>Experiments</u>		
Does moisture collect on the outside of a glass (or a polished metal cup) soon after it is filled with ice water?	19	1 X
Does dew form more readily and remain longer on the outside of a glass of ice water when the humidity is high or low?	17	2 D
Does cold water poured over an inverted closed flask of steam and water near the boiling point cause vigorous boiling action in the flask?......	16	3.5 D
Can a liquid be separated from a solution by distillation and condensation? If common salt is dissolved in water can the water be obtained from the solution by heating the solution in a flask and condensing the vapors with a Liebig condenser or by passing the vapors into a test tube set in ice?.....	16	3.5 X
93. A change in state of a substance from gas to liquid, liquid to solid, or <u>vice versa</u>, or from solid to gas or <u>vice versa</u>, is usually accompanied by a change in volume.		
<u>Experiments</u>		
Does water expand or contract in volume when it freezes? What happens if a cork is tied into a bottle exactly full with water and the bottle is placed under a mixture of cracked ice and salt for an hour or so?...........................	20	1 D

TABLE IV (CONTINUED)

Experiments Allocated to Principles	Value	Rank	
What happens when a small amount of water is heated in a flask or a thick-walled test tube which is corked?.......	19	2	D
Will a closed "steel bomb" (or a closed pipe) filled with water burst when immersed in a mixture of salt and ice?..................................	18	3	D
Can the walls of potato cells be broken by subjecting them to the temperature of boiling water?.................	16	4.5	D
Do solids such as camphor, iodine, and moth balls slowly disappear due to evaporation (sublimation)?.............	16	4.5	D
94. The presence of a non-volatile substance will cause the resulting solution to boil at a higher temperature and to freeze at a lower temperature than pure water.			
Experiment			
How does dissolving a solid (potassium nitrate; common salt) in a liquid (water) affect the freezing point and the boiling point of the liquid?........	20	1	X
95. The volume of an ideal gas varies inversely with the pressure upon it, providing the temperature remains constant.			
Experiments			
How does the volume of a confined gas vary with the pressure upon it if the temperature remains constant? What happens to the volume of a confined gas in a Boyle's law apparatus if the temperature remains constant and the pressure upon it is increased and decreased by pumping air into an appropriate commercial apparatus and letting it out?..................................	20	1	D

TABLE IV (CONTINUED)

Experiments Allocated to Principles	Value	Rank
If an inflated balloon is placed under a bell jar on a pump plate, what happens to the balloon as the air pressure in the bell jar is decreased?......	18	2 D
96. Whenever an opaque object intercepts radiant energy traveling in a particular direction, a shadow is cast behind the object. Experiment If a spotlight (the sun) is directed against one side of a basketball (the earth) in a darkened room, what is the appearance of a tennis ball (the moon) as it is moved into, across, and out of the shadow of the basketball (eclipse of the moon)?..............................	16	1 D
97. The dispersion of white light into a spectrum by a prism is caused by unequal refraction of the different wave lengths of light. Experiment Is a beam of light bent out of its original path as it passes through a prism to form a band of colors? If so, what are the colors in order from the one that is bent the least to the one that is bent the most?..................	17	1 L
98. Positively charged ions of metals may be deposited on the cathode, as atoms, when a direct current is sent through an electrolyte.		

Experiments Allocated to Principles	Value	Rank	
Experiments			
Can an old spoon (or carbon rod or graphite letter) be copper plated by passing direct current through an electrolytic cell in which the object to be plated is the cathode, the metal to be plated is the anode (copper) and the solution (copper sulfate) is the salt of that metal?.....................	19	1	L
If two pieces of copper screen of the same size are used for the anode and the cathode in the process of electroplating, does the anode or the cathode become smaller? Become larger?	18	2	X
99. In a transformer the ratio between voltages is the same as that between the number of turns.			
Experiment			
If one end of a soft iron rod (or part of a ring) is wrapped with five turns of insulated copper wire (the primary), in series with a switch and dry cells, and the other end (or part of a ring) is wrapped with ten and then twenty turns of similar wire (the secondary) in series with a galvanometer, how much less or more is the galvanometer needle deflected as the switch in the primary circuit is closed when the number of turns in the secondary is doubled?...	20	1	L
100. Energy in kilowatt hours is equal to the product of amperes, volts, and time (in hours) divided by one thousand.			
Experiment			
What is the cost of operating a home electrical appliance for one hour as determined by using readings taken from a voltmeter connected in parallel across the terminals of the appliance and an ammeter in series with it?.......	20	1	D

TABLE IV (<u>CONTINUED</u>)   185

Experiments Allocated to Principles	Value	Rank
101. The mass of an atom is concentrated almost entirely in the nucleus.		
102. Atoms of all elements are made up of protons, neutrons, and electrons, and differences between atoms of different elements are due to the number of protons and neutrons in the nucleus and to the configuration of electrons surrounding the nucleus.		
103. Earthquakes are produced by the sudden slipping of earth materials along faults. <u>Experiment</u> If three sets of six differently colored thick layers of cloth are placed side by side, where are faults, synclines and anticlines produced when the set on the left is raised from its bottom near the junction with the middle set? When both the middle set and the set on the right are raised simultaneously from their bottoms near their junction?......................	19	1 D

(Table IV is continued in Appendix B, page 214.)

Findings

1. Twenty-five, or 11.7 percent, of the 214
principles had no experiments assigned to them. Of
the twenty-five, 7 had been deemed essential by all
judges.

2. Eleven hundred seventy-seven assignments of
experiments, which were defensibly made to 189 principles, were given positive values by the 5 evaluators
for inclusion in an integrated course of physical
science for senior high school.

3. Of the assignments of experiments which had
been made to 34 of the 40 principles deemed essential
by all the judges, 125 were considered by all the
judges, to be either ideally or well suited for inclusion in the course and for the development of an
understanding of the principle, or principles, to
which they had been assigned.

4. Of the assignments to the 103 principles to
each of which an aggregate value of 13, 14, or 15[*]
had been assigned, 286 were deemed by all the judges
to be either ideally or well suited. Thus, an
average of 2.78 experiments was assigned to each of
these highly valued principles.

----

[*]In order for one of these principles to have
received one of these values, at least 3 judges considered it to be essential; no more than 2 considered
it merely desirable; and none of the 5 considered it
undesirable.

5. Twenty of these 103 principles each had assigned to it at least one experiment which was deemed by every judge to be ideally suited for inclusion in the course and for the development of an understanding of the principle. Eighty-five of the 103 principles had from 1 to 14 experiments which were considered by every judge to be either ideally or well suited. Of these 85 principles, 61 had 2 or more assignments of such experiments, and 41 had 3 or more.

6. Of the 286 experiments judged to be ideally or well suited for inclusion in the course and for the development of an understanding of one or more of the 103 principles, 159, or 55.6 percent, were deemed by 3 or more of the 4 judges to be more appropriately done as demonstrations than as laboratory experiments; 84, or 29.4 percent, were deemed to be more appropriately done as laboratory experiments than as demonstrations; and 43, or 15.0 percent, were judged to be equally appropriate for performance by either method. Comparable data for the 125 experiments assigned to the forty principles which had been deemed essential by all judges were: 64, or 51.2 percent, as demonstrations; 46, or 36.8 percent, as laboratory experiments; and 15, or 12 percent, as equally appropriate for performance by either method.

CHAPTER IV

SUMMARY, CONCLUSIONS, AND RECOMMENDATIONS

Statement of the Problem

The purpose of this investigation is (1) to
determine the relative importance of the principles
of physical science which are desirable for inclusion
in an integrated course of physical science for senior
high school; and (2) to determine the relative values
of the experiments which are desirable for inclusion
in such a course, and whether each of those experiments would more appropriately be done as a laboratory experiment or as a demonstration.

Methods Used

The list of principles chosen as the basis
of the study was that of Wise. This list of 272
principles was submitted to 5 specialists in the field
of the teaching of science, each of whom independently
evaluated every principle with respect to whether it
was essential, desirable, or undesirable for inclusion
in a high-school course of integrated physical science.
Numerical values were arbitrarily assigned to each of

188

the degrees of desirability. The principles were then
arranged in descending order of the algebraic sums of
these values assigned to each by the 5 evaluators.

Seventy-three sources including textbooks, laboratory manuals, and reports of research studies deemed
to contain materials appropriate to physical science
in the high school were analyzed page by page for
experiments. Duplications were eliminated from the
resulting lists and the remaining experiments were
assigned to the various principles.

The experiments were then evaluated on a five-
point scale by 4 specialists in the teaching of science
who indicated their individual judgments with respect
to the degree to which each experiment is suitable for
inclusion in the course and contributes to the development of an understanding of the principle, or principles,
of physical science to which it had been assigned; and
whether each of these experiments would more appropriately be performed as a laboratory experiment or as
a demonstration, or would be equally appropriate for
performance by either method.

The experiments for each principle were then arranged
in descending order of their relative values, or the algebraic sums of the values assigned to each experiment by
the 4 evaluators, for the development of an understanding
of the principle, and ranks were assigned to the experiments. The method of performance of each experiment
which was preferred by a majority of the judges was
indicated.

Conclusions

1. It is obvious that there is an abundant
number of principles well suited for inclusion in
the integrated course of physical science. (TABLE I)

2. The data presented indicate that there is
an abundance of experiments suitable for developing
understandings of most of the principles, and for most
of these principles there is a considerable choice of
such experiments. (TABLE IV)

3. The fact that about two-thirds of the
"important" principles were from the field of physics
(including astronomy and meteorology); one-fourth
from chemistry; and one-tenth from geology emphasizes
the difficulty of providing a course which is well
balanced among the different fields of the physical
sciences. This statement emphasizes the necessity
for the curriculum maker to make optimal use of those
principles, different aspects of which can be developed by an assortment of experiments and of other
materials provided from as many as possible of these
different fields of physical science. (TABLE I)

4. It should be noted that the number of experiments deemed by the judges to be more appropriately
done as laboratory experiments rather than as demonstrations is more than half the number deemed more

appropriately done as demonstrations (29.4 percent laboratory as compared with 55.6 percent demonstration); and that the remaining 15 percent were judged to be equally appropriate for performance by either method. (TABLE IV) It seems obvious, therefore, that the teacher has available an ample selection of experiments for use with either method.

5. It is likely that many of the experiments discovered, including those which were discarded as not being well suited to the development of understandings of principles, might, nevertheless, be indispensable and prove of great value for the development of skills in the use of the elements of scientific method, or the inculcation of scientific attitudes.

6. The 25 principles for which there were no experiments (primarily ones dealing with atomic structure and/or nuclear physics) present a challenge to those who are developing courses of physical science to devise experiments suitable for the inductive development of understandings of these principles. (TABLE IV)

Recommendations

1. Further studies should be made for the
purpose of supplementing the lists of experiments
useful in developing the understandings of the
important principles of physical science. It is
recognized, of course, that the problem of determining the important principles of physical science
and the ways by which understandings of them may be
developed can and should be attacked with other
techniques than those employed in this investigation.

2. The relatively small number of principles
for the development of which the lists of experiments revealed by this study are limited, provides
a major challenge to future workers, to increase
and refine these lists.

BIBLIOGRAPHY

A Program for Teaching Science. Thirty-first Yearbook
of the National Society for the Study of Education,
Part I. Bloomington, Illinois: Public School
Publishing Company, 1932. Pp. xii+364. (Distributed by The University of Chicago Press)

Agger, John. Grade Placement of Science Topics and
Principles in the High School. Unpublished
Master's thesis, University of Chicago, 1933.

Aiken, Wilford M. "An Adventure in American Education," California Journal of Secondary Education,
XVII (March, 1942), 138-143.

American Association for the Advancement of Science,
The Cooperative Committee on Science Teaching,
"Preparation of High School Science and Mathematics
Teachers," School Science and Mathematics, XLVI
(February, 1946), 107-118.

Anderson, Harold H. "Domination and Integration in
the Social Behavior of Young Children in an Experimental Play Situation," Genetic Psychology Monographs, XIX (August, 1937), 343-408.

Anibal, F. G. "Generalized Science Instruction in the
Secondary Schools," California Journal of Secondary
Education, X (November, 1935), 482-485.

Arnold, Herbert J. The Selection, Organization, and
Evaluation of Localities Available for Unspeciali-
zed Field Work in Earth Science in the New York
City Region. Doctor's dissertation, Columbia
University, 1936. Pp. vi+222. (Published as a
George Peabody College for Teachers Contribution
to Education)

Ashford, Theodore A. "A Physical Science General
Course for Grades 11 and 12," Journal of Chemical
Education, XVII (April, 1940), 157-159.

BIBLIOGRAPHY (CONTINUED)

Baird, Hal. "A Functional Course in the Physical Sciences," Curriculum Journal, VIIᵀ (January, 1937), 13-16.

Baird, Hal. "Teaching the Physical Sciences from a Functional Point of View," Educational Methods, XVI (May, 1937), 407-412.

Beauchamp, Wilbur L. Instruction in Science, U.S. Office of Education, Bulletin, 1932, No. 17, National Survey of Secondary Education, Monograph No. 22. Washington: Government Printing Office, 1933. Pp. vi+63.

Bergman, George J. "A Determination of the Principles of Entomology of Significance in General Education. I," Science Education, XXXI (February, 1947), 23-32; II, Science Education, XXXI (April, 1947), 144-157.

Bibliography of Research Studies in Education, 1926-1927. Department of the Interior, Bureau of Education, Bulletin, 1928, No. 22. Washington: Government Printing Office, 1929. Pp. vii+162. through Bibliography of Research Studies in Education, 1938-1939. Federal Security Agency, U.S. Office of Education, Bulletin, 1940, No. 5. Washington: Government Printing Office, 1940. Pp. xiv+404.

Blanchet, Waldo Emerson. A Basis for the Selection of Course Content for Survey Courses in the Natural Sciences. Unpublished Doctor's dissertation, University of Michigan, 1946. Pp. vii+339.

Boyles, Ernest E. "A Beginning Course Based on the Principles of Chemistry," Journal of Chemical Education, VII (June 1930), 1317-1319.

Brown, H. Emmett. "Science in the New Secondary School," Teachers College Record, XXXV (May, 1934), 694-707.

Brown, H. Emmett. The Development of a Course in the Physical Sciences for the Senior High School of the Lincoln School of Teachers College. New York: Bureau of Publications, Teachers College, Columbia University, 1939. Pp. ix+205.

BIBLIOGRAPHY (CONTINUED)

Brown, H. Emmett. "The Development of a Course in the Physical Sciences for the Senior High School of the Lincoln School," Science Education, XXIII (March, 1939), 145-157.

Burnett, R. Will. "The Science Teacher and His Objectives," Teachers College Record, XLV (January, 1944), 241-251.

Bush, Norris F. "Functional Science for Grade Ten," Curriculum Journal, X (November, 1939), 324-325.

Caldwell, Otis W. "Preliminary Report of the Committee on a Unified High School Science Course," School Science and Mathematics, XIV (February, 1914), 166-168.

Caldwell, Otis W. "The Next Ten Years in Science Education," Science Education, XXI (April, 1937), 61-64.

Carleton, Robert H. "Physical Science for General Education," The Science Counselor, VII (March, 1941), 7-9 ; VII (June, 1941), 48-51; VII (September, 1941), 81-83.

Carleton, Robert H. "The Acceptability of Physical Science as a College-Entrance Unit," Science Education, XXX (April, 1946), 127-132.

Carlson, A. J. "Footnotes on the Science Core in Liberal Education," School Science and Mathematics. XLVI (February, 1946), 119-124.

Cederstrom, J. A. "Retention of Information Gained in Courses in College Zoology," The Pedagogical Seminary and Journal of Genetic Psychology, XXXVIII (December, 1930), 516-517.

Craig, Gerald S. Certain Techniques Used in Developing a Course of Study in Science for the Horace Mann Elementary School, Teachers College Contributions to Education, No. 276. New York: Columbia University Press, 1927. Pp. vii+23.

BIBLIOGRAPHY (CONTINUED)

Craig, Gerald S. and Lockhart, Alton I. "The Program of Science in the Horace Mann School," Teachers College Record, XXXVI (May, 1935), 688-698.

Cummings, Frank L. "Practices in Fusion of Subject Matter in Various Courses," California Journal of Secondary Education, X (October, 1934), 13-18.

Cumulative Book Index. Vol. 49, No. 10, November, 1946. Pp. vi+215. New York: The H. W. Wilson Company, 1946, and all preceding volumes including The United States Catalogue. Books in print January 1, 1928. New York: The H. W. Wilson Company, 1928. Pp. 3164.

Curtis, Francis D. A Digest of Investigations in the Teaching of Science in the Elementary and Secondary Schools. Philadelphia: P. Blakiston's Son and Company, 1926. Pp. xvii+341.

Curtis, Francis D. Second Digest of Investigations in the Teaching of Science. Philadelphia: P. Blakiston's Son and Company, Inc., 1931. Pp. xx+424.

Curtis, Francis D. Third Digest of Investigations in the Teaching of Science. Philadelphia: P. Blakiston's Son and Company, Inc., 1939. Pp. xvii+419.

Dart, Alfred E. "A Fused Physical Science Course," Secondary Education, VIII (May, 1939), 153-156.

Doctoral Dissertations Accepted by American Universities, Volumes I-XIII, 1933-1934 through 1945-46. New York: The H. W. Wilson Company, 1934-1946.

Doss, Charles Lester. Generalized Physical Science in the Senior High School. Unpublished Master's thesis, University of Southern California, 1937. Pp. viii+94.

Downing, Elliot R. "Teaching Units in Biology -- An Investigation," North Central Association Quarterly, V (March, 1931), 453-470.

Eastman, Durward Wells. A Study of Important Principles of Physical Science Developed in Grades Seven Through Twelve of a Town in Massachusetts With Applications of Those Principles in Seven Local Industries. Unpublished Master's thesis, Boston University, 1947. Pp. vi+108.

Eckels, Charles G. "Principles Which Govern the Selection of Materials and Methods for the Physical Science Survey Course," California Journal of Secondary Education, X (March, 1935), 243-246.

Edmiston, Arnold J. An Evaluation of the Relative Importance of Certain Principles as Goals of Instruction in High School Physics. Unpublished Master's thesis University of Nebraska, 1942. Pp. iv+59.

Education Index, The. January, 1929. New York: The H. W. Wilson Company, 1932. Pp. xi+1891 through Education Index. Vol. 18, No. 9, May, 1947.

Educational Abstracts. Vol. I (January, 1936) through and including the continuation in the 1943 numbers of the Phi Delta Kappan.

Educational Policies Commission. Education for All American Youth. Washington: National Education Association, 1944. Pp. ix+421.

Edwards, Elmo W. The Selection of Principles Suitable as Goals of Instruction in High School Physics. Unpublished Master's thesis, Colorado State College of Education, 1935. Pp. vi+50.

Ehret, William F. "Postwar Teaching Problems in the Sciences," Journal of Chemical Education, XXII (January, 1945), 49-50; XII (February, 1945), 102-104.

Ehrlich, Murray. Development of the Physical Sciences in the Public Secondary Schools in New York State. Unpublished Doctor's dissertation, New York University, 1943. Pp. 389.

Featherstone, W. B. "The Place of Subjects in an Integrated Curriculum," California Quarterly of Secondary Education, IX (April, 1934), 235-246.

Federer, George A., Jr. "The Teaching of Integrated Physical Science in the West Virginia University High School," Educational Method, XIII (February, 1934), 271-273.

Ferguson, William Clarence, Instruction Problems of Generalized Science in the Senior High School. Unpublished Doctor's dissertation, George Peabody College for Teachers, 1939. Pp. xii+190. (Available as Peabody Contribution to Education No. 239)

BIBLIOGRAPHY (<u>CONTINUED</u>)

Ferguson, William C. "Instructional Problems of Generalized Science in the Senior High School," <u>Science</u> <u>Education</u>, XXIV (February, 1940), 72-75.

Fitzpatrick, Frederick L. and Edmiston, Vivian. "Teaching of Science in Senior High School and Junior College," <u>Review of Educational Research</u>, XII (October, 1942), 412-424.

Fleish, Sylvia. The Formulation of the Science Principles That Should Become the Objectives of General Science Teaching in the Junior High School. Unpublished Master's thesis, Boston University, 1945. Pp. iii+126.

Fordemwalt, Fred. "A Reorganization of Secondary School Science," <u>Journal of Chemical Education</u>, XVII (November, 1940), 541-542.

Frutchey, Fred P. "Measuring the Ability to Apply Chemical Principles," <u>Educational Research Bulletin</u> (Ohio State University), XII (December 13, 1933), 255-260.

Frutchey, F. P. "Retention in High-School Chemistry," <u>Educational Research Bulletin</u> (Ohio State University), XVI (February 17, 1937), 34-37.

<u>General Education in a Free Society</u>, Report of the Harvard Committee. Cambridge: Harvard University Press, 1945. Pp. xix+267.

Good, Carter V. (editor). <u>Dictionary of Education</u>. New York: McGraw-Hill Book Company, Inc., 1945. Pp. xxxix+495.

Hartmann, George W., and Stephens, Dean T. "The Optimal Teaching Sequences for Elementary Physical Principles Based on a Composite Scale of Pleasure-Value and Difficulty of Insight," <u>The Journal of Educational Psychology</u>, XVIII (September, 1937), 414-436.

Havighurst, Robert J. "Survey Courses in the Natural Sciences," <u>The American Physics Teacher</u>, III (September, 1935), 97-101.

BIBLIOGRAPHY (CONTINUED)

Heidel, Robert H. "A Comparison of the Outcomes of
Instruction of the Conventional High School Physics
Course and the Generalized High School Senior
Science Course," Science Education, XXVIII (March,
1944), 88-89.

Herriott, M. E., and Nettels, Charles H. "Functional
Physical Science," Curriculum Journal, XIII
(December, 1942), 362-364.

Hitchcock, Richard C. Demonstration Experiments for
Courses in Physics for General Education. Unpublished Doctor's dissertation, New York University,
1939. Pp. 513.

Hodge, Vernon. A Critical Analysis of the Aims, Content, and Organization of Upper Grade High School
Science. Unpublished Master's thesis, University
of Southern California, 1936. Pp. 92.

Hogg, John C. "Science in Schools," Journal of Chemical Education, XXI (March, 1944), 130-132.

Hogg, John C. "The Physical Sciences Course -- Its
Justification and Sequence," School Science and
Mathematics, XXXIX (February, 1939), 172-177.

Hollinger, John A., Amon, J. Clyde, Hoopes, Edgar N.
and Manwiller, Charles E. "Physical Science in
Senior High School," Science Education, XXVIII
(April-May, 1944), 130-135.

Howard, Bailey W. "Physical Science for the Eleventh
Year," The Science Teacher, Yearbook Supplement,
IX (December, 1942), 17-21.

Hunter, George W. "Six Hundred Teachers Look at
Science Trends," Science Education, XXVIII
(February, 1944), 15-25.

Hunter, George W. and Spore, Leroy. "Science Sequence
and Enrollments in Secondary Schools of the United
States," Science Education, XXV (December, 1941),
359-370; XXVI (February, 1942), 66-77.

BIBLIOGRAPHY (<u>CONTINUED</u>)

Hyde, Jay. Vitalizing High School Physics. Unpublished Master's thesis, University of Arizona,
1939. Pp. iv+90.

Ivens, H. J. The Determination and Evaluation of Some
Scientific Principles as Found in Six Widely Used
Textbooks of Physics. Unpublished Master's thesis,
University of Michigan, 1933. Pp. v+114.

James, Edward W. The Principles of Chemistry for Secondary Science Instruction. Unpublished Master's
thesis, Colorado State College of Education, 1935.
Pp. viii+54.

Johnson, Palmer O. "The Permanence of Learning in
Elementary Botany," <u>The Journal of Educational
Psychology</u>, XXI (January, 1930), 37-47.

Johnson, Palmer O. "The Scientific Study of Problems
in Science Education," <u>Science Education</u>, XXIX
(October, 1945), 175-180.

Johnson, Philip G. "A Science Program for All Students," <u>Science Education</u>, XXIV (October, 1940),
285-286.

Jones, Ruth V. A Study of the Principles of Science
Found in Ninth-Grade Textbooks of General Science.
Unpublished Master's thesis, University of Michigan,
1946. Pp. iv+61.

Joseph, Alexander. A Source Book of Extra-curricular
Activities in Physical Science for Senior High
Schools. Unpublished Doctor's dissertation, New
York University, 1941. Pp. ii+229.

Joseph, Alexander. "Developing a Sourcebook of Extra-
curricular Activities in Physical Science for
Senior High Schools," <u>Science Education</u>, XXVI
(February, 1942), 84-93.

Keeslar, Oreon. "A Survey of Research Studies Dealing
With the Elements of Scientific Method as Objectives of Instruction in Science," <u>Science Educa-
tion</u>, XXIX (October, 1945), 212-216.

BIBLIOGRAPHY (CONTINUED)

Keeslar, Oreon. "The Elements of Scientific Method," Science Education, XXIX (December, 1945), 273-278.

Keeslar, Oreon. "Contributions of Instructional Films to the Teaching of High School Science," Science Education, XXX (March, 1946), 82-88; XXX (April, 1946), 132-136.

Keeslar, Oreon Pierre. Contributions of Instructional Films to the Teaching of High School Science. Unpublished Doctor's dissertation, University of Michigan, 1945. Pp. vii+258.

Kerner, A. N. "A Survey of the Status of Physical Science in New York City High Schools," High Points, XX (March, 1938), 14-18.

Kilgore, William Arlow. Identification of Ability to Apply Principles, Teachers College Contribution to Education, No. 840. New York: Bureau of Publications, Teachers College, Columbia University, 1941. Pp. 34.

Knapp, Roy A. "Reorganization of High School Science Instruction," California Journal of Secondary Education, X (November, 1935), 485-488.

Leonelli, Renato E. Principles of Physical and Biological Science Found in Eight Textbooks of General Science for Grade Eight. Unpublished Master's thesis, Boston University, 1947. Pp. v+80.

Long, Edward L. "Functional Science for Grade Eleven," Curriculum Journal, XI (May, 1940), 209-212.

Lurensky, Maurice Leon, A Determination of the Applications of the Principles of Biology Found in Four Textbooks of Biology for the Senior High School. Unpublished Master's thesis, Boston University, 1947. Pp. v+147.

Martin, William Edgar. A Determination of the Principles of the Biological Sciences of Importance for General Education. Unpublished Doctor's dissertation, University of Michigan, 1944. Pp. vii+386.

BIBLIOGRAPHY (<u>CONTINUED</u>)

Martin, W. Edgar. "A Chronological Survey of Published Research Studies Relating to Biological Materials in Newspapers and Magazines," <u>School Science and Mathematics</u>. XLV (June, 1945), 545-550.

Martin W. Edgar. "A Chronological Survey or Research Studies on Principles as Objectives of Instruction in Science," <u>Science Education</u>, XXIX (February, 1945), 45-52.

Martin, W. Edgar. "A Determination of the Principles of the Biological Sciences of Importance for General Education," <u>Science Education</u>, XXIX (March, 1945), 100-105; XXIX (April-May, 1945), 152-163.

Matson, Virginia F. and Pierce, Paul R. "Science in the Core Curriculum," <u>School Review</u>, LIV (February, 1946), 83-89.

McGrath, Guy Dean. An Investigation of the Relative Significance and Use of Principles and Generalizations of Chemistry in General Education. Unpublished Doctor's thesis, University of Colorado, 1946. Pp. xv+ 168.

Monroe, Walter S., and Shores, Louis. <u>Bibliography and Summaries in Education to July, 1935</u>. New York: The H. W. Wilson Company, 1936. Pp. 470.

Nesbitt, Margaret. Adult-Child Relationships: Student and Child Relationships in the Nursery School. Unpublished Doctor's dissertation, University of Michigan, 1942. Pp. xii+204.

Nesbitt, Margaret. "Student and Child Relationships in the Nursery School," <u>Child Development</u>, XIV (September, 1943), 143-166.

Nettels, Charles H., Devine, Paul F., Nourse, Walter L., and Herriott, M. E. <u>Physical Science</u>, Boston: D. C. Heath and Company, 1942. Pp. xxiv+442.

Nettels, Charles H., and others. <u>Teacher's Manual [for] Physical Science</u>. Boston: D. C. Heath and Company, 1942. Pp. 60.

Noll, Victor H. "What About Integration in Science?," <u>School Science and Mathematics</u>, XLI (March, 1941), 241-248.

BIBLIOGRAPHY (CONTINUED)

North Central Association of Colleges and Secondary
Schools, The General Education Committee of the
Commission on Curricula of Secondary Schools and
Institutions of Higher Education, General Educa-
tion in the American High School, Chicago: Scott,
Foresman and Company, 1942. Pp. xvi+315.

Olson, Willard C., and Wilkinson, Muriel M. "The
Measurement of Child Behavior in Terms of Its
Social Stimulus Value," Journal of Experimental
Education, I (1932), 92-95.

Owens, J. Marold. Investigation of the Ability to
Recognize and Apply Scientific Principles to New
Situations: An Experimental Investigation in High
School Biology and Chemistry. Unpublished Doctor's
dissertation, New York University, 1944.

Peterson, Shailer. The Comparison of the Achievement
of Students in the Traditional High School Physics
and Chemistry Courses Each of One Year's Duration
With the Achievement of Students in the Integrated
Course in Physics and Chemistry Over a One Year
Period. Unpublished Doctor's dissertation, University of Minnesota, 1944. Pp. xvii+257.

Peterson, Shailer. "The Evaluation of a One-Year
Course, the Fusion of Physics and Chemistry, With
Other Physical Science Courses," Science Education,
XXIX (December, 1945), 255-264.

Peterson, Shailer A. "Advocating a Fusion of Physics
and Chemistry," School Science and Mathematics,
XXXVII (April, 1937), 449-457.

Powers, Samuel Ralph and Blick, David James. "Teach-
ing of Science in Senior High School and Junior
College," Review of Educational Research, XV
(October, 1945), 301-309.

Powers, Samuel Ralph, and Edmiston, Vivian. "Overview
of the Period," Review of Educational Research,
XII (October, 1942), 363-368.

Progressive Education Association, Commission on Secondary School Curriculum, Science in General Education. New York: D. Appleton-Century Company,
Inc., 1938. Pp. xiii+591.

BIBLIOGRAPHY (<u>CONTINUED</u>)

Progressive Education Association, Publications Com-
mission on the Relation of School and College,
Adventure in American Education, Volume V: <u>Thirty</u>
<u>Schools Tell Their Story</u>. New York: Harper and
Brothers, 1943. Pp. xxiii+795.

Pruitt, Clarence Martin. <u>An Analysis, Evaluation, and</u>
<u>Synthesis of Subject-Matter Concepts and Generali-</u>
<u>zations in Chemistry</u>. Doctor's dissertation,
Teachers College, Columbia University, 1935. Pp.
176. (Distributed through <u>Science Education</u>)

<u>Readers' Guide to Periodical Literature</u> [Cumulated],
Volume I, 1900-1904. Minneapolis: The H. W.
Wilson Company, 1907. Pp. ix+1640 through <u>Readers'</u>
<u>Guide to Periodical Literature</u>, Vol. 46, No. 22
(April 10, 1947). New York: The H. W. Wilson
Company, 1947.

Reek, Doris Lucille. A Study of the Principles of
Science Found in Four Series of Textbooks of
Elementary Science. Unpublished Master's thesis,
University of Michigan, 1943. Pp. v+183.

Riddle, Oscar, Fitzpatrick, F. L., Glass, H. B.,
Gruenberg, B. C., Miller, D. F., and Sinnott, E. W.
<u>The Teaching of Biology in Secondary Schools of the</u>
<u>United States</u>. The Committee of the Teaching of
Biology of the Union of American Biological Socie-
ties, 1942. Pp. 76.

Robertson, Martin L. A Basis for the Selection of
Course Content in Elementary Science. Unpublished
Doctor's dissertation, University of Michigan, 1933.
Pp. ix+264.

Robertson, Martin L. "The Selection of Science Principles Suitable as Goals of Instruction in the
Elementary School," <u>Science Education</u>, XIX (February, 1935), 1-4; XIX (April, 1935), 65-70.

Robinson, Myra Z. "The Contributions of a Fused
Science Course to General Education." <u>The School</u>
<u>Review</u>, LIV (April, 1946), 215-221.

BIBLIOGRAPHY (<u>CONTINUED</u>)

Rosenlof, George W. and Wise, Harold E. "Experimenting with a Course in Combined Physical Science,"
<u>School Review</u>, XLVI (May, 1938), 349-356.

<u>School Life</u>, Vol. 24 (July, 1939) until temporarily
discontinued with Vol. 27 (February, 1942);
<u>Education for Victory</u>, Vol. 1 (March 3, 1942) until
discontinued with Vol. 3 (June 20, 1945); <u>School
Life</u> from resumption of publication with Vol. 28,
No. 1, (October, 1945) to November, 1946.

<u>Science Education in American Schools</u>. Forty-sixth
Yearbook of the National Society for the Study of
Education, Part I. Chicago: The University of
Chicago Press, 1947. Pp. xii+300.

<u>Science Instruction in Elementary and High-School
Grades</u> by Members of the Faculty of the Laboratory
Schools of the University of Chicago. Chicago:
The University of Chicago, 1939. Pp. viii+227.

Slayton, Wilfred G. An Evaluation of a Course in
Integrated Physical Science for the Senior High
School. Unpublished Master's thesis, University
of Nebraska, 1937. Pp. ii+118.

Skinner, Selby M. "A Two-Year Physical Science Course
in the University of Chicago," <u>School Science and
Mathematics</u>, XL (October, 1940), 631-642.

<u>The Publisher's Trade List Annual</u>, 1945. New York:
R. R. Bowker Co., 1945

Todd, Robert B., Jr. "Fusion in Practical Physical
Science -- An Experimental Course," <u>School Science
and Mathematics</u>, XXXVII (January, 1937), 92-96.

Tyler, Ralph W. "Ability to Use Scientific Method,"
<u>Educational Research Bulletin</u> (Ohio State Univer-
sity), XI (January 6, 1932), 1-9.

Tyler, Ralph W. "Permanence of Learning," <u>Journal of
Higher Education</u>, IV (April, 1933), 203-204.

Tyler, Ralph W. "What High-school Pupils Forget."
<u>Educational Research Bulletin</u> (Ohio State Univer-
sity), IX (November 19, 1930), 490-492.

BIBLIOGRAPHY (<u>CONTINUED</u>)

Ward, William T. Practical Laboratory Exercises in Elementary Chemistry. Unpublished Master's thesis, University of Alabama, 1938. Pp. iii+130.

Watson, Donald R. Survey Courses in Physical Science: Their Status, Trends, and Evaluation. Unpublished Doctor's dissertation, University of Southern California, 1940. Pp. 425.

Watson, Donald R. "Survey Courses in Physical Science," The Junior College Journal, XI (February, 1941), 325-327.

Watson, Donald R. "A Comparison of the Growth of Survey Courses in Physical Science in High Schools and in Colleges," Science Education, XXIV (January, 1940), 14-20.

Watson, Donald R. "The Fused Physical Science Course." California Journal of Secondary Education, XV (May, 1940), 292-296.

Watson, Donald R. "The Training and Experience of Instructors in Survey Courses in Physical Science," Science Education, XXV (February, 1941), 80-84.

Watson, D. R. "Objectives of Survey Courses in Physical Science," School Review, XLVIII (November, 1940), 685-692.

Wert, James E. "Twin Examination Assumptions," Journal of Higher Education, VIII (March, 1937), 136-140.

Wise, Harold E. A Determination of the Relative Importance of Principles of Physical Science for General Education. Unpublished Doctor's dissertation, University of Michigan, 1941. Pp. iv+767.

Wise, Harold E. "A Determination of the Relative Importance of Principles of Physical Science for General Education -- I," Science Education, XXV (December, 1941), 371-379; II, XXVI (January, 1942), 8-12.

BIBLIOGRAPHY (CONCLUDED)

Wise, Harold E. "A Synthesis of the Results of Twelve Curricular Studies in the Field of Science Education -- I," Science Education, XXVII (February, 1943), 36-40; II, XXVII (September-October, 1943), 67-76.

Wise, Harold E. A Proposed Course in Integrated Physical Science for the Senior High School -- Restricted to Physics and Chemistry. Unpublished Master's thesis, University of Nebraska, 1935. Pp. iii+205.

Wise, Harold E. "An Integration of Physics and Chemistry," Science Education, XX (April, 1936), 68-72.

Wise, Harold E. "The Measurement of the Ability to Apply Principles of Physics in Practical Situations," Science Education, XXXI (April, 1947), 130-144.

Wiser, James Eldred. Demonstrations in Colloid Chemistry for High-School Students. Unpublished Master's thesis, George Peabody College for Teachers, 1940. Pp. viii+158.

APPENDIX A

PRINCIPLES CONSIDERED UNDESIRABLE FOR INCLUSION
IN AN INTEGRATED COURSE OF PHYSICAL SCIENCE
FOR SENIOR HIGH SCHOOL[*]

Principles

1. Centrifugal force is directly proportional to the square of the velocity, to the mass, and inversely proportional to the radius of rotation.

2. The period of a pendulum swinging through short arcs is independent of the weight of the bob but varies directly as the square root of the length and inversely as the square root of the acceleration of gravity.

3. When a mixture of gases is confined, each exerts its own pressure without reference to the pressure exerted by others.

4. The speed of diffusion of gases varies inversely with the square root of their densities.

5. The height to which a liquid rises in a capillary tube is directly proportional to the surface tension of the liquid and inversely proportional to the density of the liquid and to the radius of the tube.

6. A liquid will rise in a capillary tube if the contact angle between the liquid and the side of the tube is less than 90 degrees and will be depressed if the contact angle is greater than 90 degrees.

7. In moving air, wind pressure increases as the square of the velocity.

8. Fluids have no elastic limit for compression.

[*]The algebraic sum of the individual evaluations of the five judges on the scale for essential (+3), desirable (+2), and undesirable (-2) was negative for each of these principles.

9. Smooth surfaced tubes may be employed to confine the direction of sound waves and thus prevent the rapid decrease of intensity with distance from source, which would otherwise take place.

10. The velocity of sound is directly proportional to the square root of the elasticity modulus and inversely proportional to the square root of the density of the transmitting medium.

11. The rate of vaporization decreases with an increase of concentration of the vapor in the gas in contact with the liquid, the temperature remaining constant.

12. Equal amounts of heat raise equal numbers of atoms of all elements in the solid state through nearly equal intervals of temperature.

13. The specific heats of many elements are approximately inversely proportional to their atomic weights.

14. The force of attraction or repulsion between two small charged bodies varies directly as the product of the two charges and inversely as the square of the distance between the charges.

15. The mass of any substance set free by electrolysis is proportional to the current flowing and the time of flow; if the quantity of electricity is kept constant, the masses of the various substances set free are proportional to their electro-chemical equivalents.

16. By means of high frequency generators or vacuum-tube oscillators, sustained or continuous oscillations can be produced in a condenser circuit. Their intensity is made to vary with audio-frequency currents in a transmitter circuit to produce radio waves.

17. Two electro-magnetic waves having the same frequency and amplitude and traveling in nearly the same direction will interfere, constructively or destructively, depending upon whether they are in phase or out of phase.

18. In a tube which contains gas at low pressure subject to an intense electric field, cathode rays, streams of electrons, move away from the negatively charged terminal at high speed.

19. Electrons have both a magnetic and an electric field.

20. Radioactivity is independent of all physical conditions; heat, cold, pressure and chemical state.

21. Electrons change energy levels emitting or absorbing energy.

22. Each element has its own characteristic x-ray spectrum.

23. The distances of successive electron shells from the nucleus of an atom and from each other are much greater than the dimensions of the nucleus itself.

24. Each vibrating particle in the wave front of any wave motion may be considered as a secondary source of spherical wavelets which spread out from their sources with the velocity of the primary wave.

25. When light is incident upon a medium in which it will travel faster and when the angle of incidence is greater than the critical angle, it is totally reflected.

26. The speed of light in any given substance bears a constant ratio to the speed of light in air.

27. The sum of the reciprocals of the conjugate focal lengths of a lens or mirror equals the reciprocal of the principal focal length.

28. The curvature of a wave front will be changed a given amount by a lens; namely, $1/F$.

29. When a body which emits a bright line spectrum is moving toward or away from the observer, the lines are shifted toward the short or long wave length end of the spectrum, respectively.

30. When white light passes through a substance that absorbs some waves and not others, certain bands of color are missing with the production of an absorption spectrum.

31. A beam of light may become plane polarized as result of any circumstance which results in the suppression of one of the rectilinear components of the vibration without affecting the components at right angles to it.

32. A pure chemical substance may be prepared from raw materials through utilization of their physical and chemical properties.

33. Enzymes, vitamins, and hormones chemically regulate the reactions that occur in living organisms.

34. The gravimetric composition of a compound may be found by multiplying the atomic weights of the elements by their subscripts in the formula of the compound.

35. If stress is applied to a reversible chemical system, there will be a readjustment in the system to relieve the stress.

36. Surface reactions predominate in all non-homogeneous reactions.

37. Reactions occurring at ordinary temperatures are predominately exothermic.

38. When a chemical change takes place without the addition of heat from an external source, that substance which has the greatest heat of formation will tend to form.

39. Simple ionic reactions are typically rapid reactions.

40. Whenever the product of the concentrations of any two ions in a mixture exceeds the value of the ion-product in a saturated solution of the compound formed by their union, this compound will be precipitated.

41. In a saturated solution, the product of the molar concentrations of the ions is constant.

42. Whenever the product of the concentration of any two ions, in a mixture is less than the value of the ion-product in a saturated solution of the compound formed by their union, this compound, if present in the solid form, will be dissolved.

43. Chemical reactions may be carried more nearly to completion by any condition that establishes an unusually low concentration of one of the products.

44. Any substance soluble in two immiscible liquids will distribute itself between the two in proportion to its solubility in the two liquids.

45. If the vapor pressure of the water of hydration is greater than that of the moisture of the air, crystals will gradually yield up water to the air and vice versa.

46. The boiling point of hydrocarbons increases with an increase in molecular weight.

47. Unsaturated hydrocarbons are active chemically and form many compounds by addition.

48. Saturated hydrocarbons are relatively inactive chemically but form compounds by substitution.

49. Alcohols react with acids to form esters and ethers.

50. Molecules of some compounds undergo polymerization.

51. Alcohols oxidize to aldehydes, ketones, and acids.

52. Colloids show greater chemical activity than the solid substances in mass, since rates of reaction are proportional to the surface area of the solid, other factors being equal.

53. Colloids have the property of adsorption to an unusual degree.

54. Colloidal particles may carry electrical charges.

55. Temperature changes, pressure changes, the presence of electrolytes or the presence of oppositely charged particles may cause colloids to precipitate.

56. Elements and compounds to which the cells of living organisms react specifically produce physiological effects.

57. Continual erosion results in decreasing the average density of continental masses and continual deposition in increasing the average density of rocks under the ocean

58. The transporting power of streams varies approximately as the fifth power of the velocity.

TABLE IV (<u>CONTINUED</u>)

THE RELATIVE VALUES AND RANKS OF LABORATORY AND DEMONSTRATION EXPERIMENTS ALLOCATED TO THE PRINCIPLES OF PHYSICAL SCIENCE DESIRABLE FOR INCLUSION IN AN INTEGRATED COURSE OF PHYSICAL SCIENCE FOR SENIOR HIGH SCHOOL

Experiments Allocated to Principles	Value	Rank
Principles Deemed Essential by All Evaluators		

1. Energy can never be created or destroyed (except in nuclear physics); it can be changed from one form to another only with exact equivalence.

Experiments
    Do kinetic and potential energy change back and forth when a simple pendulum swings?............................... | 14^{*} | 6.5 | D[**]
    How does the speed of rotation of the vanes of a Crookes' radiometer vary with the intensity of light (shade and bright sunlight)? With the intensity of radiant heat (hot and cold metal)?... | 14 | 6.5 | D
    Does a wire free to swing between the poles of a U-shaped magnet move when a current is passed through the wire (motor)?.............................. | 13 | 8 | D
    What is the efficiency of an electric grill or heater as determined by calculating the heat absorbed (heat output) by a known weight of water in a

[*]The numerical values assigned to the experiments are the sums of the individual evaluations of the four judges on the scale of 1-5.

[**]The symbol L or D following a rank indicates, respectively, that the experiment was considered by the four evaluators as being more appropriately performed as a laboratory experiment or as a demonstration. X indicates equal appropriateness for either method.

APPENDIX B

TABLE IV (CONTINUED)

Experiments Allocated to Principles	Value	Rank	
weighed container and the heat input by measuring the average ammeter and voltmeter readings and the time of operation for the heating device?..................	12	13.5	X
What is the electrical equivalent of heat energy, that is, how many watt-seconds (Joules) are required to produce one calorie of heat when an electric bulb or heating coil is used in water?..	12	13.5	X
When a beaker of water containing an insulated coil of copper wire with a flashlight bulb in series is set on the end of a large coil of coarse insulated copper wire connected to a 110-volt A.C. circuit with a lamp in series, does the temperature of the water rise (induction heating)? Does the bulb light?....	12	13.5	D
Is a short length of small copper wire (no. 30) heated more by the greater current from two dry cells in series than by the smaller current from one cell?.................................	12	13.5	L
Will the current from two dry cells melt (overload) a short piece of small (no. 30) copper wire? The same length of larger wire (no. 14) used for wiring homes?.................................	12	13.5	L
If weights are suspended by means of a copper or an iron wire over a cake of ice, does the wire cut its way downward through the ice without leaving two separate pieces of ice?..............	12	13.5	D
As direct current is sent through a small lead storage cell consisting of two bright lead plates separated by a dilute solution of sulfuric acid, does one plate become unlike the other? When the two plates are disconnected from the direct current source and connected to a small electric bell (or buzzer), does the bell ring? Do the plates become more alike or more unlike as the bell rings (cell discharges)?......................	12	13.5	D

TABLE IV (CONTINUED)

Experiments Allocated to Principles	Value	Rank	
Is an electric current produced in a closed circuit when two dissimilar elements are immersed in an electrolyte? Does a galvanometer register current when connected to an iron nail and a copper wire sticking in a lemon? To a penny and a dime separated by a piece of blotting paper which has been dipped in salt water?........................	12	13.5	L
If a battery, photoelectric cell and relay magnet form one circuit and the relay armature, a battery and an electric bell form a second circuit, does the bell ring when a flashlight shines upon the photoelectric cell?.....................	12	13.5	D
If three dry cells and a galvanometer are connected in series with a telephone transmitter, does the galvanometer needle remain motionless, move in the same direction, or move in opposite directions when pressure is applied gently to the diaphragm of the transmitter and then released? When a telephone receiver is substituted for the galvanometer, can words spoken into the transmitter be heard from the receiver in an adjacent room?.................................	12	13.5	D
If a piece of iron wire is inserted in a circuit of copper wire of similar diameter, does the iron or copper wire become hot more readily when current passes through the circuit?.............	11	20	D
If an iron wire and a copper wire of the same diameter and length are connected to an 110-volt A.C. circuit, do paper riders on the iron and copper wires burn when the wires are in series? In parallel?........................	11	20	D
How is an electric bell constructed, and what makes it ring?.................	11	20	L

Experiments Allocated to Principles	Value	Rank	
What is the electrical equivalent of heat energy, that is, how many watt-seconds (Joules) are required to produce one calorie of heat when an electric bulb or heating coil is used in water?..	10	23	X
If three dry cells and a telephone receiver (or earphones) are connected in series with a transmitter made by laying a pencil lead across two razor blades on edge in one side of an empty crayon box, can words spoken into the crayon box be heard from the receiver in an adjacent room? Can the ticking of a watch upon the box be heard from the receiver?.....	10	23	D
Do cathode rays produce an intense heat effect when they bombard a tungsten target?...............................	10	23	D
Are much heat and light produced when a new photoflash lamp is used? Do the materials in the lamp undergo a marked change?.........................	9	26.5	D
Does a small electric bell ring when its two terminals are connected to the zinc (amalgamated) and copper (or carbon) electrodes, respectively, of a Voltaic cell containing dilute sulfuric acid as the electrolyte? Does the bell ring when the two electrodes are the same element?...............................	9	26.5	L
Is a taste noticed when a clean penny and a clean dime, one under the tongue and the other over it, touch beyond the end of the tongue?.............	9	26.5	L
Does fog produced in a flask (lowland) disappear more quickly if exposed to radiant energy (sunlight or Bunsen flame)?........................	9	26.5	D

Experiments Allocated to Principles	Value	Rank	
2. A gas always tends to expand throughout the whole space available.			
Experiments			
If a large bottle partly filled with water has a glass tube extending through its stopper deep into the water, does the volume of air confined in the bottle increase or decrease as the water is "sucked out" of the bottle?.............	10	5	D
Can an ant nest be eradicated by closing the hole into which carbon disulfide is poured on a warm day?......	10	5	D
How is water softened and treated by aeration, sedimentation, precipitation, filtration, and chlorination in a city water treatment plant (a field trip)?...	10	5	D
3. When there is a gain in mechanical advantage by using a simple machine, there is a loss in speed and vice versa.			
Experiment			
What is the actual mechanical advantage of a bicycle? Is effort gained at the expense of speed or vice versa? What is the effect on the speed when a bicycle with dual gears is changed from high to low gear and vice versa?	14	6	X
4. In the lever the force times its distance from the fulcrum equals the weight times its distance from the fulcrum.			
Experiments			
What is the correct procedure for balancing a platform balance? Beam balance?...............................	12	4.5	D

Experiments Allocated to Principles	Value	Rank
What is the actual and theoretical mechanical advantage and the efficiency of a wheel and axle? Does the effort times the effort arm equal the resistance times the resistance arm? How does the ratio of the resistance to the effort compare with the ratio of the radius of the wheel to the radius of the axle? Is effort gained at the expense of speed or *vice versa* when the force is applied to the wheel? To the axle as in a belt system?..	12	4.5 D
Is the mechanical advantage of a first-, second-, and third-class lever, respectively, less than one, one, or more than one?...........................	11	6.5 X
Can the actual mechanical advantage of a wheel and axle be increased by increasing or decreasing the diameter of the axle with respect to that of the wheel?....................................	11	6.5 D
How may the center of gravity of an irregular lever (meter stick with a clamp at one end) be found by experiment? If the irregular lever is balanced about a fulcrum after a known weight is placed near its lighter end, what is the weight of the lever from moments and how does this weight compare with that on a beam balance?...................................	10	8.5 L
If a uniform meter stick is suspended horizontally by two vertical spring balances the same distance from each end, what is the resultant (equilibrant) of the two parallel forces acting in the same direction but different paths and where is its point of application? What relation exists between the sizes of the parallel forces and their equilibrant? Their distances from the equilibrant?...................................	10	8.5 D

220

Experiments Allocated to Principles	Value	Rank	
How great is the thrust exerted by a boom and how great is the pull exerted by the tie rope when a crane is used to support a weight on the boom as determined by graphic solution or the method of moments? Does the pull exerted by the tie rope increase or decrease as the crane is lowered toward the horizontal by lowering the upper end of the tie rope?......	9	13	D
Is a brick harder to push over when on its end or on its side, that is, is the stability of an object increased or decreased by enlarging the base and by having the center of gravity as low as possible?...............................	9	13	L
Is a "four-by-four" wooden block harder to push over when standing on a slanting end or on an end sawed at right angles?...........................	9	13	L
Does a roly-poly doll weighted at the bottom return to its original upright position after being turned on its side?	9	13	D
Will an oil can with a heavy base right itself when overturned?...........	9	13	D
Will two Florence flasks, one weighted with lead shot and paraffin which has hardened while upright and the other similarly weighted while the flask is inclined obliquely, return to their original upright and oblique positions after displacement from such position?..	9	13	D
Can a pocket knife be stuck in a pencil so that the pencil will stand vertically on its point without support?	9	13	D

5. The work obtained from a simple machine is always equal to the work put into it less the work expended in overcoming friction.

TABLE IV (CONTINUED)

Experiments Allocated to Principles	Value	Rank	
Experiment If a uniform meter stick supported by a spring balance at its midpoint has a resistance (weight) added near one end while at the same distance from the other end a string fastened to the meter stick from below holds it horizontal, how does the work done on the lever compare with the work done by the lever as the spring balance is moved upward some fixed distance?................................	15	3	X
6. Sound is produced by vibrating matter and is transmitted by matter.			
Experiments Does sound travel better through a gas or a solid? Is the sound of an automobile engine or electric motor carried to the ear better through an iron rod or air? When a spoon on a string is swung against a chair, is the sound carried to the ears better through the string or through air alone or with its base touched to a tooth?....................	15	3.5	L
If the tines of a table fork held on end on a table are compressed and suddenly released, can the vibration be heard?	15	3.5	D
Is the intensity of sound increased or decreased by increasing the amplitude of a vibrating body such as plucking a tightly stretched string and striking a tuning fork harder?....................	13	5.5	D
Is the intensity of a sound increased or decreased by increasing the area of the vibrating body such as holding the stem of a vibrating tuning fork on a chalk box and then on a table top?	13	5.5	D

APPENDIX B

TABLE IV (CONTINUED)

Experiments Allocated to Principles	Value	Rank	
Does sound travel better through a gas or a liquid? Is the tick of a watch heard better through a filled hot-water bottle held to the ear or through the same distance of air?.....................	12	7	L
Do sounds travel better through some solids than through others? Are sounds of the voice carried better over a string or a wire between two tin cans? Can the ticking of a watch be heard better through a length of iron or a similar piece of wood when the ear and a watch are at opposite ends of the solid?......	10	8	L

7. Solids are liquefied and liquids are vaporized by heat; the amount of heat used in this process, for a given mass and a given substance, is specific and equals that given off in the reverse process.

Experiments

	Value	Rank	
Does the process of cooling liquids and solids and the process of changing a substance from the liquid state to the solid state (freezing) give off or absorb heat from the surroundings? If a stationary thermometer in melted crystals of acetamide (or naphthalene) in a test tube in air is read every half minute as the temperature changes from ninety-five to fifty degrees Centigrade, does the temperature fall, remain the same, or rise during the cooling of the liquid? At the instant crystals begin to form? While solidification continues? During the cooling of the solid?..............	15	8	L
Does gasoline in a cloth on a thermometer held in front of a fan absorb heat and lower the thermometer reading as the gasoline evaporates?............	13	9	D

Experiments Allocated to Principles	Value	Rank	
If a finger is dipped in water (or alcohol) and is then waved back and forth several times, does the finger feel cooler or warmer?	12	10	L
Can a mixture of water and alcohol be separated by fractional distillation and condensation?	11	11	D
Can the solid, liquid and vapor states of sulfur be produced by heating and cooling?	10	13	D
Will a beaker placed on water on a board be frozen to the board if air is blown into ether in the beaker? If a watch glass is placed on water in a small hole in a cork and air is blown across ether in the glass, what is observed when the watch glass is picked up?	10	13	D
If a test tube of ether is placed in a slightly larger test tube of water, does the water between the two tubes freeze when air is bubbled through the ether?	10	13	D
If cold water, in a watch glass or shallow metal lid resting over a flat dish of sulfuric acid, is under a small bell jar from which the air is being evacuated, does the water freeze (to ice) as it boils rapidly?	9	15	D

8. Most bodies expand on heating and contract on cooling, the amount of change depending upon the change in temperature.

Experiments Allocated to Principles	Value	Rank	
Experiments			
Does a solid body expand or contract when it is heated? When it is cooled? If a thin narrow strip of sheet iron about one foot long is securely fastened at its ends to a block of wood by means of nails, what change occurs in the shape of the iron as it is heated with a Bunsen flame? As it cools?...........................	15	14	D
What is the result of unequal heating when boiling water is poured quickly into a thick-walled glass tumbler?......	14	15.5	D
Does a glass rod heated in a flame crack when immersed in cold water?......	14	15.5	X
Will a "Pyrex" dish resting on ice break on being subjected to a hot flame? Will a hot "Pyrex" beaker and ordinary glass tubing break when placed in cold water?...................................	13	18	D
Does a solid body expand or contract when it is heated? Does a long "horizontal" iron wire expand and sag or contract in length when the temperature of the wire is increased by sending current from an 110-volts A.C. circuit through the wire? Decreased by turning off the current?.......................	13	18	D
Does water expand or contract in volume when it freezes? What happens if a cork is tied into a bottle exactly full with water and the bottle is then placed under a mixture of cracked ice and salt for an hour or so?......................	13	18	D
If one-hole stoppers with a long glass tube are inserted into two flasks filled with alcohol and water, respectively, and set into a vessel of warm water, do the different liquids expand at a different rate for the same rise in temperature? Do the liquids expand faster than the solid (glass flask)?........	12	21	D

Experiments Allocated to Principles	Value	Rank	
Does stretched rubber (a chain made of rubber bands under a load) and unstretched rubber lengthen or shorten when heated?......................	12	21	D
Does the mercury in a clinical thermometer move "upward" past a constriction in the capillary when placed in the mouth? Does the mercury move "downward" past the constriction when cooled in ice? Can the mercury be "shaken down" by a quick thrust of the arm and hand?......................	12	21	X
How does the compound bar open and close the electrical circuits of a thermostat when an electric bulb, in series with the electrical circuit and lighted at room temperature, is held near the thermostat?......................	11	23	D
If a heated glass rod is held just above the bulb of an air thermometer, is sufficient heat energy radiated from the rod to cause the air in the bulb to expand and push the liquid downward?.......	10	24.5	D

9. Heat is liberated when a gas is compressed, and is absorbed when a gas expands.

Experiments

	Value	Rank	
Does a body of air expand or contract when it is heated? When it is cooled? Is there more or less than a flaskful of air after an inverted flask, fitted with a delivery tube which extends through a vessel of water into an inverted drinking glass entirely full of water, is heated with a Bunsen flame? After the air in the flask is cooled?............	12	5	D

Experiments Allocated to Principles	Value	Rank	
Does the air in a flask expand or contract when heated? When cooled? If an inverted flask of air with a glass tube through the stopper dips into water, does the water inside the tube move down to indicate expansion of the air or up to indicate contraction of the air when a warm hand is held on the flask? When a cloth wet with cold water is placed on the flask?......................	12	5	D
How are cold storage plants cooled (a field trip)?..................	12	5	D
Does a body of air expand or contract when it is heated? If the open end of a deflated balloon is placed over the only outlet to a flask of air, does the balloon become inflated when the flask of air is heated?..............	10	7	D
Does a body of air expand or contract when it is heated? If two balloons inflated with air are the same size, does one held over an electric hot plate increase or decrease more in size than one not held over the plate?..............	9	8.5	D
Does a body of air expand or contract when it is heated? When it is cooled? If an inflated balloon is adjusted between two rings on a stand so that the balloon just touches the rings, does the balloon expand or contract when hot water is poured over it? When cold water is poured over it?..............	9	8.5	D
Does ice form on a cloth bag held over the open valve through which gas passes from a cylinder of liquid carbon dioxide?.....................	8	10	D
10. Atmospheric pressure decreases as the altitude increases.			

TABLE IV (<u>CONTINUED</u>)

Experiments Allocated to Principles	Value	Rank	
11. The higher the temperature of the air, the greater is the amount of moisture required to saturate it.			
<u>Experiments</u> Does moisture collect on the outside of a glass (or polished metal cup) soon after it is filled with ice water?......	15	4	L
What is the relative humidity of the air in the classroom as determined by the use of a hygrodeik or a hair hygrometer?.............................	14	5	D
How are the washing, the heating and cooling, and the humidity of air controlled in an air-conditioning unit (cutaway model or a field trip)?........	13	6.5	D
Is "live steam" invisible, that is, does a cloud of "steam" disappear when the cloud is heated with a Bunsen flame?	13	6.5	D
12. Bodies of land heat up and cool off more rapidly than bodies of water.			
13. The principal cause of wind and weather changes is the unequal heating of different portions of the earth's surface by the sun; thus all winds are convection currents caused by unequal heating of different portions of the earth's atmosphere, and they blow from places of higher atmospheric pressure to places of lower atmospheric pressure.			

TABLE IV (CONTINUED)

Experiments Allocated to Principles	Value	Rank	
Experiments What is the relation between the barometric pressure and some of the elements of weather such as temperature, wind velocity, relative humidity and precipitation?......................	14	1	X
What are the causes of the differences in the amount of rainfall in different areas of the United States?...	10	2	D
14. If a beam of light falls upon an irregular surface, the rays of light are scattered in all directions.			
Experiments If a cardboard is placed between the eyes and a clear-glass lamp while a book is being read, does holding a piece of frosted glass between the lamp and book reduce the glare? Is it possible to hold the book in such a position that there will be no glare?.....................	13	1	L
If a sharp shadow is cast by a rod near a clear-glass electric lamp, what effect does using one frosted bulb have upon the sharpness of the shadow? Is the sharpness of the shadow increased, decreased, or eliminated entirely by turning on a cluster of lights on both sides of the clear-glass lamp?.........	12	2	D
15. Dark, rough or unpolished surfaces absorb or radiate energy more effectively than light, smooth or polished surfaces.			

Experiments Allocated to Principles	Value	Rank	
Experiments			
Does a black dull surface lose (radiate) heat more quickly than a light smooth surface, or <u>vice versa</u>? Is the rise in temperature greater for a thermometer near the black dull half of a tin can containing boiling water than for one near the light smooth half of the same can, or <u>vice versa</u>?	15	5	D
Does a Leslie's cube used with a differential thermometer show that a black surface radiates heat faster than a white one, or <u>vice versa</u>?.............	14	6.5	D
If an opaque board shades a light meter from an electric lamp in a box in which the interior walls are of different colors, what color gives the highest light readings? The poorest light readings?...............................	14	6.5	D
How does the speed of rotation of the vanes of a Crookes' radiometer vary with the intensity of light (shade and bright sunlight)? With the intensity of radiant heat (hot and cold metal)?......	13	8	D
Is radiant energy (heat and light) absorbed more rapidly by a dark dull surface or a light smooth surface? If an electric heating unit is placed equidistant from two inverted glass flasks (which serve as bulbs for air thermometers), one covered with lamp-black and the other left unchanged, does the blackened surface absorb the energy radiated by the heating unit faster than the bright surface as shown by the expansion of the air which pushes the liquid down in the tube?................	12	9	D
If a white-tipped match held at the focal point of light rays does not ignite, will it ignite after being darkened with a soft pencil lead?.......	11	10	D

TABLE IV (CONTINUED)

Experiments Allocated to Principles	Value	Rank	
16. The colors of objects depend upon the wave lengths of the light rays they transmit, absorb or reflect.			
Experiments Do colored lights add or subtract certain colors? What colors are observed on a white paper flat on a table and midway between two electric light bulbs of different colors such as red and green or yellow and blue (mixing lights)? Do colored pigments add or subtract certain colors? If a printed picture of red and green colors is placed under a microscope, what is observed where each color predominates (mixing pigments)?.....................	13	4	D
What are the effects of mixing the different primary colored lights as shown by the use of Von Nardoff's color apparatus?.....................	11	5	D
Does a disc painted in a particular manner with spectral colors appear white on rotation?.....................	10	6	D
17. Light travels in straight lines in a medium of uniform optical density.			
Experiments What is observed on a screen of wax paper at the end of an oatmeal box when a small hole in the other end faces a well lighted object (pinhole camera)? Is the probable path of the rays a curved or straight line?.....................	14	2	D

Experiments Allocated to Principles	Value	Rank	
If a narrow beam of strong light passes downward at a forty-five degree angle through a hole in a piece of metal hanging over the edge of glass tank partly filled with water made cloudy with soap solution, does the beam continue straight, bend toward, or bend away from the normal on passing from the less dense to the more dense medium (air to water) and vice versa? Does the light appear to travel in a curved or straight line in air? In water?......................	13	3	D
If in a darkened room a small hole is made in a window shade facing a building or landscape, what is observed on white paper as it is brought closer to the hole?........................	12	4	D
If a spotlight (the sun) is directed against one side of a basketball (the earth) in a darkened room, what is the appearance of a tennis ball (the moon) as it is moved into, across, and out of the shadow of the basketball (eclipse of the moon)?........................	11	6	D
If a person holding a very small ball about one foot in front of the one open eye moves backward or forward until the ball (moon) just covers the view of the bright circle of light from a spotlight or a strong flashlight (sun), what is the appearance of the circle of light as the ball is moved horizontally across it (eclipse of the sun)?................	11	6	L
If a person holds a basketball (the moon) a little higher than his head in a line between the head (the earth) and a flashlight or floorlamp (the sun) and then turns entirely around toward his left, how much of the half of the moon facing him is lighted when it has been turned one-fourth, half, three-fourths and all the way around?...........................	11	6	L

Experiments Allocated to Principles	Value	Rank	
Can an object be seen around a corner?.....................................	9	8	L
Does the shadow cast by an opaque object in front of a light which is not a point source have both an umbra and a penumbra? If so, why?..................	8	9	D

18. Waves travel in straight lines while passing through a homogeneous or uniform medium.

19. When light is reflected, the angle of incidence is equal to the angle of reflection.

20. Like electrical charges repel and unlike electrical charges attract.

Experiments

	Value	Rank	
If a proof-plane (a penny on the end of a stick of sealing wax) is brought near a pith ball after the proof-plane is touched to a negatively charged rod, does the proof-plane attract or repel the pith ball in the same manner that the negatively charged rod alone does, that is, does an uncharged object in contact with a charged body receive the same kind of charge that is on the body?.....	15	16	D
Does a pith ball suspended on silk thread between two bells, one grounded and the other connected by a chain to one terminal of a static machine, ring the bells alternately when the machine is in operation?.......................	15	16	D

TABLE IV (CONTINUED)

Experiments Allocated to Principles	Value	Rank	
When a charged body is brought near a neutral body is the opposite kind of electricity developed (induced) on the nearer side of that body and the same kind on the remote side, that is, if a positively charged rod is held near one end of a neutral body does a proof-plane touched to the remote end of the body attract or repel a positively charged pith ball?................................	15	16	D
Does an inflated rubber balloon "stick" to the under side of an uncharged book before and after being rubbed with flannel? To a wall before and after the balloon is rubbed against the wall?.....	13	19	D
If each end of a neutral "conduction cylinder" is touched by a suspended neutral pith ball, do the pith balls move away from the cylinder when a charged rod is brought near one of its ends?.................................	13	19	D
If a positively charged metal ball is suspended by an insulating thread in a metal vessel, are the inner and outer surfaces of the vessel neutral, positive or negative (as shown by using a proof plane), that is, are charges of opposite kinds induced on opposite surfaces of a conductor by a charged body on one side of the conductor?......................	13	19	D
Does salt water (an electrolyte) cause the precipitation and settling of a colloidal dispersion such as fine clay in water (river delta)?.................	12	21	L
Can an old spoon (or copper rod or graphite letter) be copper plated by passing direct current through an electrolytic cell in which the object to be plated is the cathode, the metal to be plated is the anode (copper) and the solution (copper sulfate) is the salt of that metal?........................	11	22	D

Experiments Allocated to Principles	Value	Rank	
Does a small electric bell ring when its two terminals are connected to the zinc (amalgamated) and copper (or carbon) electrodes, respectively, of a Voltaic cell containing dilute sulfuric acid as the electrolyte? Does the bell ring when the two electrodes are the same element?	10	23	L
Can hydrogen and oxygen be obtained by passing direct current through an acid solution of water in a Hoffman or similar apparatus? What gas bubbles "rise" from the anode? Cathode? What is the ratio of the volume of the gas collected at the cathode to that collected at the anode, that is, what is the composition of water by volume?...............................	9	24.5	D
If direct current is passed through a saturated solution of sodium chloride in a U-tube, do red and blue litmus paper indicate a base, an acid, or a bleaching agent at the anode? Cathode?............	9	24.5	L

21. A magnet always has at least two poles and is surrounded by a field of force.

Experiments

	Value	Rank	
Is the polarity of the ends of a nail held near one end of a bar magnet reversed when the magnet is reversed?...	15	5.5	L
What is the shape of the magnetic field surrounding an isolated bar (or U-shaped) magnet as determined by moving a small tracing compass several times from one pole to the other pole of the magnet?.........................	15	5.5	L
How is an electric bell constructed, and what makes it ring?...............	12	7.5	L
How is a simple telegraph system connected, and what happens to the relay and the sounder when the key is depressed and released?.........................	12	7.5	D

TABLE IV (CONTINUED)

Experiments Allocated to Principles	Value	Rank	
Can a magnetic pole strong enough to pick up iron filings be developed at a spot about two inches from the end poles of a magnetized steel needle by heating the needle red hot and twisting it with demagnetized pliers?.....................	10	9	D
22. Like magnetic poles always repel each other and unlike magnetic poles always attract each other.			
Experiments			
If the armature of a St. Louis motor is in series with a rheostat and two dry cells, how is the rotation affected by reversing only the connections of the dry cells? By reversing only the polarity of the magnets? By reversing both the polarity of the magnets and the direction of the current through the armature? By decreasing the resistance in the rheostat?	14	8	D
How is an electric bell constructed, and what makes it ring?................	13	9.5	X
How is a simple telegraph system connected and what happens to the relay and the sounder when the key is depressed and released?.....................	13	9.5	X
What is the declination (angle between true north and the direction in which a compass needle actually points) at this locality as determined by placing a compass needle over a true north-and-south line found by using a plumb line, the North Star, and the middle star of the handle of the Great Dipper?........	12	11	X
Is the polarity of the ends of a nail held near one end of a bar magnet reversed when the magnet is reversed?	8	12	X
What is the shape of the magnetic field surrounding an isolated bar (or U-shaped magnet as determined by moving a small tracing compass several times from one pole to the other pole of the magnet?..............................	8	13	X

Experiments Allocated to Principles	Value	Rank	
What is the shape of the magnetic field surrounding an isolated bar (or U-shaped) magnet as determined by shaking iron filings across blueprint paper over a horizontal magnet and exposing the paper to light in a partly darkened room?	8	13	X
What is the shape of the magnetic field surrounding an isolated bar (or U-shaped) magnet as determined by shaking iron filings across a cardboard over a horizontal magnet and tapping the cardboard?.....................................	7	15.5	L
Can a mixture and a compound be separated into their constitutents by physical means? Can a mixture of iron filings and powdered sulfur be separated by passing a magnet through it? By adding carbon disulfide and pouring the solution through a filter? Can the compound formed by heating iron with sulfur be separated by passing a magnet over it? By adding carbon disulfide?.............	7	15.5	D

23. Pieces of iron, steel, cobalt or nickel may become magnetized by induction when placed within a magnetic field.

<u>Experiments</u>

	Value	Rank	
How do copper, soft iron and air compare in their "ability to concentrate magnetic lines of force" (permeability) between two opposite kinds of magnetic poles as determined by shaking iron filings on paper over the arrangement?	15	7	D
Does a compass show that most iron radiators, steam pipes, and water pipes have polarity?...........................	14	8	D

TABLE IV (<u>CONTINUED</u>)

Experiments Allocated to Principles	Value	Rank	
Is a steel knitting needle magnetized (given polarity) by stroking it in one direction with one end of a bar magnet? If a magnetized steel knitting needle is cut into several pieces are there always at least two opposite kinds of poles for each piece?...............................	12	12.5	L
What is the relationship between the strength of an electromagnet and the amount of current through its coil, the number of turns of wire around the core, and the kind of core? If an electromagnet is made by sending direct current through insulated copper wire wrapped around a large nail, is the number of small nails (or iron tacks) which can be picked up by one end of the electromagnet about the same, halved, or doubled when the current is doubled by using two dry cells instead of one? When the number of turns of wire around the core is doubled (five to ten)? When a wooden core (pencil) replaces the iron core (nail)?..........................	12	12.5	X
How is a simple telegraph system connected, and what happens to the relay and the sounder when the key is depressed and released?...........................	12	12.5	L
What is the shape of the magnetic field surrounding an isolated bar (or U-shaped) magnet as determined by shaking iron filings across blueprint paper over a horizontal magnet and exposing paper to light in a partly darkened room?........	11	15	L
Which parts of a bar (or U-shaped) magnet have the greatest concentration of magnetic lines of force and therefore pick up the greatest number of nails?...	10	16	L

TABLE IV (CONTINUED)

Experiments Allocated to Principles	Value	Rank	
Can a mixture and a compound be separated into their constituents by physical means? Can a mixture of iron filings and powdered sulfur be separated by passing a magnet through it? By adding carbon disulfide and pouring the solution through a filter? Can the compound formed by heating iron with sulfur be separated by passing a magnet over it? By adding carbon disulfide?.............	9	17	X
What is the shape of the magnetic field surrounding an isolated bar (or U-shaped) magnet as determined by moving a small tracing compass several times from one pole to the other pole of the magnet?...................................	8	19	L
If one end of a soft iron rod (or part of a ring) is wrapped with five turns of insulated copper wire (the primary), in series with a switch and dry cells, and the other end (or part of a ring) is wrapped with ten and then twenty turns of similar wire (the secondary) in series with a galvanometer, how much less or more is the galvanometer needle deflected as the switch in the primary circuit is closed when the number of turns in the secondary is doubled?............	8	19	X
If three dry cells and a galvanometer are connected in series with a telephone transmitter does the galvanometer needle remain motionless, move in the same direction, or move in opposite directions when pressure is applied gently to the diaphragm of the transmitter and then released? When a telephone receiver is substituted for the galvanometer, can words spoken into the transmitter be heard from the receiver in an adjacent room?.....................................	8	19	D

Experiments Allocated to Principles	Value	Rank	

24. An electric current may be produced in three ways: by rubbing or friction, chemical action, and using a magnetic field.

Experiments
   If a flat rectangular coil of insulated wire (no. 26), in series with a galvanometer (zero center), is rotated quickly past a straight line between the poles of a U-shaped magnet, is the galvanometer needle deflected? If the coil, rotated in the same direction, quickly passes between the poles again, is the needle deflected in the same or in the opposite direction (electric generator)?   **15**   **6**   **L**

   When two coils of wire on separate closed circuits are placed side by side or one within the other, does current flow in one coil (the secondary) when current is started, stopped, varied or steady in the other coil (the primary), that is, when the number of magnetic lines of force (flux) passing through the secondary coil is changed or steady?   **14**   **7**   **D**

   Is a taste noticed when a clean penny and a clean dime, one under the tongue and the other over it, touch beyond the end of the tongue?............   **13**   **8**   **L**

   Can different kinds of electric charges be produced by rubbing silk on glass and fur (or woolen cloth) on hard rubber (or sealing wax), that is, if the leaves of an electroscope stand apart when the knob of the electroscope is touched with glass rubbed with silk, do they collapse when the knob is touched with hard rubber rubbed with fur?.......   **11**   **9**   **X**

TABLE IV (CONTINUED)

Experiments Allocated to Principles	Value	Rank	
Can 110-volt 60-cycle alternating current flowing through a coil of wire cause a small electric bulb in a separate coil to light, that is, can electrical energy be transferred without wires?....	10	10	D
As direct current is sent through an electrolytic cell consisting of two lead plates separated by a dilute solution of sulfuric acid, does one plate become unlike the other? When the two plates are disconnected from the direct current source and connected to a small electric bell, does the bell ring?...............	9	11	D
Does the deflection of a galvanometer needle indicate that the current taken from a model generator (Cowan type or St. Louis type) is direct or alternating current when the coil of the armature terminates in solid slip rings? In a commutator (a split ring)?................	8	12	D

25. An electric current will flow in the external circuit when two metals of unlike chemical activity are acted upon by a conducting solution, the more active metal being charged negatively.

Experiments

	Value	Rank	
As direct current is sent through a small lead cell consisting of two bright plates separated by a dilute solution of sulfuric acid, does one plate become unlike the other? When the two plates are disconnected from the direct current source and connected to a small electric bell (or buzzer), does the bell ring? Do the plates become more alike or more unlike as the bell rings (cell discharges?.................................	14	4	D
Is a taste noticed when a clean penny and a clean dime, one under the tongue and the other over it, touch beyond the end of the tongue?......................	11	5	L

Experiments Allocated to Principles	Value	Rank
26. An electromotive force is induced in a circuit whenever there is a change in the number of the lines of magnetic force passing through the circuit.		
Experiments		
If a bell-ringing transformer connected to an 110-volt A.C. circuit has a door bell connected to its secondary coil, is the voltage and amperage, respectively, in the secondary coil more or less than in the primary coil?.......	15	7 L
If a flat stationary coil of wire is placed parallel to a similar lightweight coil suspended from a high point and free to move, is the suspended coil attracted or repelled by the stationary coil when direct current in the latter is started? Stopped? Is the direction of the current induced in the movable coil always such as to produce a polarity for the movable coil which will oppose the building up and dying out of the magnetic field of the stationary coil, that is, whenever a change is made in an electrical system is there always brought into existence something which opposes that change (Lenz's law)?.......	12	8.5 X
If one end of a soft iron rod (or part of a ring) is wrapped with five turns of insulated copper wire (the primary), in series with a switch and dry cells, and the other end (or part of a ring) is wrapped with ten and then twenty turns of similar wire (the secondary) in series with a galvanometer, how much less or more is the galvanometer needle deflected as the switch in the primary circuit is closed when the number of turns in the secondary is doubled?............	12	8.5 X

APPENDIX B

TABLE IV (CONTINUED)

Experiments Allocated to Principles	Value	Rank	
Can 110-volt 60-cycle alternating current flowing through a coil of wire cause a small electric bulb in a separate coil to light, that is, can electrical energy be transferred without wires?....	11	10	D
Can an induction coil increase the voltage of an intermittent direct current in its primary sufficiently to produce a spark across a gap in its secondary?.............................	9	11	X

27. Elements are made up of small particles of matter called atoms which are alike in the same element (except for occasional differences in atomic weight; i.e., isotopes) but different in different elements.

Experiment
Can hydrogen and oxygen be obtained by passing direct current through an acid solution of water in a Hoffman or similar apparatus? What gas bubbles "rise" from the anode? Cathode? What is the ratio of the volume of the gas collected at the cathode to that collected at the anode, that is, what is the composition of water by volume?..... **10 1 D**

28. All substances are made up of small particles called molecules which are alike in the same substance (except for variations in molecular weight due to isotopes) but different in different substances.

Experiments Allocated to Principles	Value	Rank	
Experiments Can hydrogen and oxygen be obtained by passing direct current through an acid solution of water in a Hoffman or similar apparatus? What gas bubbles "rise" from the anode? Cathode? What is the ratio of the volume of the gas collected at the cathode to that collected at the anode, that is, what is the composition of water by volume?.........	10	1.5	D
Is matter composed of exceedingly small particles? Can salt dissolved in water be tasted? Be seen with an ordinary microscope?....................	10	1.5	L
29. All matter is composed of single elements or combinations of several elements.			
Experiments Can hydrogen chloride be synthesized by combining equal volumes of hydrogen and chlorine?.......................	13	2	D
Can chlorine gas be prepared by passing direct current through hydrochloric acid in a Hoffman or similar apparatus?............................	11	3	D
Can the compound copper sulfide be synthesized from its elements by heating?............................	10	4	X
30. Every pure sample of any substance, whether simple or compound, under the same conditions will show the same physical properties and the same chemical behavior.			

Experiments Allocated to Principles	Value	Rank	
Experiments			
How is a ferric salt distinguished from a ferrous salt, that is, what color is characteristic of a ferric salt with potassium ferrocyanide? With potassium sulfocyanate? Of a ferrous salt with potassium ferricyanide?..................	12	4	L
How are the color changes alike and different when ammonia water is added to a cupric salt and to a cuprous salt in solution?..............................	11	5.5	L
Can a large crystal of copper sulfate be grown by placing one well-shaped crystal of copper sulfate in a fresh (daily) saturated solution of copper sulfate for several weeks?.......	11	5.5	D
Are the water solutions of non-metallic oxides such as carbon dioxide or sulfur dioxide acid or basic? Are the water solutions of metallic oxides such as calcium oxide or magnesium oxide acid or basic?......................	10	7	L
Do sodium sulfate crystals, calcium chloride granules, and sodium hydroxide pellets readily gain or lose weight on exposure to air while counterpoised on a balance?..............................	7	8	L
31. The materials forming one or more substances, without ceasing to exist, may be changed into one or more new and measurably different substances.			
Experiments			
Can a salt be prepared by the neutralization of a base with an acid (sodium hydroxide solution and hydrochloric acid) followed by evaporation of the liquid?................................	15	4	L

Experiments Allocated to Principles	Value	Rank	
What is the silver nitrate test for the presence of a chloride? Is a white precipitate formed when clear solutions of silver nitrate and sodium chloride are mixed?..............................	15	4	L
When a new photoflash lamp is used, are the new materials produced plainly different from those of the original materials?..............................	14	6	D
Can a salt be prepared by the substitution of a metal for the hydrogen of an acid as occurs on dropping a piece of sodium or mossy zinc into a dilute solution of hydrochloric acid?...........	14	6	L
Can hydrogen and oxygen be obtained by passing direct current through an acid solution of water in a Hoffman or similar apparatus? What gas bubbles "rise" from the anode? Cathode? What is the ratio of the volume of the gas collected at the cathode to that collected at the anode, that is, what is the composition of water by volume?.....	13	11.5	D
What product condenses on and falls from the inside of a beaker held over a flame of hydrogen burning in air?.......	13	11.5	L
Will ammonia gas and hydrogen chloride fumes from two reagent bottles react at room temperature to produce a white solid?..............................	13	11.5	X
Does a chemical reaction "run to an end" or "go to completion" when an insoluble gas is formed? (Pour hydrochloric acid on baking soda). When an insoluble precipitate is formed? (Pour silver nitrate solution in hydrochloric acid). When an un-ionized or very slightly ionized product (water) is formed? (Mix a solution of sodium hydroxide and hydrochloric acid)........	13	11.5	L
Are carbon dioxide and water products of common oxidation such as breathing and the burning of paper?....................	13	11.5	L

Experiments Allocated to Principles	Value	Rank	
Can an acid be prepared by heating a salt (sodium chloride) of the acid to be prepared (hydrochloric) with sulfuric acid? By passing an acid anhydride such as sulfur dioxide into water?...........	13	11.5	L
Are the water solutions of non-metallic oxides such as carbon dioxide or sulfur dioxide acid or basic? Are the water solutions of metallic oxides such as calcium oxide or magnesium oxide acid or basic?...............................	13	11.5	L
Can an insoluble base (ferric hydroxide) be prepared by treating a soluble salt of some metal (ferric chloride) with some soluble base (sodium hydroxide)?....	13	11.5	L
When a small piece of sodium is placed on the surface of water is hydrogen liberated? Does the residue give a basic or acid reaction with litmus paper?......	12	20	D
Can hydrochloric acid be prepared by heating sodium chloride with sulfuric acid and bubbling the gas formed through water?..................................	12	20	L
Is copper oxide reduced when heated with carbon forming free copper and carbon dioxide?...............................	12	20	L
Does carbon dioxide gas issue from a fire extinguisher in which concentrated sulfuric acids pours into a solution of sodium bicarbonate?......................	12	20	D
Do solutions of aluminum sulfate and sodium bicarbonate react to release carbon dioxide gas in a fire extinguisher of the foam type?......................	12	20	D
Is sugar converted into alcohol and carbon dioxide when yeast is placed in a solution of corn syrup or molasses and kept warm?.............................	12	20	D
Is carbon dioxide liberated when hydrochloric acid is added to carbonates such as limestone and marble or bicarbonates such as baking soda and "alkalizers"?	12	20	L

TABLE IV (CONTINUED)

Experiments Allocated to Principles	Value	Rank	
Can an insoluble salt be prepared by the interaction of two soluble salts (solutions of silver nitrate and sodium chloride or sodium sulfate and barium chloride)? By the interaction of a soluble salt and an acid (solutions of barium chloride and sulfuric acid or silver nitrate and hydrochloric acid?...	12	20	L
Does egg contain sulfur? Does the yolk of an egg tarnish silver?..........	12	20	D
Does iron oxidize more readily in relatively dry air or in more moist air?	11	28	D
What is the ratio by volume in which hydrogen and oxygen combine in an eudiometer to form water?..................	11	28	D
Can the compound copper sulfide be synthesized from its elements by heating?	11	28	L
What change occurs in a clear solution of limewater when carbon dioxide is passed into it?.......................	11	28	L
Does clear limewater turn milky on standing in air? Does air contain carbon dioxide?......................	11	28	L
Does carbon dioxide gas bubbled into cold water form an acid or a base? Does the gas given off by an "alkalizer" form an acid or a base as the gas bubbles in water?..............................	11	28	L
Do the oxides or some metals (sodium and calcium) unite with water to form bases?.............................	11	28	L
Does a candle or hydrogen gas continue to burn in chlorine gas?...........	10	35	L
Can dry hydrogen reduce hot copper oxide to metallic copper?...............	10	35	L
Can copper sulfate crystals be prepared by adding dilute sulfuric acid to cupric oxide?.......................	10	35	L
Is the odor of ether evident after shaking ethyl alcohol with a concentrated sulfuric acid?........................	10	35	L

TABLE IV (CONTINUED)

Experiments Allocated to Principles	Value	Rank	
What gas is evolved when an acid (acetic) is poured on baking soda? Is the same gas evolved when water is added to baking powders? When yeast is mixed with flour and water and allowed to stand in a warm place?...............	10	35	L
Can the silver halides be precipitated by adding a soluble halogen salt such as sodium chloride to a solution of silver nitrate?.........................	10	35	L
As direct current is sent through a small lead cell consisting of two bright lead plates separated by a dilute solution of sulfuric acid, does one plate become unlike the other? When the two plates are disconnected from the direct current source and connected to a small electric bell (or buzzer), does the bell ring? Do the plates become more alike or more unlike as the bell rings (cell discharges)?......................	10	35	D
Can nitrogen be prepared by heating ammonium chloride and sodium nitrite? Does nitrogen burn? Support Combustion?	9	41.5	L
Can sulfur dioxide be prepared by burning sulfur in air? By the decomposition of sulfites (sodium sulfite) by the action of hydrochloric or sulfuric acid? By heating copper and concentrated sulfuric acid?...............	9	41.5	L
What evidence is there of chemical change when a match is burned?..........	9	41.5	L
Can a salt be prepared by the direct union of elements as in burning a piece of sodium in chlorine gas?..............	9	41.5	D
What change occurs in the appearance of a silver coin when sulfur is rubbed on it?..................................	9	41.5	D
Do all baking powders contain starch? Baking soda?...................	9	41.5	L

APPENDIX B

TABLE IV (CONTINUED)

249

Experiments Allocated to Principles	Value	Rank
Can sulfuric acid be prepared by using potassium permanganate to oxidize sulfurous acid prepared by burning sulfur in a bottle of air and dissolving the product, sulfur dioxide, in water?......	8	47.5 L
Does concentrated sulfuric acid dehydrate sugar, wood, paper, or cotton leaving carbon as a residue?............	8	47.5 L
Is carbon dioxide present in greater amount in a bottle of oxygen or a bottle of oxygen in which charcoal has been burned?.................................	8	47.5 L
Can a salt be prepared by the inter-action of a metallic oxide with an acid (cupric oxide and dilute nitric or sul-furic acid, or sodium oxide and hydro-chloric acid)?........................	8	47.5 L
Is starch changed to glucose (Fehling's test) by saliva? By pancreatin? By diastase?......................	8	47.5 L
What color appears when a solution of iodine in alcohol is added to a cold starch solution?......................	8	47.5 L

32. Oxidation always involves the re-moval or sharing of electrons from the element oxidized while the reduction always adds or shares with the element reduced.[1]

33. Oxidation and reduction occur simultaneously and are quantitatively equal.[1]

[1]Since each experiment which contributes to an understanding of Principle number 32 would also contrib-ute to an understanding of Principle number 33, and vice versa, the experiments which are here listed under Principle 33 are considered to be listed also under Principle 32, and the evaluation given each experiment is considered to apply equally to both principles.

Experiments Allocated to Principles	Value	Rank	
Experiments			
Can oxygen be prepared by heating potassium chlorate with a catalyst, manganese dioxide, or by heating red mercuric oxide or by dripping water on sodium peroxide?......................	15	4.5	L
Will oxygen burn in hydrogen?.......	15	4.5	D
Can an electric current (electrons) reduce brownish-yellow ferric chloride to colorless ferrous chloride? Oxidize ferrous to ferric chloride?.............	15	4.5	D
What product condenses on and falls from the inside of a beaker held over a flame of hydrogen burning in air?.......	15	4.5	L
Are carbon dioxide and water products of common oxidation such as breathing and the burning of paper?..............	14	8	L
What difference is there in the action of metals above and below hydrogen in the "activity or replacement series for metals" on dilute and concentrated sulfuric acid, respectively?............	14	8	D
Can a salt be prepared by the substitution of a metal for the hydrogen of an acid as occurs on dropping a piece of sodium or mossy zinc into a dilute solution of hydrochloric acid?..........	14	8	L
When a small piece of sodium is placed on the surface of water is hydrogen liberated? Does the residue give a basic or acid reaction with litmus paper?.....	13	11	D
Can lead be changed to yellow lead oxide or tin to stannic oxide in the oxidizing flame of a blowpipe?..........	13	11	D
Is lead oxide in contact with carbon reduced to lead when heated by gases taken by a blow pipe from the tip of the luminous cone in a Bunsen flame?........	13	11	D
Does oxygen burn? Does oxygen support combustion, that is, does wood or sulfur burning in air continue to burn in oxygen? What effect is observed when a glowing wooden splint or a red-hot iron picture wire is moved from air into oxygen?.................................	12	14.5	L

TABLE IV (<u>CONTINUED</u>)

Experiments Allocated to Principles	Value	Rank	
Is the valence of iron increased by oxidation, that is, does potassium permanganate solution lose its color slowly as it oxidizes ferrous to ferric irons?	12	14.5	X
Can dry hydrogen reduce hot copper oxide to metallic copper?................	12	14.5	D
Can a salt be prepared by the direct union of elements as in burning a piece of sodium in chlorine gas?.............,.	12	14.5	D
Can chloride gas be prepared by using manganese dioxide to oxidize hydrogen chloride as it is made by heating a mixture of sodium chloride and sulfuric acid?	11	17	D
Can sulfur dioxide be prepared by burning sulfur in air? By the decomposition of sulfites (sodium sulfite) from the action of hydrochloric or sulfuric acid? By heating copper and concentrated sulfuric acid?................	10	18	L
Is concentrated nitric acid a strong oxidizing agent? Does hot charred sawdust in an evaporating dish take fire instantly when concentrated nitric acid is poured on it or does a glowing piece of charcoal dropped into nitric acid continue to glow after it touches the acid?	9	20	L
Is hydrogen sulfide a reducing agent, that is, when hydrogen sulfide is bubbled through hydrogen peroxide is the latter reduced to water? Is sulfur precipitated?	9	20	D
How is a spot or stain removed from washable and non-washable cloth if the spot or stain is grease or oil, chocolate or coffee, ink, paint, fruit, grass, iron rust, milk, lipstick, nail polish, chewing gum, or blood?........................	9	20	L
Can spontaneous combustion occur at room temperature to a filter paper removed from a solution of yellow phosphorus in carbon disulfide? To white phosphorus covered with a small amount of boneblack? To a mixture of a drop of glycerine on a small cone of powdered potassium permanganate?................	8	23.5	D

Experiments Allocated to Principles	Value	Rank	
Does the color of potassium permanganate solution disappear in water containing decaying plant or animal matter? In tap water?..................	8	23.5	D
Does ferrous chloride change to brownish-yellow ferric chloride on exposure to air?.........................	8	23.5	D
Can cupric nitrate be prepared from copper turnings and concentrated nitric acid?.....................................	8	23.5	L
What are the approximate percentages of oxygen and of nitrogen in air as determined by the decrease in a volume of air when yellow phosphorus or moist iron filings are introduced into a graduated cylinder or test tube inverted over water?	7	27.	D
Does iron oxidize more readily in relatively dry air or in more moist air?	7	27	X
Will a kitchen knife left moist overnight rust if made of ordinary steel? Stainless steel?......................	7	27	X

34. The exchange of the negative and positive ions of acids and bases results in the formation of water and a salt.

Experiments

Can an acid spilled on cloth be prevented from eating a hole in the cloth by application of ammonium hydroxide without delay?.................................	13	3.5	L
Is the conductivity of a solution a minimum with excess acid or excess base or when neutralization is complete (sulfuric acid from a burette into a solution of barium hydroxide)?..........	13	3.5	X

Experiments Allocated to Principles	Value	Rank	
Does a chemical reaction "run to an end" or "go to completion" when an insoluble gas is formed? (Pour hydrochloric acid on baking soda) When an insoluble precipitate is formed? (Pour silver nitrate solution in hydrochloric acid) When an un-ionized or very slightly ionized product (water) is formed? (Mix a solution of sodium hydroxide and hydrochloric acid.)..................	12	5	D
Can dilute solutions of hydrochloric acid and sodium hydroxide be mixed in an evaporating dish in proportions so that the mixture has no effect on litmus paper? What characteristic taste does the residue have?.................................	11	6	L
Is cotton cloth harmed less if lye spilled on it is removed with water or vinegar?.................................	10	7	L
How do volumes of basic and acid solutions required for neutralization vary with the concentrations of the respective solutions?....................	8	8	D

35. Electrolytes dissolved in water exist partially or completely as electrically charged particles called ions.

Experiments

	Value	Rank	
Do different electrolytes (solutions of sodium carbonate, common salt, hydrochloric acid, sulfuric acid) in a Voltaic cell produce different voltages?..........	13	2.5	D
What characteristic color does a solution of copper sulfate show?..........	13	2.5	L
What color change occurs when direct current is passed through an electrolytic cell containing a solution of potassium iodide with starch as an indicator?.......	12	4	X

Experiments Allocated to Principles	Value	Rank	
Is an electric current produced in a closed circuit when two dissimilar elements are immersed in an electrolyte? Does a galvanometer register current when connected to an iron nail and a copper wire sticking in a lemon? To a penny and a dime separated by a piece of blotting paper which has been dipped in salt water?	11	6	X
If direct current is passed through a saturated solution of sodium chloride in a U-tube, do red and blue litmus paper indicate a base, an acid, or a bleaching agent at the anode? Cathode?...........	11	6	X
Can an old spoon (or copper rod or graphite letter) be copper plated by passing direct current through an electrolytic cell in which the object to be plated is the cathode, the metal to be plated is the anode (copper) and the solution (copper sulfate) is a salt of that metal?.............................	11	6	D
Can chlorine gas be prepared by passing direct current through hydrochloric acid in a Hoffman or similar apparatus?..............................	10	8	D

36. All matter is made up of protons, neutrons, and electrons.

37. The electrons within an atom form shells about the nucleus, each of which contains a definite number of electrons.

38. When elevations or depressions are created upon the surface of the earth, the elevations are usually attacked by the agents of erosion, and the materials are carried to the depressions.

TABLE IV (CONTINUED)

Experiments Allocated to Principles	Value	Rank	
Experiments			
What are some of the features of the coastal plains and their shore lines?..	15	2	L
What are some changes in surface relief brought about by river deposition and floods (the Salton Sea Quadrangle)?	14	3	L
What are some of the features of the shoreline of an emerging continental shelf (sea Isle Sheet)?................	13	4	L
39. Streams, generally, are lowering the surface land in some places and building it up in other places.			
Experiments			
What are some of the features of the coastal plains and their shore lines?...	15	6	L
Does salt water (an electrolyte) cause the precipitation and settling of a colloidal dispersion such as fine clay in water (river delta)?................	14	7	D
What are the depths of water for a typical section of a continental shelf?	10	8	D
40. Rocks may be formed by the compacting and cementing of sediments.			

Principles Having a Total Assigned Value of Fourteen[*]

41. A fluid has a tendency to move from a region of higher pressure to one of lower pressure; the greater the difference, the faster the movement.		

[*]The numerical values assigned to the principles are the sums of the individual evaluations of the five judges on the scale for essential (+3), desirable (+2), and undesirable (-2). These principles are therefore judged essential by all evaluators except one who considered them to be desirable for inclusion in the integrated course if time permitted.

TABLE IV (CONTINUED)

Experiments Allocated to Principles	Value	Rank	
Experiments			
If an inflated balloon is placed under a bell jar on a pump plate, what happens to the balloon as the air pressure in the bell jar is decreased?......	14	15.5	D
Are convection currents set-up in a model of a hot-water heating system? If a glass tube, rectangular in shape has an outlet from a lower corner deep into a flask (boiler) which is closed except for a high funnel filled with water (overflow tank), through what path does wet sawdust in the flask circulate as heat is applied to the flask?...............	14	15.5	D
What happens if air is taken from the upper end of a tube set in an open beaker of mercury (Torricelli's experiment) or any liquid?.................	13	18.5	D
If the stopper to an inverted flask of ammonia gas contains a medicine dropper and a tube with a jet at its upper end extending into the flask from a beaker of water, what happens after a few drops of water are projected into the flask from the medicine dropper (ammonia fountain)?..................	13	18.5	D
If a lighted candle is placed under one of two lamp chimneys over openings in the top of a closed box, what happens to smoke produced at the opening to the other chimney?..............	13	18.5	D
If a divider extends down a lamp chimney to the edge of the flame of a candle in a pan of water, what happens to smoke produced at the top of the chimney on the side of the divider opposite the candle?....................	13	18.5	D
Can a gas be collected by the displacement of water from a bottle inverted in water?........................	12	22.5	X

Experiments Allocated to Principles	Value	Rank	
After a test tube, half filled with water and with a slightly smaller test tube pushed down into it until the water just rises to the top of the larger tube, is inverted while both tubes are held in this position and the inner tube is re-leased as the water begins to run out, what is observed?.....................	12	22.5	D
Does a body of air expand or contract when it is heated? When it is cooled? Is there more or less than a flaskful of air after an inverted flask, fitted with a delivery tube which extends through a vessel of water into an inverted drinking glass entirely full of water, is heated with a Bunsen flame? After the air in the flask is cooled?............	12	22.5	X
When air in the jacket of a model of a hot-air furnace is heated, does smoke move through the jacket when the smoke is held at the top or at the bottom of the jacket?...........................	12	22.5	D
What happens when a small amount of water is heated in a flask or a thick-walled test tube which is corked?.......	11	27	D
What is the relation between the barometric pressure and some of the elements of weather such as temperature, wind velocity, relative humidity and precipitation?......................	11	27	L
Is a better circulation of air (smoke) secured through a shoe box (bedroom) when a flap (window) is opened at the bottom, at the top, or at both the bottom and top?......................	11	27	D
What is the path of circulation in a model of a hot-water heating system? If a lower flask and an upper flask (inverted aspirator) filled with water have large glass tubing extending from their respective stoppers deep into the other flask, in what path does ink placed in the upper flask circulate?.............	11	27	D

TABLE IV (CONTINUED)

Experiments Allocated to Principles	Value	Rank	
Does a pinwheel start rotation when held above a room radiator or over a Bunsen flame?......................	11	27	D
What are satisfactory locations in a room for the "intake" and "outlet" of a hot-air heating system? If a room (square box) has stoppered holes near the top and near the bottom of two walls and near the center and edges of the floor so that a flexible metal tube containing an electrical heating unit near one end can be connected at any two holes, which connections provide the best circulation of air as shown by a smoking stick held at different places within the room?.....................	10	30.5	D
Does a lift pump or a force pump (glass models) give a steadier supply of water at the outlet? Does the volume of air in the "air dome" increase or decrease as the piston moves down? Up?...	10	30.5	D
Does a body of air expand or contract when it is heated? If the open end of a deflated balloon is placed over the only outlet to a flask of air, does the balloon become inflated when the flask of air is heated?.................	9	32	D
If a mailing tube rests over one of two holes opposite each other in the top of a gallon can, what is observed if the can is heated after a few drops of oil or some sawdust or scraps of paper are dropped into the can?..................	8	34.5	D
If a Bunsen flame is applied below a crystal of potassium permanganate (or sawdust) at one edge of a beaker of water, does the color (or sawdust) circulate in a uniform direction?.......	8	34.5	L

TABLE IV (CONTINUED)

Experiments Allocated to Principles	Value	Rank	
May air in motion produce reduced pressure on one side of an object? If a strip of cardboard bent to the shape of the front and upper surface of a wing section is hung over a pencil, does the strip move toward or away from the stream of air blown from a small glass tube past the convex side of the strip?..................................	8	34.5	D
Does a stream of air over a wing section (of heavy paper hinged to a board at the leading edge by gummed paper) cause the trailing edge to rise or remain against the board when the chord of the airfoil section is at a slight angle to the relative wind?.................	8	34.5	D
Does a body of air expand or contract when it is heated? When it is cooled? If an inflated balloon is adjusted between two rings on a stand so that the balloon just touches the rings, does the balloon expand or contract when hot water is poured over it? When cold water is poured over it?.................	7	37	D

42. Any two bodies attract one another with a force which is directly proportional to the attracting masses and inversely proportional to the square of the distance between their centers of mass.

Experiments

	Value	Rank	
How is water softened and treated by aeration, sedimentation, precipitation, filtration, and chlorination in a city water treatment plant (a field trip)?...	12	1	D
Where do the finest particles settle after sand and small gravel are stirred vigorously in water?.....................	11	2.5	X
Do fine particles or coarse particles settle more rapidly from a muddy mixture of sand and water and are therefore found at the bottom of the container?...	11	2.5	X

Experiments Allocated to Principles	Value	Rank	
How do comets curve around the sun when they come near it and why do they make such paths? If a ball bearing (one-half inch in diameter) rolls down a grooved inclined plane which may have its lower end directed toward or away from the end of the core of an electro-magnet (current from a storage battery) on a level with and near the bottom of the grooved plane, what is the path of the "comet" (ball) when not near the sun (Current is off.)? With the current on, can the trough be aimed closer and closer to the magnet so that the "comet" (ball) will go around the "sun" (magnet) and come back almost in the same direction from which it came?..................................	10	5.5	D
What relation, if any, is there between the time of spring and neap tides and the phases of the moon?.............	10	5.5	L
How is sewage treated in a modern sewage-disposal plant (a field trip)?...	10	5.5	D
Can insoluble suspended matter (calcium carbonate, sand, or flour in water) be separated slowly from the liquid by decantation (allowing the suspended matter to settle and pouring off the liquid)?........................	10	5.5	L
Does most of the suspended matter in muddy water settle out on standing?..	9	8	X
What happens to a miniature parachute rolled up with a weight and thrown into the air?...................	6	9	D

43. Movements of all bodies in the solar system are due to gravitational attraction and inertia.

TABLE IV (CONTINUED)

Experiments Allocated to Principles	Value	Rank
44. The pressure in a fluid in the open is equal to the weight of the fluid above a unit area including the point at which the pressure is taken; it therefore varies with the depth and average density of the fluid.		
Experiments If a cardboard disk is held against the bottom of a glass cylinder by means of a string until the cylinder is partly submerged and then the string is released, how long can water be poured slowly into the cylinder before the disk is pushed loose, that is, what is the relation between the upward and the downward pressure of water at the same depth; also, what is the relation between the pressure and the depth of a liquid? If vessels of different shapes but with the same size opening at the bottom are used, do equal depths produce equal or different pressures independent of or dependent on the shape of the vessel?.....................................	14	5 D
How can water be made to run faster through one siphon than through another siphon? How is the rate of flow of a siphon affected by the kind of liquid? The internal diameter of the tube? The difference in height (pressure, not weight) between the upper water level, and the lower water level or end open to air?.....................................	13	6 X
If the upward force on an aluminum rod is suspended in a liquid from one arm of a beam balance and counterpoised, what is the relation of the pressure (on the bottom of the rod) to the depth below the surface of the liquid? To the density of the liquid (water and salt water or gasoline) for a given depth?...	11	7 X

APPENDIX B

TABLE IV (<u>CONTINUED</u>)

Experiments Allocated to Principles	Value	Rank	
If a test tube (with shot and solidified paraffin at its bottom) floating in water or salt water or gasoline) contains a ruler to measure its changes in depth as more weights are added in the tube, how does the pressure (weights added) change with depth? With the density of the liquid for a given depth?................................	10	8	X
As the piston of a model glass lift pump is moved upward is water moved higher than its immediate source?............	9	9	D
45. Bodies in rotation tend to fly out in a straight line which is tangent to the arc of rotation.			
<u>Experiment</u> What happens to a metal hoop free to move about a central axis as the speed of rotation is increased? Decreased?......	13	5	D
46. A body immersed or floating in a fluid is buoyed up by a force equal to the weight of the fluid displaced.			
<u>Experiments</u> Does a fresh egg sink or float when placed in fresh water? What happens to the egg when salt water is mixed with the fresh water? When more fresh water is added?...............................	15	11.5	D
Will an iron ball float or sink in mercury?.............................	15	11.5	D
What is the specific gravity of any solid? Is the specific gravity of any solid, heavier or lighter than water, always equal to the weight of the solid in air divided by its apparent loss of weight in any liquid (the buoyant force) multiplied by the specific gravity of that liquid?................................	14	14.5	L

Experiments Allocated to Principles	Value	Rank	
What is the specific gravity of any solid? Is the specific gravity of any solid, heavier or lighter than water, always equal to the weight of the solid in air divided by the weight of water displaced by it when it is submerged?...	14	14.5	X
What is the specific gravity of any liquid? Is the specific gravity of any liquid always equal to the apparent loss of weight of a solid in that liquid divided by the apparent loss of weight of the same solid in water (loss of weight method)?......................	14	14.5	X
What is the specific gravity of any liquid? Is the specific gravity of any liquid always equal to the weight of a given volume of the liquid divided by the weight of the same volume of water (bottle method)?......................	14	14.5	D
Will a sunken bottle (submarine) filled with water rise or go deeper as air is blown into the bottle to replace the water?............................	13	17.5	D
Do some floating objects such as balsa wood, cork, maple and ice sink more deeply than others?...............	13	17.5	D
Does a hollow metal ball, which is counterpoised on a beam balance after the air is taken from the ball, remain balanced, go up, or go down as air enters the ball? Why?......................	11	19.5	D
What is the specific gravity of a liquid as determined by the hydrometer method?................................	11	19.5	D
47. The pressure at a point in any fluid is the same in all directions.			

Experiments Allocated to Principles	Value	Rank	
Experiment			
If a cardboard disk is held against the bottom of a glass cylinder by means of a string until the cylinder is partly submerged and then the string is released, how long can water be poured slowly into the cylinder before the disk is pushed loose, that is, what is the relation between the upward and the downward pressure of water at the same depth; also, what is the relation between the pressure and the depth of a liquid? If vessels of different shapes but with the same size opening at the bottom are used, do equal depths produce equal or different pressures independent of or dependent on the shape of the vessel?................................	12	3	D
48. Heat is conducted by the transfer of kinetic energy from molecule to molecule.[1]			
49. When two bodies of different temperature are in contact, there is a continuous transference of heat energy from the body of higher temperature to the one of lower temperature, the rate of which is directly proportional to the difference of temperature.[1]			

[1]Since each experiment which contributes to an understanding of Principle number 48 would also contribute to an understanding of Principle number 49, and vice versa, the experiments which are here listed under Principle 49 are considered to be listed also under Principle 48, and the evaluation given each experiment is considered to apply equally to both principles.

TABLE IV (CONTINUED)

Experiments Allocated to Principles	Value	Rank	
Experiments			
If a piece of ice is held in the bottom of a test tube by a lead weight, can the water in the upper part of the test tube be heated to the boiling point without melting the ice?...............	15	7	X
If a test tube nearly full of water is heated near the top of the water with the bottom of the tube held in the hand, does the water at the top of the tube boil before heat is conducted down to the hand?..............................	14	8	L
Will a beaker placed on water on a board be frozen to the board if air is blown into ether in the beaker? If a watch glass is placed on water in a small hole in a cork and air is blown across ether in the glass, what is observed when the watch glass is picked up?	13	10.5	D
What sensation is felt when a liquid such as water, alcohol, or ether, placed on only one hand, is blown upon?........	13	10.5	L
When "dry ice" is placed on water, what evidence is there of a change from solid to gaseous carbon dioxide?........	13	10.5	D
If similar marbles (or B-B shot) are held by paraffin at regular intervals along an iron rod and one end of the rod is heated, in what order do the marbles fall, that is, does an iron rod conduct heat from the hot toward the colder portions of the rod, or vice versa?.....	13	10.5	D
If a test tube of ether is placed in a slightly larger test tube of water, does the water between the two tubes freeze when air is bubbled through the ether?..................................	12	14	D
Will a thermos bottle keep hot liquids hot and cold liquids cold for a few hours?..............................	12	14	D

TABLE IV (CONTINUED)

Experiments Allocated to Principles	Value	Rank	
If a thermometer is placed in a test tube of water in a mixture of cracked ice and salt, does the temperature (thermometer reading) rise, fall, or remain the same until ice begins to form? While ice is being formed? After all water has changed to ice? If the mixture of ice and salt is removed and the thermometer is read while the ice is melting, is the melting point of ice the same temperature as the freezing point of water?...	12	14	X
How is ice made in a commercial plant (a field trip)?...................	11	16.5	D
What is the result of unequal heating when boiling water is poured quickly into a thick-walled glass tumbler?......	11	16.5	D
Will "dry ice" freeze mercury in a test tube around which ether and "dry ice" are placed?......................	9	19.5	D
Does the air in a flask expand or contract when heated? When cooled? If an inverted flask of air with a glass tube through the stopper dips into water, does the water inside the tube move down to indicate expansion of the air or up to indicate contraction of the air when a warm hand is held on the flask? When a cloth wet with cold water is placed on the flask?................	9	19.5	D
Does a body of liquid expand or contract when it is heated? When it is cooled? If colored water fills a flask and is part way up in a glass tube inserted in the stopper to the flask, does the level of water in the tube rise or fall as the flask is heated? As the flask is cooled?........................	9	19.5	D
Does a glass rod heated in a flame crack when immersed in cold water?......	9	19.5	L

TABLE IV (<u>CONTINUED</u>)

Experiments Allocated to Principles	Value	Rank	
Does a body of air expand or contract when it is heated? When it is cooled? If an inflated balloon is adjusted between two rings on a stand so that the balloon just touches the rings, does the balloon expand or contract when hot water is poured over it? When cold water is poured over it?.....	8	22	D
50. The lower the temperature of a body, the less the amount of energy it radiates; the higher the temperature, the greater is the amount of energy radiated.			
51. Heat is transferred by convection in currents of gases or liquids, the rate of transfer decreasing with an increase in the viscosity of the circulating fluid.			
Experiments If a mailing tube rests over one of two holes opposite each other in the top of a gallon can, what is observed if the can is heated after a few drops of oil or some sawdust or scraps of paper are dropped into the can?..................	15	8.5	D
When air in the jacket of a model of a hot-air furnace is heated, does smoke move through the jacket when the smoke is held at the top or at the bottom of the jacket?............................	15	8.5	D
If a model of a hot water tank is made by inserting deep into a laboratory-type boiler (the tank) a tube connected to the side outlet of an inverted aspirator with a air-tube up through its center and by connecting an outlet tube just through the stopper of the tank, how does the temperature of the water that flows from the heated tank compare with that flowing into the tank?........................	13	10.5	D

268

APPENDIX B

TABLE IV (CONTINUED)

Experiments Allocated to Principles	Value	Rank	
Does a pinwheel start rotation when held above a room radiator or over a Bunsen flame?......................	13	10.5	D
What are satisfactory locations in a room for the "intake" and "outlet" of a hot-air heating system? If a room (square box) has stoppered holes near the top and near the bottom of two walls and near the center and the edges of the floor so that a flexible metal tube containing an electrical heating unit near one end can be connected at any two holes, which connections provide the best circulation of air as shown by a smoking stick held at different places within the room?....	11	13	D
How is ice made in a commercial plant (a field trip)?....................	11	13	D
How are cold-storage plants cooled (a field trip)?....................	11	13	D
If a moth ball on a sheet of metal is heated gently over a Bunsen flame, until half the ball is melted, and is then covered with a tall cool glass, what is the direction of circulation of the sparkling flakes (and air) which appear?	10	15	D

52. Every pure liquid has its own specific boiling and freezing point.

Experiments

If a thermometer is placed in a test tube of water in a mixture of cracked ice and salt, does the temperature (thermometer reading) rise, fall, or remain the same until ice begins to form? While ice is being formed? After all water has changed to ice? If the mixture of ice and salt is removed and the thermometer is read while the ice is melting, is the melting point of ice the same temperature as the freezing point of water?..........	15	3	L

Experiments Allocated to Principles	Value	Rank	
Do solutions of different anti-freezes, namely, methyl alcohol, de-natured alcohol, glycerine and "Prestone," boil away at the same or different temperatures?..............	14	4	D
If a solid (citric acid, cane sugar, naphthalene, lead) is placed in glass tubing which is tapered and closed at the end, and the tube with a thermometer attached is suspended in melted paraffin which is being heated, at what temperature does the solid begin to melt?.....	10	5	D

53. The higher the pitch of a note, the more rapid the vibrations of the producing body and vice versa.

Experiment
If an open or closed organ pipe produces its lowest or fundamental tone when blown into, does blowing harder result in a tone of higher frequency or pitch?............................ 9 3 D

54. Musical tones are produced when a vibrating body sends out regular vibrations to the ear while only noises are produced when the vibrating body sends out irregular vibrations to the ear.

55. Energy is often transmitted in the form of waves.

56. When waves strike an object, they may be absorbed, transmitted, or reflected.

APPENDIX B

TABLE IV (CONTINUED)

Experiments Allocated to Principles	Value	Rank	
Experiments			
On what does the color of an opaque object depend? What color does white, red, and blue cloth, respectively, appear to be when held separately in white, red, and blue light?........................	14	2.5	X
On what does the color of transparent objects depend? Does a piece of transparent red glass (also green) transmit or absorb to a high degree white light? Red light? Green light?..................	14	2.5	X
Is common glass, wax paper or a book, transparent, translucent or opaque?......	12	4	X
Do colored lights add or subtract certain colors? What colors are observed on a white paper flat on a table and midway between two electric light bulbs of different colors such as red and green or yellow and blue (mixing lights)? Do colored pigments add or subtract certain colors? If a printed picture of red and green colors is placed under a microscope, what is observed where each color predominates (mixing pigments)?.........	9	5	D
If a person holds a basketball (the moon) a little higher than his head in a line between the head (the earth) and a flashlight or floorlamp (the sun) and then turns entirely around toward his left, how much of the half of the moon facing him is lighted, when it has been turned one-fourth, half, three-fourths and all the way around?................	8	6.5	D
Are particles of chalk dust in the path of a beam of light in a darkened room visible to the naked eye? Do the dust particles exhibit random motion?.........	8	6.5	D

57. When light rays are absorbed, some of the light energy is transformed into heat energy.

TABLE IV (CONTINUED)

Experiments Allocated to Principles	Value	Rank	
58. The darker the color of a surface, the better it absorbs light.			
Experiments			
If two thermometer bulbs, one wrapped in black cloth and the other in white cloth, are held in bright white light, which thermometer registers the greater rise in temperature?.....................	15	3	L
Is radiant energy (heat and light) absorbed more rapidly by a dark surface or by a similar surface of lighter color? Does snow (or finely cracked ice) melt more rapidly under a piece of black metal (or cloth) exposed to sunlight (or a Bunsen flame) than under a similar piece of metal (or cloth) of lighter color, or vice versa?...........................	15	3	X
If an opaque board shades a light meter from an electric lamp in a box in which the interior walls are made different colors, what color gives the highest light readings? The poorest light readings?......................	15	3	D
If a white-tipped match held at the focal point of light rays does not ignite, will it ignite after being darkened with a soft pencil lead?..........	12	5	D
How does the speed of rotation of the vanes of a Crookes' radiometer vary with the intensity of light (shade and bright sunlight)? With the intensity of radiant heat (hot and cold metal)?...	10	6	D
59. The intensity of illumination decreases as the square of the distance from a point source.			
60. Radiant energy travels in waves along straight lines, its intensity at any distance from a point source is inversely proportional to the square of the distance from the source.			

Experiments Allocated to Principles	Value	Rank	
Experiment What is the candle power of an electric lamp measured by using a paraffin-block (Joly) photometer and a lamp of known candle power (Assume a forty-watt lamp to be thirty-two candle power)?..............................	12	1	D
61. When light rays pass obliquely from a rare to a more dense medium, they are bent or refracted toward the normal and when they pass obliquely from a dense to a rarer medium, they are bent away from the normal.			
Experiment If one triangular glass prism disperses white light into a color band, can a second prism placed alongside the first one to make a parallelogram, recombine those colors to produce white light?....	10	6	D
62. An image appears to be as far back of a plane mirror as the object is in front of the mirror and is reversed.			
63. Parallel light rays may be converged or focused by convex lenses or concave mirrors; diverged by concave lenses or convex mirrors.			
Experiment Does a convex (and a concave) lens converge or diverge parallel light rays (Hart's optical disk)?.................	14	3	D
64. Protons and neutrons only are found in the nucleus of an atom.			

Experiments Allocated to Principles	Value	Rank
65. In an unchanged body there are as many protons as electrons and the charges neutralize each other while a deficiency of electrons produces a plus charge on a body and an excess of electrons produces a negative charge.		

Experiments
   Do two inflated rubber balloons suspended almost side-by-side attract or repel each other when they are given the same kind of charge by rubbing them with flannel? When they are given different kinds of charges by rubbing one balloon with flannel and the other with sulfur? — 14 — 8 — D

   Does a pith ball suspended on silk thread between two bells, one grounded and the other connected by a chain to one terminal of a static machine, ring the bells alternately when the machine is in operation?...................... — 13 — 10.5 — D

   Can pith dolls (or balls) be made to "dance" between two parallel metal plates connected to a static machine?... — 13 — 10.5 — D

   If a suspended uncharged pith ball is grounded with the finger while a charged rubber rod is under, but not touching, the ball, is the pith ball more or less strongly attracted by the rod than before touching the ball with the finger? Does a charged glass rod attract or repel the pith ball, that is, when a negatively charged object is used to charge a body by induction, what charge results in the body?............. — 13 — 10.5 — D

   If a positively charged metal ball is suspended by an insulating thread in a metal vessel, are the inner and outer surfaces of the vessel neutral, positive or negative (as shown by using a proof plane), that is, are charges of opposite surfaces of a conductor by a charged body on one side of the conductor?.......... — 13 — 10.5 — D

—kinds induced on opposite

Experiments Allocated to Principles	Value	Rank	
Are electrons liberated as a metal is dissolved in a solvent? When the zinc terminal of a battery of six small Voltaic cells is connected to a lower metal disc on a leaf electroscope and the copper terminal is connected to an upper disc insulated from the lower one with shellac, does removing the connections and then the upper disc leave the electroscope negatively charged with electrons liberated at the zinc terminal as a result of chemical action?......................	12	13.5	D
If a Leyden jar is charged by grounding the outside metal and connecting the inside metal with one pole of a static machine, does a spark discharge occur when an insulated metal conductor touching the outside metal of the jar is brought near the knob connected with the inside metal?..................	12	13.5	D
Does salt water (an electrolyte) cause the precipitation and settling of a colloidal dispersion such as fine clay in water (river delta)?..................	11	15	L
If a conical linen bag (a conductor), charged negatively by contact, is fastened at its large end to an insulated metal ring and a long silk thread extends through the apex, does a proof-plane (penny at the end of a stick of sealing wax) show a negative charge on the inner and outer surfaces of the bag before and after the thread is pulled to turn the bag "inside out", that is, do charges on an isolated conductor tend to reside on the outside surface?..................	9	16	D
Does a saturated solution of common salt coagulate a colloidal dispersion of soap in water which settles on standing?	7	17	X

TABLE IV (CONTINUED)

Experiments Allocated to Principles	Value	Rank
66. An electrical charge in motion produces a magnetic field about the conductor, its direction being tangential to any circle drawn about the conductor in a plane perpendicular to it.		
Experiments Does a coil of wire have at its ends a north and a south pole like a bar magnet when a direct current passes through the wire? If so, does reversing the direction of the current in the wire also reverse the polarity?...............	14	6.5 L
If a flat stationary coil of wire is placed parallel to a similar lightweight coil suspended from a high point and free to move, is the suspended coil attracted or repelled by the stationary coil when direct current in the latter is started? Stopped? Is the direction of the current induced in the movable coil always such as to produce a polarity for the movable coil which will oppose the building up and dying out of the magnetic field of the stationary coil, that is, whenever a change is made in an electromagnetic system is there always brought into existence something which opposes that change (Lenz's law)?..............	14	6.5 D
Does a wire free to swing between the poles of a U-shaped magnet move when a current is passed through the wire (motor)?................................	13	9 L
How is an electric bell constructed, and what makes it ring?................	13	9 L
When two coils of wire on separate closed circuits are placed side by side or one within the other, does current flow in one coil (the secondary) when current is started, stopped, varied or steady in the other coil (the primary), that is, when the number of magnetic lines of force (flux) passing through the secondary coil is changed or steady?.....	13	9 D

Experiments Allocated to Principles	Value	Rank
What is the shape of the magnetic field of a helix as determined by shaking iron filings on a horizontal surface which dissects the helix lengthwise?....	12	11.5 X
How is a simple telegraph system connected and what happens to the relay and the sounder when the key is depressed and released?................................	12	11.5 X
If the armature of a St. Louis motor is in series with a rheostat and two dry cells, how is the rotation affected by reversing only the connections of the dry cells? By reversing only the polarity of the magnets? By reversing both the polarity of the magnets and the direction of the current through the armature? By decreasing the resistance in the rheostat?......................	11	13 X
Is the shape of the magnetic field about the two vertical sides of each of two rectangular loops of wire at right angles to each other a figure "8" when excited with direct current (instead of alternating current as in a loop-antenna range station)?......................	9	14 D
If three dry cells and a galvanometer are connected in series with a telephone transmitter, does the galvanometer needle remain motionless, move in the same direction, or move in opposite directions when pressure is applied gently to the diaphragm of the transmitter and then released? When a telephone receiver is substituted for the galvanometer, can words spoken into the transmitter be heard from the receiver in an adjacent room?................................	7	15 D

67. All materials offer some resistance to the flow of electric current, and that part of the electrical energy used in overcoming this resistance is transformed into heat energy.

Experiments Allocated to Principles	Value	Rank	

Experiments

What is the efficiency of an electric grill or heater as determined by calculating the heat absorbed (heat output) by a known weight of water in a weighed container and the heat input by measuring the average ammeter and voltmeter readings and the time of operation for the heating device?...................... | 15 | 5 | D

When a beaker of water containing an insulated coil of copper wire with a flashlight bulb in series is set on the end of a large coil of coarse insulated copper wire connected to an 110-volt A.C. circuit with a lamp in series, does the temperature of the water rise (induction heating)? Does the bulb light?......... | 11 | 6 | D

What is the electrical equivalent of heat energy, that is, how many watt-seconds (Joules) are required to produce one calorie of heat when an electric bulb or heating coil is used in water? | 10 | 7 | X

68. The resistance of a metallic conductor depends on the kind of material from which the conductor is made, varies directly with the length, inversely with the cross sectional area, and increases as the temperature increases.

Experiments

Will the current from two dry cells melt (overload) a short piece of small (no. 30) copper wire? The same length of larger wire (no. 14) used for wiring homes?................................. | 14 | 5 | D

If a piece of iron wire is inserted in a circuit of copper wire of similar diameter, does the iron or copper wire become hot more readily when current passes through the circuit?............. | 13 | 6 | X

278

Experiments Allocated to Principles	Value	Rank	
If five feet of iron wire, wound on a glass rod, is in series with a dry cell and an ammeter, is the current increased or decreased after the coil at room temperature is heated with a Bunsen flame, that is, does the resistance of a metallic conductor increase (less current) or decrease (more current) with a rise in temperature?..........................	12	7	X
69. The electrical current flowing in a conductor is directly proportional to the potential difference and inversely proportional to the resistance.			
Experiments How are a voltmeter and an ammeter correctly and safely used to measure voltage and current?....................	12	3.5	D
Does a series or a parallel arrangement of cells (non-polarizing or Daniell) give greater current when the external resistance is much larger than the total internal resistance of the cells and vice versa?..............................	12	3.5	X
If a flat iron and a lighted electric lamp in parallel are connected in series with an ammeter and a source of 110-volt A.C., is there an increase or a decrease, when the iron is turned on, of the current in the main line, the voltage across the lamp, and the brightness of the lamp?.................................	10	5	D
If an iron wire and a copper wire of the same diameter and length are connected to an 110-volt A.C. circuit, do paper riders on the iron and copper wires burn when the wires are in series? In parallel?.................................	9	7.5	D

TABLE IV (<u>CONTINUED</u>)

Experiments Allocated to Principles	Value	Rank	
If current (from a storage battery or dry cells) passes for a very short time through equal lengths (100 cms) of different kinds of wire (German silver and copper) of the same size, do different materials of the same size and length have different resistances (calculated by using voltmeter and ammeter readings in Ohm's Law)?.........	9	7.5	X
If current (from a storage battery or dry cells) passes for a very short time through fifty and then 100 centimeters of the same kind of wire (no. 30 copper wire or the wire on a Wheatstone bridge), what is the relation between the resistance of the uniform wire (calculated by using voltmeter and ammeter readings in Ohm's Law) and its length?..........	9	7.5	X
If current (from a storage battery or dry cells) passes for a very short time through equal lengths (100 cms) of the same kind of wire (copper) of different cross-sectional area (The diameter of B and S no. 18 is twice that of no. 21.), what is the relation between the resistance of wire (calculated by using voltmeter and ammeter readings in Ohm's Law) and its cross-sectional area?......	9	7.5	X

70. Electrical power is directly proportional to the product of the potential difference and the current.

Experiments
How do mazada lamps compare with fluorescent lamps of comparable candle power with respect to power consumption?	14	3	D
What is the cost of electrical energy for a home for one month?...............	13	4	X
Does an electric toaster or iron use the wattage listed on the device?.......	12	5	L

Experiments Allocated to Principles	Value	Rank
71. When a current-carrying wire is placed in a magnetic field, there is a force acting on the wire tending to push it at right angles to the direction of the lines of force between the magnetic poles, providing the wire is not parallel to the field.		
Experiments		
How is a simple electric motor constructed and made to run?...............	13	2.5 L
If a flat rectangular coil of insulated wire (no. 26) is suspended by a thread with its edges between and in line with the north and south poles of a U-shaped magnet, is the coil deflected when current is passed through it (D'Arsonval galvanometer)? Does an increase of current through the coil cause greater deflection? Does reversing the direction of the current through the coil also reverse the direction of its deflection?...........................	13	2.5 X
If the armature of a St. Louis motor is in series with a rheostat and two dry cells, how is the rotation affected by reversing only the connections of the dry cells? By reversing only the polarity of the magnets? By reversing both the polarity of the magnets and the direction of the current through the armature? By decreasing the resistance in the rheostat?	11	4 L
72. The atoms of all radioactive elements are constantly disintegrating by giving off various rays (alpha, beta, and gamma) and forming helium and other elements.		

TABLE IV (CONTINUED)

Experiments Allocated to Principles	Value	Rank	
Experiment			
Are separate flashes of light visible when the zinc sulfide screen in a spinthatiscope is examined in the dark?....................................	15	2	L
73. The solubility of solutes is affected by heat, pressure, and the nature of the solute and solvent.			
Experiments			
Does a saturated solution of sugar dissolve salt just as readily as plain water?..................................	15	7	L
Can so much of a solid (alum; common salt) be dissolved in water at room temperature that an additional amount of the same solid does not dissolve but settles to the bottom and remains there?	14	9	L
Do crystals form more rapidly when a supersaturated solution of sodium acetate or sodium thiosulfate ("hypo") in a flask is allowed to cool without moving the flask or when the solution is disturbed by stirring or by suspending a small crystal of the same substance on a string in the solution? Does the flask feel warmer or cooler as crystallization proceeds?.................................	14	9	D
Can tincture of iodine be prepared more readily by placing crystals of iodine and potassium iodide in grain alcohol or in water?....................	14	9	L
Does warm or cold water possess a greater cleansing power?...............	13	14	L
Can an insoluble salt be prepared by the interaction of two soluble salts (solutions of silver nitrate and sodium chloride or sodium sulfate and barium chloride)? By the interaction of a soluble salt and an acid (solutions of barium chloride and sulfuric acid or silver nitrate and hydrochloric acid)?..	13	14	L

Experiments Allocated to Principles	Value	Rank	
What is the relative solubility of carbon in dilute acids and bases, alcohol, and water?.....................	13	14	L
Are most metallic oxides soluble in water?...................................	13	14	L
Are the nitrates of all metals soluble in water?......................	13	14	L
Can India ink (carbon), blue ink (washable dye) and blue-black ink (iron; permanent) be removed both before and after the ink dries by the use of water alone? Soap and water? A reducing agent (solution of oxalic acid or lemon juice)? An oxidizing agent ("Clorox")?	13	14	L
How can a model limestone cave be demonstrated? If a rectangular box with a glass window on one side contains the following layers slanting upward to the left from bottom to top: sand, plaster of Paris (thin dough), rock salt, plaster of Paris (with holes at the lower end for an outlet), and sand, what is the path of the water which drips slowly upon the sand at the top left for several hours? In what material does the water "eat out" a cave?................................	13	14	D
Can an insoluble base (ferric hydroxide) be prepared by treating a soluble salt of some metal (ferric chloride) with some soluble base (sodium hydroxide)?	12	19.5	L
Does boiling soften water of temporary and permanent hardness? Does soap solution form suds more readily with water of temporary hardness (containing calcium bicarbonate) before or after boiling the water? With water of permanent hardness (containing magnesium sulfate) before or after boiling the water?......	12	19.5	L
Does common soap or "soapless soap" (Dreft) form more suds in hard water? Do the "soapless soaps" lather just as freely in hard water as in soft water?...	12	19.5	L

TABLE IV (CONTINUED)

Experiments Allocated to Principles	Value	Rank	
Will a higher percentage of equal weights of orange pekoe or pekoe tea dissolve in hot water?.................	12	19.5	L
Does the ammonia fountain indicate a high or low degree of solubility of ammonia in water at room temperature?.....	11	22.5	D
Will limestone or marble dissolve in tap water? Rain water?.................	11	22.5	L
Can the speed at which a solid (copper sulfate) dissolves in a solvent (water) be increased by stirring? By pulverizing the solid to increase the surface area?......................	10	25	L
Does starch form a paste when put in cold water? Hot water?................	10	25	L
How can painted surfaces, varnished or oiled surfaces, and windows be safely cleaned?.............................	10	25	L
Can the taste be restored to boiled water by pouring it from one vessel to another several times?.................	9	29.5	L
Are rubbing alcohol, glycerine, and carbon tetrachloride, respectively, soluble in water on shaking?............	9	29.5	L
Is bromine more soluble in water or carbon tetrachloride? In water or carbon disulfide?.............................	9	29.5	D
Can ink be eradicated with a solution of equal parts by weight of tartaric and citric acid in twenty times their combined weight of water?.................	9	29.5	L
Can "spirits of camphor" be prepared by placing camphor gum in grain alcohol?	9	29.5	L
Does acetone remove both shellac and varnish from wood?......................	9	29.5	I
Does a small amount of soap solution form a curdy precipitate or a lasting suds with soft water (distilled water or water containing sodium sulfate)? With hard water (water containing calcium or magnesium sulfate)? With tap water?....	8	33.5	L

Experiments Allocated to Principles	Value	Rank
How is a spot or stain removed from washable and non-washable cloth if the spot or stain is grease, chocolate or coffee or oil, ink, paint, fruit, grass, iron rust, milk, lipstick, nail polish, chewing gum, or blood?.................	8	33.5 L
Which more readily forms suds with soap, distilled water or hard water? Does distilled water require more or less soap solution than hard water to produce a lather which lasts?....................	7	35.5 L
What percentage of a given sample of soil is acid-insoluble matter? Acid-soluble matter or reserve plant food?.....	7	35.5 L
74. The valence of an atom is determined by the number of electrons it gains, loses or shares in chemical reactions.[1]		
75. Most atoms have the property of losing, gaining or sharing a number of out shell electrons.[1]		

[1]Since each experiment which contributes to an understanding of Principle number 74 would also contribute to an understanding of Principle number 75, and <u>vice versa</u>, the experiments which are here listed under Principle 75 are considered to be listed also under Principle 74, and the evaluation given each experiment is considered to apply equally to both principles.

Experiments Allocated to Principles	Value	Rank
Experiments Which metals (sodium, magnesium, aluminum, lead, copper) displace hydrogen from dilute hydrochloric or sulfuric acid? Does a metal displace hydrogen from the acid if the metal is above hydrogen in the "activity or replacement series for metals?" If the metal is below hydrogen in the series? Is the chemical reaction faster if the metal and hydrogen are farther apart or closer together in the series?................	14	4.5 D
If strips of zinc and copper, respectively, are placed in separate sets of six solutions, namely, dilute hydrochloric acid, lead nitrate, silver nitrate, nitric acid, copper sulfate, and aluminum sulfate, what elements does zinc replace from the compounds in solution? Not replace? What elements does copper replace from the compounds in solution? Not replace? Do metals higher in the "activity or replacement series of metals" displace metals lower in the series from solutions of their compounds or <u>vice versa</u>?................................	14	4.5 D
Is an electric current produced in a closed circuit when two dissimilar elements are immersed in an electrolyte? Does a galvanometer register current when connected to an iron nail and a copper wire sticking in a lemon? To a penny and a dime separated by a piece of blotting paper which has been dipped in salt water?.........................	12	6 D
76. The energy shown by atoms in completing their outer shell by adding, losing or sharing electrons determines their chemical activity.		

Experiments Allocated to Principles	Value	Rank	
Experiments Is an electric current produced in a closed circuit when two dissimilar elements are immersed in an electrolyte? Does a galvanometer register current when connected to an iron nail and a copper wire sticking in a lemon? To a penny and a dime separated by a piece of blotting paper which has been dipped in salt water?............................	12	3	D
Are electrons liberated as a metal dissolves in a solvent? When the zinc terminal of a battery of six small Voltaic cells is connected to a lower metal disc on a leaf electroscope and the copper terminal is connected to an upper disc insulated from the lower one with shellac, does removing the connections and then the upper disc leave the electroscope negatively charged with electrons liberated at the zinc terminal as a result of chemical action?.........	11	4	D
As direct current is sent through a small lead storage cell consisting of two bright lead plates separated by a dilute solution of sulfuric acid, does one plate become unlike the other? When the two plates are disconnected from the direct-current source and connected to a small electric bell (or buzzer), does the bell ring? Do the plates become more alike or more unlike as the bell rings (cell discharges)?................	10	5.5	X
Does a small electric bell ring when its two terminals are connected to the zinc (amalgamated) and copper (or carbon) electrodes, respectively, of a Voltaic cell containing dilute sulfuric acid as the electrolyte? Does the bell ring when the two electrodes are the same element?................................	10	5.5	D

Experiments Allocated to Principles	Value	Rank	
If direct current is passed through a saturated solution of sodium chloride in a U-tube, do red and blue litmus paper indicate a base, an acid, or a bleaching agent at the anode? Cathode?	9	7	D
77. The properties of the elements show periodic variations with their atomic numbers.			
78. Each combustible substance has a kindling temperature which varies with its condition but may be greater or less than the kindling temperature of some other substance.			
Experiments			
Does the flame of a gas ignited above a wire gauze, placed horizontally several inches above a Bunsen burner, go below the gauze?..............................	12	4	X
If a petri dish containing kerosene is floated on a pan of water being heated gradually, at what temperature does a flame moved across the surface of the kerosene first "flash" and disappear?...	12	4	D
Does the tip of a file have to be hotter to ignite yellow phosphorus or to ignite red phosphorus?....................	12	4	D
Will the unburned gas from the inner cone of a flame burn?....................	10	6	D
Can a candle flame be extinguished by holding a copper spiral in the flame?	9	7	D
What is the "flash point" and fire point for each of three different brands of lubricating oils of the same S.A.E. rating?............,.....................	8	8	D

APPENDIX B

TABLE IV (CONTINUED)

Experiments Allocated to Principles	Value	Rank
79. Matter may be transformed into radiant energy and radiant energy into matter; in either case, the mass is unchanged.		
80. The total mass of a quantity of matter is not altered by any chemical or physical changes occurring among the materials composing it. (except in nuclear physics).		
81. The rates of many reactions are affected by the presence of substances which do not enter into the completed chemical reaction.		
Experiments		
Can glucose (Fehling's test) be prepared by boiling starch in water with a few drops of dilute hydrochloric acid to act as a catalyst?...................	15	3.5 D
Can sucrose (cane and beet sugar) be converted to glucose (Fehling's test) by boiling sucrose in water with a few drops of dilute hydrochloric acid to act as a catalyst?..............................	15	3.5 D
82. Acids and bases in water solution ionize to give hydrogen and hydroxyl ions, respectively, from their constituent elements.		
Experiments		
What is the characteristic taste and feel of very dilute acids? Of very dilute bases?.............................,.	15	1 L
Is a sample of soil acid, that is, does a paste of the soil turn blue litmus red or does a red color appear when a sample of dry soil is added to a solution of potassium thiocyanate dissolved in alcohol?................................	10	3 D

TABLE IV (CONTINUED)

Experiments Allocated to Principles	Value	Rank	
Which of the following are good electrolytes (cause an electric lamp in series to glow brightly), poor electrolytes, and non-electrolytes, respectively: distilled water, tap water, dry sodium chloride; separate solutions of sodium chloride, hydrochloric acid, sulfuric acid, ammonium hydroxide, glycerine, sugar, alcohol; carbon tetrachloride?.................	10	3	X
Will a pint of alcohol mixed with a pint of water make a quart of the mixture?.............................	10	3	D
Does slaked lime give an acid or a basic reaction with litmus?...........	9	5	L

83. The ingredients of a solution are homogeneously distributed through each other.

84. When different amounts of one element are found in combination with a fixed weight of another element (in a series of compounds) the different weights of the first element are related to each other by ratios which may be expressed by small whole numbers.

85. The earth's surface may be elevated or lowered by interior forces.

Experiments

	Value	Rank	
What are some characteristic features of the topography of the Rocky Mountains?	13	2	L
What are some of the features of a region of former volcanic activity (Crater Lake Quadrangle)?................	11	3	L

Experiments Allocated to Principles	Value	Rank	
What are the effects of movements of the earth's crust on the topography of the folded Appalachian Mountains?.......	10	4	L
What are some of the features of the shoreline of an emerging continental shelf (Sea Isle Sheet)?................	9	5	L
What are some of the topographic features formed in a region by its re-elevation (The Antietam Quadrangle)?	8	6	L

86. Strata of rocks occur in the earth's crust in the order in which they were deposited, except in the case of over-thrust faults.

Experiment
If three sets of six differently colored thick layers of cloth are placed side by side, where are faults, synclines and anticlines produced when the set on the left is raised from its bottom near the junction with the middle set? When both the middle set and the set on the right are raised simultaneously from their bottoms near their junction?......   12   1   D

Principles Having a Total Assigned Value of Thirteen

87. The energy which a body possesses on account of its position or form is called potential energy and is measured by the work that was done in order to bring it into the specified condition.

APPENDIX B

TABLE IV (CONTINUED)

Experiments Allocated to Principles	Value	Rank	
Experiments			
As direct current is sent through a small lead cell consisting of two bright lead plates separated by a dilute solution of sulfuric acid, does one plate become unlike the other? When the two plates are disconnected from the direct current source and connected to a small electric bell (or buzzer), does the bell ring? Do the plates become more alike or more unlike as the bell rings (cell discharges)?.....................	13	3	D
Do kinetic and potential energy change back and forth when a simple pendulum swings?.....................	11	4	D
If weights are suspended by means of a copper or an iron wire over a cake of ice, does the wire cut its way downward through the ice without leaving two separate pieces of ice?............	7	5	D
88. When the resultant of all the forces acting on a body is zero, the body will stay at rest if at rest, or it will keep in uniform motion in a straight line if it is in motion.			
Experiments			
Can a paper under a tall cylinder of water open at the top be jerked away quickly without overturning the cylinder?	14	8	D
If a heavy metal ball is suspended by a thread just strong enough to hold it and a similar thread attached below the ball is given a quick jerk downward, what happens? What happens when a steady pull is used instead of a quick jerk?...	11	9	D
Can a large block of wood be balanced on the head of a vertical nail?	10	10.5	D

Experiments Allocated to Principles	Value	Rank	
If a piece of chalk stands upright on writing paper over the edge of a table, does the chalk fall or remain upright when the paper projecting off the table is held in one hand as the other hand strikes the paper a sharp blow between the hand and the table?....	10	10.5	D
89. When one body exerts a force on a second body, the second body exerts an equal and opposite force on the first.			
Experiments			
What is the reaction of rubber tubing suspended from a faucet to a strong stream of water? What happens when the flow of water is increased?............	12	2.5	D
If a small balloon with a short piece of glass tubing in its neck is inflated and released with the tubing under water, what is observed?....................	12	2.5	D
How does a mercurial barometer measure atmospheric pressure?...........	11	4.5	D
What facts about centrifugal force can be felt or observed as a blackboard eraser is whirled around at the end of a weak string?......................	11	4.5	L
What happens when water escapes from the openings of a rotary lawn sprinkler?	10	6	D
If a person is sitting on a chair on a scale, does he weigh more or less as he gets up quickly? Sits down quickly?	9	7	D
90. When pressure is applied to any area of a fluid (liquid or gas) in a closed container, it is transmitted in exactly the same intensity to every area of the container in contact with the fluid.			

Experiments Allocated to Principles	Value	Rank	
If a small bottle or test tube nearly full of water is inverted in the water of a larger full bottle with flat, thin walls and tightly stoppered, what happens to the inner bottle (Cartesian diver or bottle imp) when pressure applied to the sides of the outer bottle is alternately increased and decreased?.................	15	3	D
Is pressure transmitted equally in all directions or in only one direction by water? By a solid? Does a rubber diaphragm at the lower end of a vertical cylinder bulge only downward or equally in all directions when water is poured into the cylinder? When a glass rod is pushed against the rubber from above?...	14	4	D

91. The average speed of molecules increases with the temperature and pressure.

Experiments

	Value	Rank	
Does a body of air expand or contract when it is heated? When it is cooled? Is there more or less than a flaskful of air after an inverted flask, fitted with a delivery tube which extends through a vessel of water into an inverted drinking glass entirely full of water is heated with a Bunsen flame? After the air in the flask is cooled?.............	14	1	D
Does a body of air expand or contract when it is heated? If the open end of a deflated balloon is placed over the only outlet to a flask of air, does the balloon become inflated when the flask of air is heated?.......................	13	2	D
Does a body of liquid expand or contract when it is heated? When it is cooled? If colored water fills a flask and is part way up in a glass tube inserted in the stopper to the flask, does the level of water in the tube rise or fall as the flask is heated? As the flask is cooled?................................	12	3.5	X

Experiments Allocated to Principles	Value	Rank
Does the air in a flask expand or contract when heated? When cooled? If an inverted flask of air with a glass tube through the stopper dips into water, does the water inside the tube move down to indicate expansion of the air or up to indicate contraction of the air when a warm hand is held on the flask? When a cloth wet with cold water is placed on the flask?..............................	12	3.5 L
Does a body of air expand or contract when it is heated? When it is cooled? If an inflated balloon is adjusted between two rings on a stand so that the balloon just touches the rings, does the balloon expand or contract when hot water is poured over it? When cold water is poured over it?................	11	5.5 D
If the same pressure is maintained, how does the volume of an enclosed gas vary as its temperature is increased and decreased? If a little mercury is near the middle of an open horizontal glass tube which has one end connected through a one-hole stopper to a flask of air set in a water bath, is the mercury moved in a manner to indicate an increase or a decrease in the volume of the confined air as the temperature of the water bath (and the confined air) is raised? Lowered?..............................	11	5.5 D
Does a body of air expand or contract when it is heated? If two balloons inflated with air are the same size, does one held over an electric hot plate increase more in size than one not held over the plate?........................	10	7.5 D
Can a liquid be separated from a solution by distillation and condensation? If common salt is dissolved in water can the water be obtained from the solution by heating the solution in a flask and condensing the vapors with a Liebig condenser or by passing the vapors into a test tube set in ice?.....	10	7.5 D

Experiments Allocated to Principles	Value	Rank	
92. Condensation will occur when a vapor is at its saturation point if centers of condensation are available and if heat is withdrawn.			
Experiments			
Is fog formed more readily by evacuation of a flask containing air and water than by evacuation of a similar flask containing only dry air?	14	5	D
Can fog be produced by blowing air into a large closed bottle containing some water and then suddenly releasing the pressure by removing the stopper?..	13	6	X
Is water vapor given off from the leaves of a plant (potted geranium) and condensed on the inside of a battery jar placed over the plant?...............	12	7	D
Can iodine be crystallized on the bottom of a dish of cold water set over a heated evaporating dish containing the oxidizing agent, manganese dioxide, with sodium iodide and sulfuric acid?.......	11	9	L
What is the dew point for the air in the classroom, that is, at what average temperature does moisture first appear on and disappear from the outside of a drinking glass (or polished metal cup) after ice (and later warm water) is added to water in the cup?....................	11	9	D
How is ice made in a commercial plant (a field trip)?.......................	11	9	D
Can fractional distillation and condensation be used to separate two miscible liquids (alcohol and water) which have different boiling points?..........	9	11	L

Experiments Allocated to Principles	Value	Rank	
93. A change in state of a substance from gas to liquid, liquid to solid, or _vice versa_, or from solid to gas or _vice versa_, is usually accompanied by a change in volume.			
Experiments			
What happens to a balloon after a small piece of dry ice is placed in the balloon and the opening is tied?........	14	6	D
How does a cutaway model of a reciprocating steam engine operate "to convert heat energy to mechanical energy?"	11	7	D
How much snow (in a tall glass cylinder or rain gauge) represents an inch of rain?............................	10	8	D
94. The presence of a non-volatile substance will cause the resulting solution to boil at a higher temperature and to freeze at a lower temperature than pure water.			
Experiments			
Does one mole of an electrolyte (common salt) or one mole of a nonelectrolyte (sugar) raise the boiling point of its water solution the greater amount?................................	14	2	X
How is ice made in a commercial plant (a field trip)?...................	10	3	D
What is the relative effectiveness of equal volumes of methyl alcohol, denatured alcohol, and glycerine in lowering the freezing point of a water solution?............................	9	4.5	D
What is the relative effectiveness of equal volumes of different brands of commercial antifreezes in lowering the freezing point of a water solution?.....	9	4.5	X

Experiments Allocated to Principles	Value	Rank
95. The volume of an ideal gas varies inversely with the pressure upon it, providing the temperature remains constant.		
Experiments		
If a small bottle nearly full of water is inverted in a glass jar partly filled with water, what happens to the small bottle (Cartesian diver or bottle imp) when pressure applied to the rubber dam across the top of the jar is alternately increased and decreased?...............	15	3.5 D
If a small bottle or test tube nearly full of water is inverted in the water of a larger full bottle with flat, thin walls and tightly stoppered, what happens to the inner bottle (Cartesian diver or bottle imp) when pressure applied to the sides of the outer bottle is alternately increased and decreased?...............	15	3.5 D
How does the volume of a confined gas vary with the pressure upon it if the temperature remains constant? If a large bottle partly filled with water has a glass tube extending through its stopper deep into the water, does the volume of air confined in the bottle increase or decrease as the water is "sucked out" of the bottle (pressure on the water is decreased)?	14	5 D
How does the volume of a confined gas vary with the pressure upon it if the temperature remains constant? Can air in a tightly stoppered bottle be compressed into a smaller volume by water entering the bottle from a faucet?	13	6.5 D

Experiments Allocated to Principles	Value	Rank
How does the volume of a confined gas vary with the pressure upon it if the temperature remains constant? If a small glass tube four and one-half feet long has three arms DA, AB, and BC of lengths eighteen inches, two and one-half feet and six inches, respectively, with BC perpendicular to a horizontal board on which the other two arms at right angles to each other lie flat and if arm AB is filled with mercury before end D is sealed, what happens to the volume (length) of the air confined in arm AD by the mercury when the pressure on it is increased and decreased by raising and lowering arm BC about axis AD?...........	13	6.5 D
Does a lift pump or a force pump (glass models) give a steadier supply of water at the outlet? Does the volume of air in the "air dome" increase or decrease as the piston moves down? Up?....	9	8 D

96. Whenever an opaque object intercepts radiant energy traveling in a particular direction, a shadow is cast behind the object.

Experiments

  If a person holds a basketball (the moon) a little higher than his head in a line between the head (the earth) and a flashlight or floorlamp (the sun) and then turns entirely around to his left, how much of the half of the moon facing him is lighted when it has been turned one-fourth, half, three-fourths and all the way around?.........................

| | 15 | 2   D |

Experiments Allocated to Principles	Value	Rank	
If a person holding a very small ball about one foot in front of the one open eye moves backward or forward until the ball (moon) just covers the view of the bright circle of light from a spotlight or a strong flashlight (sun), what is the appearance of the circle of light as the ball is moved horizontally across it (eclipse of the sun)?..................	14	3	D
If a key is placed on photographic print paper which is then exposed to a strong light, where on the paper does the greatest change in color appear?....	13	4.5	X
If a vertical opaque object (board) has on one side two adjacent candle flames and on the opposite side a white screen, does the diameter of the shadow increase or decrease as the screen is moved away from the opaque object? When the screen and object are stationary, does the thickness of the penumbra increase or decrease as the light is moved farther away from the object?.....	13	4.5	L
Is an exposed and developed blueprint white or blue where little or no light reached the paper? Where much light reached the paper?.....................	8	6	D

97. The dispersion of white light into a spectrum by a prism is caused by unequal refraction of the different wave lengths of a light.

Experiments
If one triangular glass prism disperses white light into a color band, can a second prism placed alongside the first one recombine those colors to produce white light?.....................

| | 15 | 2 | D |

Experiments Allocated to Principles	Value	Rank	
If a glass prism held in sunlight (or in light from a narrow slit in front of a projection lantern) is rotated in front of a wall of light color or white paper in a darkened room, what is observed? Does white light consist of only one of many colors of light?....................................	14	3	D
What is observed when sunlight which comes from high in the sky, but not directly overhead, passes through a glass of water to white paper?.......	10	4	L
If white light is passed through a Florence flask (round bottom) filled with water, are no, only one, or are many colors seen?......................	9	5	D
98. Positively charged ions of metals may be deposited on the cathode, as atoms, when a direct current is sent through an electrolyte.			
Experiment Can copper be purified by passing direct current through an electrolytic cell in which a small piece of pure copper is the cathode, the impure copper is the anode and a solution of copper sulfate is the electrolyte?.............	8	3	D
99. In a transformer the ratio between voltages is the same as that between the number of turns.			
Experiment If a bell-ringing transformer connected to an 110-volt A.C. circuit has a door bell connected to its secondary coil, is the voltage and amperage, respectively, in the secondary coil more or less than in the primary coil?......................	14	2	X

TABLE IV (CONTINUED)

Experiments Allocated to Principles	Value	Rank
100. Energy in kilowatt hours is equal to the product of amperes, volts, and time (in hours) divided by one thousand.		
101. The mass of an atom is concentrated almost entirely in the nucleus.		
102. Atoms of all elements are made up of protons, neutrons, and electrons, and differences between atoms of different elements are due to the number of protons and neutrons in the nucleus and to the configuration of electrons surrounding the nucleus.		
103. Earthquakes are produced by the sudden slipping of earth materials along faults.		

Principles Having a Total Assigned Value of Twelve

	Value	Rank	
104. In the inclined plane, weight times height equals acting force times length, providing friction is neglected and the force is parallel to the plane.			
Experiment			
What is the actual and theoretical mechanical advantage and the efficiency of an inclined plane at a given angle of inclination? What effect does changing the angle of inclination have upon these? How does the work done in rolling a loaded car up an inclined plane compare with that done in lifting it through the same vertical distance?	19	1	L

TABLE IV (CONTINUED)

Experiments Allocated to Principles	Value	Rank	
105. When two forces act upon the same object, the resultant is the diagonal of a parallelogram whose sides represent the direction and magnitude of the two forces. A single force represented by the diagonal may be resolved into two forces represented by the sides of the parallelogram.			
Experiments			
How does the resultant of two forces acting at angles to each other compare in magnitude and direction with a third force (the equilibrant) which produces equilibrium with the two forces?........	19	1	L
If a weight hangs anywhere along a rope whose ends are fastened to a cross-bar, is the tension in any part of the rope as shown by a spring balance less than, equal to, or greater than the weight?...............................	16	2	X
If the two ends of a string which supports a book about two feet below are held side-by-side in different hands, does the pull on each hand increase or decrease as the hands are moved farther apart horizontally?....................	13	3	L
If a pencil (airplane) is moved straight the length of a sheet of paper as another sheet under it and under carbon paper is pulled out at a right angle (wind direction), what is the true course marked by a carbon line on the bottom sheet?.........................	11	4	L
How great is the thrust exerted by a boom and how great is the pull exerted by the tie rope when a crane is used to support a weight on the boom as determined by graphic solution and the method of moments? Does the pull exerted by the tie rope increase or decrease as the crane is lowered toward the horizontal by lowering the upper end of the tie rope?	10	5	D

TABLE IV (CONTINUED)

Experiments Allocated to Principles	Value	Rank	
106. At any point on the earth's surface, all bodies fall with a constant acceleration which is independent of the mass or size of the body if air resistance be neglected.			
Experiments			
Do small balls of different weights but the same size hit the floor at the same or different times when released simultaneously at the same height above the floor?......................	20	1	D
Will a coin and a feather fall side-by-side or apart in a vacuum? In air?	19	2	D
Do two metal balls of slightly different mass strike the floor at the same time if one is dropped vertically at the same instant the other is projected horizontally from the same height?..............................	18	3	D
107. Sliding friction is dependent upon the nature and condition of the rubbing surfaces, proportional to the force pressing the surfaces together and independent of area of contact.			
Experiments			
Must more, the same, or less force be exerted on a spring balance in order to pull a block of wood along a smooth table top with the same uniform motion after the surfaces in contact are rubbed with paraffin?.......................	19	1.5	L
Does the force of friction depend upon the area of the surfaces in contact as determined from the readings of a scale by which a rectangular block of wood is pulled across a table on a flat side and then on one edge? Is the scale reading doubled if a similar block is placed on top of the original block, that is, does the force of friction depend upon the force pressing the surfaces together?	19	1.5	L

Experiments Allocated to Experiments	Value	Rank	
Is more force exerted on a spring balance to pull a car along a smooth table top with uniform motion when the wheels can or cannot rotate, that is, how does sliding friction compare with rolling friction?......................	11	3	X

108. The loudness of a sound depends upon the energy of the sound waves and, if propagated in all directions, decreases inversely as the square of the distance from the source.

Experiments

	Value	Rank	
What is the difference in the intensity of the sound produced by blowing a whistle gently and then vigorously?...	17	1.5	D
If a tuning fork is struck gently and then moved one, two, and three feet away from the ear, what effect does increasing the distance between the ear and the source of the sound have upon the loudness of the sound?.................	17	1.5	L
Is the intensity of sound increased or decreased by increasing the amplitude of a vibrating body such as plucking a tightly stretched string with more force and striking a tuning fork harder?......	16	3.5	D
Is the intensity of sound increased or decreased by increasing the area of the vibrating body such as holding the stem of a vibrating tuning fork on a chalk box and then on a table top?......	16	3.5	X
If the tines of a table fork held on end on a table are compressed and suddenly released, can the vibration be heard?................................	12	5	X

109. If the same pressure is maintained, the volume of a gas is varied directly as the absolute temperature.

TABLE IV (CONTINUED)

Experiments Allocated to Principles	Value	Rank
Experiments If a Charles' law tube (air enclosed in the closed end of an open tube of uniform bore by a globule of mercury) is placed in cracked ice and then in steam, what is the relation between the volume and the absolute temperature of the enclosed gas under constant (atmospheric) pressure?..............................	19	1 D
If the same pressure is maintained, how does the volume of an enclosed gas vary as its temperature is increased and decreased? If a little mercury is near the middle of an open horizontal glass tube which has one end connected through a one-hole stopper to a flask of air set in a water bath, is the mercury moved in a manner to indicate an increase or decrease in the volume of the confined air as the temperature of the water bath (and the confined air) is raised? Lowered?.................................	16	2 D
110. If the volume of a confined body of gas is kept constant, the pressure is proportional to the absolute temperature.		
111. The boiling point of any solution becomes lower as the pressure is decreased and higher as the pressure is increased.		

TABLE IV (CONTINUED)

Experiments Allocated to Principles	Value	Rank	
Experiments			
If a boiler of the laboratory type has its side outlet closed and the top fitted with a thermometer and a J-shaped tube containing mercury (manometer), does the temperature at which the water boils increase, decrease or remain constant as the pressure increases and pushes the mercury up in the long arm of the manometer?...........................	19	1	D
If a delivery tube and a thermometer are inserted into a stopper to a flask of boiling water, does the temperature of the boiling water rise as the rubber tube is pinched so as to partly close it? (Remove the burner simultaneously.)	18	3	D
Does the temperature of water rise while it boils in an open pressure cooker? When the pressure cooker is closed and the pressure rises?..........	18	3	D
If a glass tube (inverted U) has the shorter arm in a closed flask of water and the longer arm deep in water in a hydrometer jar, does the boiling point of the water in the flask remain constant, increase, or decrease as the water pressure at the lower end of the inverted tube (and hence the pressure on the boiling water) is increased by pouring more water in the jar?..............	17	5	D
If cold water, in a watch glass or shallow metal lid resting over a flat dish of sulfuric acid, is under a small bell jar from which the air is being evacuated, does the water freeze (to ice) as it boils rapidly?.....................	15	6	D
Do potatoes cook quicker in a closed or in an open pressure cooker?..........	12	7	D

Experiments Allocated to Principles	Value	Rank	
112. The atmosphere of the earth tends to prevent the heat of the earth's surface from escaping and the earth begins to cool only when the amount of heat lost during the night exceeds that gained during the day.			
113. The more nearly vertical the rays of radiant energy the greater the number that will fall upon a given horizontal area, and the greater is the amount of energy that will be received by that area.			
Experiments			
If one end of a shoebox contains an electric lamp (the sun) and the other open end rests on a table top, does more of the light from the lamp fall upon a given unit area (the size of the end of the box) of the table top when the box is vertical or slanted?........	19	1	D
How does the inclination of the earth's axis and the earth's revolution about the sun (globe about a flashlight at the end of a mailing tube) cause the seasons? Why are there more hours of daylight than of darkness during the summer and more hours of darkness than of daylight during the winter? Why is it warmer during the summer than during the winter?............................	18	2	D
114. The dimensions of an image produced by a lens or a mirror are to the dimensions of the object as their respective distances from the lens or mirror are to each other.			

Experiments Allocated to Principles	Value	Rank	
Experiments			
If an object is gradually moved closer to a double convex lens, what relation exists between the relative size of the object to its image and their relative distances from the lens?.............................	19	1	L
How does ones image change in size as a concave shaving mirror (also a convex mirror) is moved slowly away from the face?...............	17	2	L
115. The force of attraction or repulsion between two magnetic poles varies directly as the product of the pole strengths and inversely as the square of the distance between the poles.			
Experiments			
When a motor (St. Louis type) is in operation, does moving the poles of the bar magnets closer to the ends of the armature change its speed of rotation?	19	1	D
Which parts of a bar (or U-shaped) magnet have the greatest concentration of magnetic lines of force and therefore pick up the greatest number of nails?...	16	2	X
If a pole of a bar magnet is brought near a pole of a second magnet which is free to move horizontally, does the same kind (and opposite kinds) of magnetic poles attract or repel each other?	15	3	D
Are iron filings on the ends of two separate bar (or U-shaped) magnets attracted or repelled as the same kind (and opposite kinds) of magnetic poles is brought near each other?...........	13	4	D

TABLE IV (CONTINUED)

Experiments Allocated to Principles	Value	Rank	
If the armature of a St. Louis motor is in series with a rheostat and two dry cells, how is the rotation affected by reversing only the connections of the dry cells? By reversing only the polarity of the magnets? By reversing both the polarity of the magnets and the direction of the current through the armature? By decreasing the resistance in the rheostat?	12	5	X
Does reversing the direction of the current through the armature and field magnet of a series-wound and a shunt-wound direct-current motor (St. Louis type) change the direction of rotation of the armature? Does the series or the shunt (parallel)connection give the greater speed?......................	11	6	D
If the north pole of a horizontal bar magnet beneath a pan of water is placed under a north pole of a Mayer's floating magnet (a magnetized needle thrust vertically through a cork), what path is taken by the floating magnet?	8	7	L
Can iron or steel be made a magnet by induction, that is, by merely bringing it near a magnet? Does the point of a large nail hold smaller nails before and after one pole of a strong bar magnet is brought near the head of the large nail? After the bar magnet is withdrawn?......	6	8	L

116. The magnitude of an induced electromotive force is proportional to the rate at which the number of lines of magnetic force change and to the number of turns of wire in the coil.

Experiments Allocated to Principles	Value	Rank	
Experiments Is the amount of an induced electromotive force (as indicated by the deflection of a galvanometer) increased on increasing the strength of a varying magnetic field by using two magnets instead of one or by sending more current through the primary of two coils? On increasing the rate at which the magnetic lines of force (flux) cut a coil of wire by increasing the speed of motion of a magnet with respect to a closed coil, or _vice versa_, or by "making" and "breaking" a primary circuit? On increasing the number of turns of wire in a single coil or in the secondary of an induction coil or transformer?.....................	20	1	D
If a flat coil of insulated wire (no. 26), in series with a galvanometer, is rotated between the poles of a U-shaped magnet, is the deflection of the galvanometer needle increased on increasing the strength of the magnetic field? On increasing the speed of rotation of the coil? On increasing the number of turns of wire in the coil?..............	19	2	D
Is an electromotive force (e.m.f.) induced in a coil of wire (as indicated by a current through a galvanometer in series with the coil) when a magnet is thrust into or rapidly withdrawn from the coil, that is, when magnetic lines of force (flux) cut a wire in a closed circuit?.............................	18	3.5	X
If the armature of a St. Louis-type motor-generator is connected in series with a galvanometer, how is the current output affected by slow and rapid rotation of the armature?...............	18	3.5	L

Experiments Allocated to Principles	Value	Rank	
If one end of a soft iron rod (or part of a ring) is wrapped with five turns of insulated copper wire (the primary), in series with a switch and dry cells, and the other end (or part of a ring) is wrapped with ten and then twenty turns of similar wire (the secondary) in series with a galvanometer, how much less or more is the galvanometer needle deflected as the switch in the primary circuit is closed when the number of turns in the secondary is doubled?.............................	17	5	D
Is current induced in a closed copper wire moved rapidly down or up between the poles of a U-shaped magnet?.............	16	6	X
Can an induction coil increase the voltage of an intermittent direct current in its primary sufficiently to produce a spark across a gap in its secondary?....	9	7	D

117. Charges on a conductor tend to stay on the outside surface and to be greatest on the sharp edges and points.

Experiments

	Value	Rank	
Can an electroscope be discharged more rapidly by holding the point of a needle or its other end a few inches from the knob of the electroscope?.......	19	1	D
Do electrical charges reside on the outside and the inside of a conductor, that is, are pith balls suspended inside and outside of a hollow metal cylinder affected by the charge when the cylinder is connected by a chain to a static machine?................................	17	2.5	D

Experiments Allocated to Principles	Value	Rank	
Do electrical charges reside on the outside and the inside of a charged open metal vessel, that is, if the inner vessel of a calorimeter is rubbed both inside and outside with the same charged rubber rod, what happens to the leaves of a neutral electroscope when a proof-plane (a penny at the end of a stick of sealing wax) is brought near the electroscope after touching the inside of the charged vessel? After touching the outside of the charged vessel?.............................	17	2.5	X
If an electroscope is placed inside a closed screen box, is the electroscope affected by any charged objects brought near it or by connecting the wire screen to a static machine, that is, is the interior of a hollow conductor shielded from external electrical disturbances?...	13	4.5	D
If charges of opposite kinds are induced on the inside and outside surfaces of a metal vessel (as shown by using a proof-plane) by suspending a positively charged metal ball in the vessel and the ball is then touched to the inner surface and withdrawn from the vessel, is the ball, the inner surface, and the outer surface, respectively, neutral, positive, or negative (as shown by using a proof-plane); that is, do charges on an isolated conductor tend to reside on the outside surface?.............................	13	4.5	D
Are spark discharges less likely from a point or a knob on metal standards of the same height placed between two insulated metal discs connected to a static machine?.............................	11	6.5	D
How is a candle flame affected when placed opposite a sharp point (and a round knob) connected to one terminal of a static machine?......................	11	6.5	D

TABLE IV (<u>CONTINUED</u>)

Experiments Allocated to Principles	Value	Rank	
In what direction does an electric whirl rotate when connected to one end of a static machine? Is a "brush discharge" visible at the points?..........	10	8	D
To what extent can the sparks be felt when the hand covered with wire screen for doors is held between the knobs of a static machine?............	9	9	L

118. Metals may be arranged in an activity series according to their tendency to pass into ionic form by losing electrons.

<u>Experiments</u>

	Value	Rank	
Which metals (sodium, magnesium, aluminum, lead, copper) displace hydrogen from dilute hydrochloric or sulfuric acid? Does a metal displace hydrogen from the acid if the metal is above hydrogen in the "activity or replacement series for metals"? If the metal is below hydrogen in the series? Is the chemical reaction faster if the metal and hydrogen are farther apart or c loser together in the series?.................................	20	1	X
If strips of zinc and copper, respectively, are placed in separate sets of six solutions, namely, dilute hydrochloric acid, lead nitrate, silver nitrate, nitric acid, copper sulfate, and aluminum sulfate, what elements does zinc replace from the compounds in solution? Not replace? What elements does c opper replace from the compounds in solution? Not replace? Do metals higher in the "activity of replacement series of metals" displace metals lower in the series from solutions of their compounds, or <u>vice versa</u>?......	20	2	L

TABLE IV (CONTINUED)

Experiments Allocated to Principles	Value	Rank	
Which of the following combinations of electrodes in a Voltaic cell with sulfuric acid as the electrolyte produces the greatest voltage: copper-zinc, copper-carbon, aluminum-zinc, aluminum-lead, lead-copper?............................	17	3	D
Does a bright nail become coated with red copper when dipped in a solution of cupric salt?.............................	16	4.5	X
Can metallic silver be thrown out of a solution of silver nitrate by plates of copper hung in it?........................	16	4.5	L
When a small piece of sodium is placed on the surface of water is hydrogen liberated? Does the residue give a basic or acid reaction with litmus paper?......	14	6	D
Can an old spoon (or copper rod or graphite letter) be copper plated by passing direct current through an electrolytic cell in which the object to be plated is the cathode, the metal to be plated is the anode (copper) and the solution (copper sulfate) is the salt of that metal?.............................	13	7.5	X
Is an electric current produced in a closed circuit when two dissimilar elements are immersed in an electrolyte? Does a galvanometer register current when connected to an iron nail and a copper wire sticking in a lemon? To a penny and a dime separated by a piece of blotting paper which has been dipped in salt water?	13	7.5	X
Can hydrogen be prepared by displacement from an acid (sulfuric or hydrochloric) by a metal("mossy" zinc)?......	12	9.5	L
Can a salt be prepared by the substitution of a metal for the hydrogen of an acid as occurs on dropping a piece of sodium or mossy zinc into a dilute solution of hydrochloric acid?...........	12	9.5	L

TABLE IV (<u>CONTINUED</u>)

Experiments Allocated to Principles	Value	Rank	
Does a small electric bell ring when its two terminals are connected to the zinc (amalgamated) and copper (or carbon) electrodes, respectively, of a Voltaic cell containing dilute sulfuric acid as the electrolyte? Does the bell ring when the two electrodes are the same element?	10	12	D
Can the tarnish be removed from copper by boiling it in salt water with a piece of zinc touching the copper?....	10	12	X
Can stannous chloride be made by dissolving tin in concentrated hydrochloric acid?.........................	10	12	L
As direct current is sent through a small lead cell consisting of two bright lead plates separated by a dilute solution of sulfuric acid, does one plate become unlike the other? When the two plates are disconnected from the direct current course and connected to a small electric bell (or buzzer), does the bell ring? Do the plates become more alike or more unlike as the bell rings (cell discharges)?.............................	9	14.5	D
Can ferrous chloride be prepared by heating iron and hydrochloric acid in the absence of air? By boiling ferric chloride with iron wool?..............	9	14.5	L
119. The solubility of a gas in an inert solvent varies directly with the pressure to which the gas is subjected.			
Experiment			
Does the gas in a bottle of soda water or "pop" come out of the liquid when the pressure on the gas is decreased by removing the cap?.....................	19	1	D

Experiments Allocated to Principles	Value	Rank	
120. Falls or rapids tend to develop in a stream bed where the stream flows over a hard stratum to a soft one.			
Experiment			
What are some of the features of the Niagara Falls Quadrangle?..........	15	1	X
121. Rocks may be folded to form mountains.			
Experiments			
Do differently colored layers of cloth or felt fold (like rocks) when pushed upon from opposite sides?........	17	1	D
What are some characteristic features of the topography of the Rocky Mountains?..............................	13	2.5	L
What are the effects of movements of the earth's crust on the topography of the folded Appalachian Mountains?.......	13	2.5	L
122. Rocks may be metamorphosed, or changed by heat, pressure and flexion.			
Experiments			
How are some common metamorphic rocks (gneiss, mica schist, slate, quartizite, marble, and anthracite coal) alike and different with respect to bands, crystalline and granular structure, and the acid test?..............................	13	1	L
How are granites (chiefly light-colored minerals, especially quartz) and gabbros (chiefly dark-colored minerals, but no quartz) -- two great classes of igneous rocks---alike and different in general appearance, type of groundness, and size of crystals?..............................	11	2	L

TABLE IV (CONTINUED)

Experiments Allocated to Principles	Value	Rank	
Principles Having a Total Assigned Value of Eleven			

123. When forces act in the same direction, the resultant is their algebraic sum.

Experiment
If a uniform meter stick is suspended horizontally by two vertical spring balances the same distance from each end, what is the resultant (equilibrant) of the two parallel forces acting in the same direction but in different paths and where is its point of application? What relation exists between the sizes of the parallel forces and their equilibrant? Their distances from the equilibrant?..................

| | 19 | 1 | X |

124. The speed gained by a body with a constant acceleration is equal to the product of the acceleration and the time.

125. The acceleration of a body is proportional to the resultant force acting on that body and is in the direction of that force.

Experiments
Is a block of wood moved farther when hit by a large or by a small steel ball rolled across a table with about the same speed?............................

| | 16 | 1 | X |

If a hand pulls horizontally on a string attached to the side of a large mass hung on a vertical wire, do increased accelerations seem to require stronger or weaker forces?.............

| | 14 | 2 | L |

126. The velocity of a wave is equal to the product of its frequency and wave length.

Experiments Allocated to Principles	Value	Rank	
Experiment As water is raised or lowered the length of a long cylinder over which a vibrating tuning fork is held, are there moments when the sound heard is distinctly loudest? What is the velocity of sound in air by the resonance method, or the frequency of a tuning fork, or the wave length of the tone given off by a tuning fork?........	17	1	L
127. When energy is transmitted in waves, the medium which transmits the wave motion does not move along with the wave, but the energy does.			
Experiments Does a wave travel up and down the length of a long coiled vertical spring fastened at its ends with a section of the spring is compressed and suddenly released? Does the individual particle, as shown by a string tied to one turn of the coil, move only a short distance up and down parallel with the direction in which the wave moves (longitudinal waves)?	19	1.5	D
If one end of a long rope is fastened to a fixed support and the hand at the other end is moved up and down, in what direction do the individual particles of the rope move as shown by a string tied at some point along the rope? In what direction do the (transverse) waves move?	19	1.5	D
When energy is transmitted in waves, does the energy and the medium which transmits the wave motion move along with the wave? If small pieces of cork float on the surface of water in a pan and the water is tapped with the finger, in what direction do the water waves move? In what direction do the corks move? By what means is the energy of the finger tapping the water transmitted?..........	18	3.5	X

Experiments Allocated to Principles	Value	Rank
If a long piece of rubber tubing stretched between two supports is struck a sharp blow, does a wave travel back and forth the length of the tube? Does the individual particle, as shown by a string tied at some point along the tube, move perpendicular to or parallel with the direction the wave travels (transverse waves)?..................................	18	3.5 D
If several metal balls are suspended in line, can energy be transmitted from ball to ball with little motion of the balls themselves?......................	16	5 D
If each of six persons in a line places the hand of a stiff arm on the shoulder of the one in front of him, which of the persons is pushed forward when the one at the rear of the line gives a sudden push? Does the energy and the individual move forward in this "wave?"	14	6 D
When energy is transmitted in waves does the energy and the medium which transmits the wave motion move along with the wave? Do waves started by blowing the breath on the surface of a tub of water pass by a partly submerged bottle or do the waves carry the bottle with them?...........................	12	7 X

128. Salts of strong acids and strong bases undergo negligible hydrolysis, while salts of inactive acids and inactive bases undergo more marked hydrolysis.

Experiments Allocated to Principles	Value	Rank	
Experiments			
Are some salts not neutral? Does the water solution of a salt (sodium chloride, potassium nitrate, sodium sulfate) derived from a strong acid and a strong base give an acid, a basic, or a neutral reaction with litmus paper? Does the water solution of a salt (sodium carbonate) derived from a strong base (sodium hydroxide) and a weak acid (carbonic) give an acid, basic, of a neutral reaction with litmus paper? Does the water solution of a salt (ferric chloride) derived from a weak base (ferric hydroxide) and a strong acid (hydrochloric) give an acid, a basic, or a neutral reaction with litmus paper?...	19	1	L
Does soap, an organic salt formed from a weak acid and a strong base, hydrolyze in water to give a neutral, an acid, or a basic reaction with litmus paper?...........................	14	2.5	L
Does aluminum sulfate or ferrous sulfate hydrolyze in turbid water to form a coagulant which takes suspended matter with it as it settles thus decreasing the turbidity?................	14	2.5	D
Does a solution of sodium carbonate and water hydrolyze to give an acidic or basic reaction with litmus?.............	12	4	L
Does a solution of copper sulfate and water hydrolyze to give an acidic or basic reaction with litmus?..........	11	5	L
Do solutions of aluminum sulfate and sodium bicarbonate react to release carbon dioxide in a fire extinguisher of the foam type?.......................	10	6	D
Does stannous chloride in water hydrolyze to form a colloidal suspension?	8	7	L

TABLE IV (CONTINUED)

Experiments Allocated to Principles	Value	Rank
129. The activity of an acid or base is proportional to the degree of ionization of the compound when in solution.		
Experiments		
Which of the following are good electrolytes (cause an electric lamp in series to glow brightly), poor electrolytes, and non-electrolytes, respectively: distilled water, tap water, dry sodium chloride; separate solutions of sodium chloride, hydrochloric acid, sulfuric acid, ammonium hydroxide, glycerine, sugar, alcohol; carbon tetrachloride?.........	12	1.5 X
Is the conductivity of a solution a minimum with excess acid or excess base or when neutralization is complete (sulfuric acid from a burette into a solution of barium hydroxide)?.................	12	1.5 D
Does the litmus test show the following substances to be acidic, basic, or neutral: vinegar, milk of magnesia, ammonia water, table salt solution, soap solution, sugar solution, lemon juice and the liquid in an automobile battery?.....	10	3.5 L
What is the effect of solutions of a variety of acids and bases, respectively, on the color of some of the following indicators: blue and red litmus paper, phenolphthalein, methyl orange, methyl violet, bromothymol blue, Congo red, a blood-red beet?......................	10	3.5 X
130. Streams, potentially, have a regular cycle; youth, maturity, and old age.		
Experiments		
What are some of the characteristics found in a given area (or on a topographic map) which indicate a region of mature drainage?......................	16	1.5 L

Experiments Allocated to Principles	Value	Rank	
What are some of the characteristics found in a given area (or on a topographic map) which indicate an old river?	16	1.5	L
What are some of the characteristics found in a given area (or on a topographic map) which indicate an early stage of stream erosion?...............	11	3	L

Principles Having a Total Assigned Value of Ten

131. The total change in length of a metal bar is equal to its coefficient of linear expansion times the original length times the change of temperature in degrees Centigrade.

Experiments
      What is the coefficient of linear expansion (increase in length per unit length for one degree increase in temperature) of a metal rod as determined by the Cowen apparatus in which steam passing through a metal tube causes the tube to roll the shaft of a pointer which is moved through an arc?................ 16   2   X
      What is the coefficient of linear expansion (increase in length per unit length for one degree increase in temperature) of a metal rod as determined by a piece of apparatus in which steam is passed through a jacket containing a metal rod, the expansion of which is measured by moving a vernier on a sphereometer at one end of the rod?..... 16   2   X
      What is the coefficient of linear expansion (increase in length per unit length for one degree increase in temperature) of a metal rod as determined by a piece of apparatus in which steam is passed through a jacket containing a metal rod which, as it expands, pushes on the shorter arm of a bent lever and moves the longer arm of the lever through an arc across a scale?........................... 16   2   L

TABLE IV (CONTINUED)

Experiments Allocated to Principles	Value	Rank	
Does a straight compound bar of brass and iron become convex on the brass side or the iron side when heated, that is, do two different metals expand at different rates when heated?.........	9	4.5	D
How does a compound bar open and close the electrical circuits of a thermostat when an electric bulb, in series with the electrical circuit and lighted at room temperature, is held near the thermostat?..................	9	4.5	D
How does a thermograph (a compound bar) operate to record temperature changes?.............................	6	6	D

132. Sound waves or other energy impulses may set up vibrations in a body the amplitude of which is increased if the impulses are exactly timed to correspond to any one of the natural periods of vibration of the body.

Experiments

If two tuning forks of the same frequency are mounted on sounding boxes a few inches apart and one fork is set in vibration, what happens to a suspended ping-pong or pith ball which touches a flat side of a tine of the other fork?	18	1	D
As water is raised or lowered the length of a long cylinder over which a vibrating tuning fork is held, are there moments when the sound heard is distinctly loudest? What is the velocity of sound in air by the resonance method, or the frequency of a tuning fork, or the wave length of the tone given off by a tuning fork?......................	16	3.5	X

APPENDIX B

TABLE IV (CONTINUED)

Experiments Allocated to Principles	Value	Rank	
If water is poured into a glass tube above which a tuning fork vibrates or as a vibrating tuning fork is held over a glass cylinder as the latter is moved up and down with one end under water, are there moments when the sound heard is distinctly loudest?.....................	16	3.5	D
Do sound waves emitted by one vibrating body impart vibration to another body of the same frequency? If a small V-shaped paper rider is placed on one of two wires tuned in unison on a sonometer, does the paper rider remain where placed or it is thrown off when the other wire is plucked?............................	16	3.5	D
Can a vibrating tuning fork which cannot be heard at a short distance be heard throughout a room when placed over a tube having an air column of the proper length?................................	16	3.5	D
If the tines of a vibrating tuning fork are held close and parallel to a second fork of the same frequency before clamping the tines of the first fork with the fingers, what is discovered when the second fork is held near an ear?........	14	6	L
If a tuning fork on a resonance box is held near an ear at the rear of a room while another one of the same frequency is set in vibration on a resonance box at the front of the room for a few seconds and then stopped, what happens to the fork at the rear of the room?................................	13	7.5	D
If a vibrating tuning fork is held near one end of a tube as it is telescoped inside another tube in air, are there moments when the sound heard is distinctly loudest?.....................	13	7.5	D

Experiments Allocated to Principles	Value	Rank	
Can energy be transmitted through a cord from one swinging pendulum to a nearby stationary pendulum suspended from the same cord when the cords are the same length or one is half as long a s the other?.....................................	10	9	D
What are the conditions for resonance with both closed and open tubes?........	9	10	D

133. The speed of sound increases with an increase in temperature of the medium conducting it.

134. A number of substances will emit electrons and become positively charged when illuminated by light.

<u>Experiment</u>
If a battery, photoelectric cell and relay magnet form one circuit and the relay armature, battery and electric bell form a second circuit, does the bell ring when a flashlight shines upon the photoelectric cell?................ 15   1   D

135. When a stream of high-speed electrons strikes a body, the atoms of that body emit x-rays.

<u>Experiment</u>
Do the bones of the hand cast a distinct shadow if the hand is placed between an x-ray tube and a photographic plate or the screen of a fluoroscope?... 17   1   D

TABLE IV (CONTINUED)

Experiments Allocated to Principles	Value	Rank	
136. Parent material for the development of soils is formed through the physical disintegration and chemical decomposition of rock particles and organic matter.			
Experiment If a small stone is immersed in a concentrated solution of sodium sulfate and hung up in the air for three days, are parts of the stone forced off when the salt crystallizes? Has the stone lost weight? (The Barrd test is used to estimate the amount of disintegration caused by frost.)......................	16	1	D

Principles Having a Total Assigned Value of Nine

	Value	Rank	
137. The energy which a body possesses on account of its motion is called kinetic energy and is proportional to its mass and the square of its velocity.			
Experiments What is the relationship between kinetic energy and speed? What difference is felt by the hand which catches a heavy pendulum at the bottom of its arc when the pendulum is released from a short distance and from a greater distance out on the arc?...........................	14	1	L
Do kinetic and potential energy change back and forth when a simple pendulum swings?........................	13	2	D
138. All liquids are compressible but only to a slight degree.			

TABLE IV (CONTINUED)

Experiments Allocated to Principles	Value	Rank	
Experiment If a cork inserted into a gallon glass jug completely filled with water is struck a sharp blow with the hand (or board or hammer), what happens?........	17	1	D
139. The atmospheric pressure decreases with increasing water vapor content, other things being equal.			
Experiment What is the relation between the barometric pressure and some of the elements of weather such as temperature, wind velocity, relative humidity and precipitation?........................	16	1	D
140. The rate of evaporation of a liquid varies with temperature, area of exposed surface, nature of the liquid itself, and saturation and circulation of the gas in contact with the liquid.			
Experiments If identical amounts of water at room temperature and water near the boiling points are placed in separate watch glasses, does the hot or the cooler water evaporate to dryness first?..............	18	2	D
If identical amounts of a volatile liquid (ether, alcohol) are placed in a small test tube and on a watch glass, does the liquid evaporate to dryness more rapidly from the larger or the small exposed surface area?.................	18	2	D
If identical amounts of a volatile liquid (ether, alcohol) are placed on two watch glasses, one covered with a beaker and the other left uncovered, does evaporation to dryness occur more rapidly in the covered or the uncovered beaker?....	18	2	D

TABLE IV (CONTINUED)

Experiments Allocated to Principles	Value	Rank	
Do identical amounts of different liquids (water, alcohol, gasoline) in similar beakers require the same or different lengths of time to evaporate to dryness?...............................	16	4.5	D
After absorbent cotton wound on the bulb of a thermometer is removed from liquid ether, does the temperature (thermometer reading) rise, fall, or remain the same?......................	16	4.5	D
If a finger is dipped into water (or alcohol) and is then waved back and forth several times, does the finger feel cooler or warmer?..................	14	6	L
Will a beaker placed on water on a board be frozen to the board if air is blown into ether in the beaker? If a watch glass is placed on water in a small hole in a cork and air is blown across ether in the glass, what is observed when the watch glass is picked up?....................................	13	7.5	D
Does gasoline in a cloth on a thermometer held in front of a fan absorb heat and lower the thermometer reading as the gasoline evaporates?.................	13	7.5	D

141. Any homogeneous body of liquid free to take its own position, will seek a position in which all exposed surfaces lie on the same horizontal plane.

Experiments

Does a liquid stand at the same or different heights in connecting vessels of different shapes, providing none have small diameters?........................	20	1	D

Experiments Allocated to Principles	Value	Rank	
What conditions are necessary in order that water may be siphoned from one vessel to another? Must the short arm and the long arm of a siphon always be entirely full of water? Must the outlet and the intake always be under water? Does the water always flow through the siphon toward the vessel which has its water level at the greater or at the smaller height above sea level?.........	12	2	D
142. Diffusible substances tend to scatter from the point of greatest concentration until all points are at equal concentration.			
Experiments			
If concentrated sulfuric acid is carefully released from a pipette at the bottom of a tall glass cylinder containing a solution of blue litmus, what is observed over a period of time?.........	19	1.5	D
Will ammonia gas from an open bottle move to all parts of a room, that is, do gases diffuse through gases?............	19	1.5	D
Will a crystal of copper sulfate or potassium permanganate diffuse upward throughout still water in a tall cylinder, that is, do molecules move from solids into liquids and diffuse through liquids?......................	18	3.5	D
If a bottle of ink with a flat glass cover is set under water in a large beaker and the cover is carefully pushed aside, what is observed over a period of time?..................................	18	3.5	D
If moth balls are placed in a large jar, smelled, then closed, and again smelled the next day, is there any evidence that molecules move from solids into gases and diffuse through gases?..................................	16	5.5	X

Experiments Allocated to Principles	Value	Rank	
If a gas jet is barely open can the odor of gas soon be detected at a considerable distance from the jet?.......	16	5.5	D
Will ammonia vapor diffuse from the bottom of a bottle upward through filter paper into a chimney on top of the bottle?..................................	12	7	D
If two drops of ammonia water and hydrochloric acid are placed in separate warm glass bottles covered with glass plates, what is observed after the bottle of ammonia is inverted on top of the other bottle and the glass plates are removed?.............................	11	8.5	D
Does a rubber balloon inflated with hydrogen or gasoline vapor remain inflated or collapse in a short time?....	11	8.5	D
Does hydrogen diffuse readily from an upper bottle of hydrogen to a lower bottle of air placed mouth to mouth?..	9	10.5	D
Do molecules of carbon disulfide move from the bottom of a bottle into a deflated balloon over the mouth of the bottle?...........................	9	10.5	D

143. The quality of a musical tone is determined by the pitch and intensity of the different simple tones or harmonics into which it may be resolved.

Experiments

If seven points divide a sonometer string into eight equal parts and v-shaped paper riders are placed at the first five points, from which points are the paper riders thrown (antinodes) and at which points do they remain (nodes) when the string is touched gently at the sixth point as it is bowed at the seventh point?.................................	14	1	D

TABLE IV (<u>CONTINUED</u>)

Experiments Allocated to Principles	Value	Rank	
If the same note is produced by a violin, cornet, and saxaphone, do the three instruments sound alike or different? If they are sounded at the same time, can their separate sounds be recognized?......................	11	2.5	D
If a sonometer string is vibrating in one big loop, in how many loops will it vibrate when it is touched in the middle? At a point one-third its length from one end?......................	11	2.5	D
If long pieces of iron, wood, lead and rubber are struck when suspended near each other, are the sounds produced alike or different?....................	8	4	D

144. In a series circuit the current is the same in all parts, the resistance of the whole is the sum of the resistance of the parts, and the voltage loss of the whole is the sum of the voltage losses of the parts.

<u>Experiments</u>
In a series circuit containing resistances of different values (two coils or electric lamps), is the current (from a storage battery, dry cells or other source of direct current) the same in all parts of the circuit? Is the voltage loss across combined resistances equal to the sum of the voltage losses across the individual resistances? Is the total resistance (of the two coils or lamps combined) equal to the sum of the individual resistances as determined by using an ohmmeter or by using the voltmeter and ammeter readings in Ohm's Law? | 20 | 1 | L

TABLE IV (CONTINUED)

Experiments Allocated to Principles	Value	Rank	
If cells are grouped in series in a closed circuit, is the current the same in all parts of the circuit? Is the total voltage across the group of cells (available electromotive force) equal to the sum of the voltages across the individual cells?......................	17	2	L
If current (from a storage battery or dry cells) passes for a very short time through a series circuit containing an ammeter and a coil of wire of unknown resistance across which a voltmeter is connected, what is the resistance of the coil of wire calculated by using volt-meter and ammeter readings in Ohm's Law? (resistance determined by the voltmeter-ammeter method)......................	16	3	L
When three electric lamps are con-nected in series to an 110-volt A.C. circuit, do the lights glow more or less brilliantly than they do when they are in the common house circuit?............	15	4	D
What is the resistance of the follow-ing automobile circuits based on ammeter readings taken when the engine is not running and the voltage of the storage battery: two headlights, two parking lights, horn?........................	13	6	D
How are a voltmeter and an ammeter correctly and safely used to measure voltage and current?......................	13	6	D
Does a series or a parallel arrange-ment of cells (non-polarizing or Daniell) give greater current when the external resistance is much larger than the total internal resistance of the cells and vice versa?......................	13	6	X
How is an electric current connected to ring two electric bells (or buzzers) with one push button? To ring one bell (and two bells) with either of two push buttons?......................	9	8	D

TABLE IV (<u>CONTINUED</u>)

Experiments Allocated to Principles	Value	Rank	
If a flat iron and a lighted electric lamp in parallel are connected in series with an ammeter and a source of 110-volt A.C., is there an increase or a decrease, when the iron is turned on, of the current in the main line, the voltage across the lamp, and the brightness of the lamp?....	7	9	D
145. In a parallel circuit, the total current is the sum of the separate currents, the voltage loss is the same for each branch, and the total resistance is less than the resistance of any one branch.			
<u>Experiments</u> If one of similar cells (new dry cells or wet cells) are in parallel branches of the same circuit, is the total current furnished by all branches equal to the sum of the currents in each branch? Is the total voltage across the terminals of the group of similar cells in parallel the same as that for a single cell?..................................	20	1.5	L
In a parallel circuit containing resistances (two coils) of different values, does the greater current (from a storage battery, dry cells or other source of direct current) flow through the branch with the higher or the lower resistance? Is the voltage loss the same for each branch and for the combined branches? Is the total resistance of the combined branches less than the resistance of any one branch as determined by using an ohmmeter or by using the voltmeter and ammeter readings in Ohm's Law?.............................	20	1.5	L

APPENDIX B

TABLE IV (CONTINUED)

Experiments Allocated to Principles	Value	Rank	
Does the reading of a galvanometer increase, decrease or remain the same for the same current when a low resistance shunt is connected across its terminals (making an ammeter)?..........	13	4	D
How are a voltmeter and an ammeter correctly and safely used to measure voltage and current?....................	13	4	D
Does a series or a parallel arrangement of cells (non-polarizing or Daniell) give greater current when the external resistance is much larger than the total internal resistance of the cells and vice versa?.............................	13	4	D
How is an electric current connected to ring two electric bells (or buzzers) with one push button? To ring one bell (and two bells) with either of two push buttons?................................	9	6	D

146. Some elements have more than one atomic weight due to differences in the neutron content of their nuclei.

147. Metals comprise a group of elements (other than hydrogen) whose atoms have a tendency to lose electrons readily and whose compounds when dissolved in polar solvents are capable of forming positive ions.

Experiments
    Which metals (sodium, magnesium, aluminum, lead, copper) displace hydrogen from dilute hydrochloric or sulfuric acid? Does a metal displace hydrogen from the acid if the metal is above hydrogen in the "activity or replacement series for metals?" If the metal is below hydrogen in the series? Is the chemical reaction faster if the metal and hydrogen are farther apart or closer together in the series?.....................................

	Value	Rank	
	17	1.5	X

TABLE IV (CONTINUED)

Experiments Allocated to Principles	Value	Rank
If strips of zinc and copper, respectively, are placed in separate sets of six solutions, namely, dilute hydrochloric acid, lead nitrate, silver nitrate, nitric acid, copper sulfate, and aluminum sulfate, what elements does zinc replace from the compounds in solution? Not replace? What elements does copper replace from the compounds in solution? Not replace? Do metals higher in the "activity or replacement series of metals" displace metals lower in the series from solutions of their compounds or vice versa?......................	17	1.5 L
When a small piece of sodium is placed on the surface of water is hydrogen liberated? Does the residue give a basic or acid reaction with litmus paper?	14	3 D
Can an old spoon (or copper rod or graphite letter) be copper plated by passing direct current through an electrolytic cell in which the object to be plated is the anode (copper) and the solution (copper sulfate) is a salt of that metal?...........................	13	4 D
As direct current is sent through a small lead cell consisting of two bright lead plates separated by a dilute solution of sulfuric acid, does one plate become unlike the other? When the two plates are disconnected from the direct-current source and connected to a small electric bell (or buzzer), does the bell ring? Do the plates become more alike or more unlike as the bell rings (cell discharges)?...........................	9	5 D

148. The natural movements of air, water and solids on the earth are due chiefly to gravity plus rotation of the earth.

APPENDIX B

TABLE IV (CONTINUED)

Experiments Allocated to Principles	Value	Rank	
Experiments			
What relation, if any, is there between the time of spring and neap tides and the phases of the moon?............	18	1	X
What deflection of wind currents is caused by the rotation of the earth? If less than a test tube of water is poured on a slate globe as it spins rapidly in a counterclockwise direction but the globe is suddenly stopped, does the water curve to the right or to the left of a meridian north and south of the equator?	16	2	D
Are there alluvial fans at the base of cliffs, or railway or highway cuts?	8	3	D
149. The rate of erosion is inversely proportional to the resistance of rocks to decomposition and disintegration.			

Principles Having a Total Assigned Value of Eight

	Value	Rank	
150. The distance a body travels, starting from rest with a constant acceleration, is one-half the acceleration times the square of the time.			
Experiment			
If a grooved board is made just deep enough so that a marble rolls down one foot the first second, what is the relationship between the distance the ball rolls and the number of seconds elapsed (uniformly accelerated motion)?	19	1	X
151. As the velocity of flow through a constricted area increases, the pressure diminishes, and _vice versa_.			

TABLE IV (CONTINUED)

Experiments Allocated to Principles	Value	Rank
Experiments		
If natural gas passes with increasing velocity into a main tube at its closed end and out at the other end and at three vertical jets of the same diameter and height, the jet at a constricted part of the tube having to its right and left jets in the wider parts of the tube, what difference is noticed in the height of the flame at the three jets? Is the pressure (judged by the height of flame) greater where the tube is wide or narrow?.......	18	1.5 D
As water flows steadily through a tube do manometers show the pressure to be greater or less in the constricted portion of the tube than in the wider portions of the tube? What happens to the pressure in the narrow and wider portions of the tube as the velocity of flow is increased?...................	18	1.5 D
Does a manometer connected to the side tube of a water-jet aspirator indicate reduced or increased air pressure inside the aspirator as the velocity of water flow is increased? If a finger is held over the side tube, in which direction does air tend to move?	17	5 D
Does increasing or decreasing the velocity of air through a constricted area increase or decrease the pressure in that area? If a card is placed on the top of a spool with a pin through the card into the hole in the spool, can the card be blown off the spool by air blown through the spool from the other end? Will a card held against the lower part of a vertical spool fall when air is blown down through the spool as the hand holding the card is removed?.......	17	5 D

APPENDIX B

TABLE IV (CONTINUED)

Experiments Allocated to Principles	Value	Rank	
When a jet of air is blown horizontally across the upper end of a tube dipping into water in an open vessel, is the water pushed up into the tube and sent forward in a fine spray (atomizer)?.....	17	5	D
May air in motion produce reduced pressure on one side of an object? If a strip of cardboard bent to the shape of the front and upper surface of a wing section is hung over a pencil, does the strip move toward or away from the stream of air blown from a small glass tube past the convex side of the strip?..........	17	5	D
May air in motion produce reduced pressure on one side of an object? When air from the mouth is blown across the top of a piece of paper held out horizontally from the chin, does the paper move toward or away from the air stream when it is released at its outer end?.........	17	5	D
Does increasing the velocity of air through a constricted area increase or decrease the pressure in that area? If an air stream is directed downward between two paper mailing tubes side-by-side a short distance apart across a set of tracks made of two pencils, what is observed?............................	16	9	D
May air in motion produce reduced pressure on one side of an object? Can a stream of air directed downward to one side of a suspended ping-pong ball hold it at a considerable angle from the vertical? Does the ball move toward or away from the air stream?..............	16	9	D
May liquids in motion produce reduced pressure on one side of an object? Can a stream of water directed downward to one side of a suspended inflated rubber balloon hold it at a considerable angle from the vertical? Does the balloon move toward or away from the stream?	16	9	D

Experiments Allocated to Principles	Value	Rank	
May air in motion produce reduced pressure on one side of an object? Can a tennis ball or a ping-pong ball be balanced in a strong upward jet of air? If so, can the ball be made to rotate by directing the jet of air to one side of the ball?.............................	15	11.5	D
May air in motion produce reduced pressure on one side of an object? If a ping-pong ball rests in a small glass funnel, can the ball be blown out of the funnel when the funnel is upright? Inverted?...................................	15	11.5	D
May air in motion produce reduced pressure in one side of an object? Can a screw driver or a ping-pong or tennis ball be supported by an upward jet of air at a considerable angle from the vertical without falling?..............	14	14	D
What effect does blowing air around a milk bottle toward a lighted candle on the opposite side have on the flame?....	12	15	D
How does the motion of a candle flame placed behind a flat surface and opposite an approaching air stream compare with that of a flame behind the trailing edge of a stream-lined object (milk bottle)?.........................	11	16	D
Does a stream of air over a wing section of heavy paper hinged to a board at the leading edge by gummed paper cause the trailing edge to rise or remain against the board when the chord of the airfoil section is at a slight angle to the relative wind?.............	10	17	D
152. When a gas expands, heat energy is converted into mechanical energy.			

TABLE IV (CONTINUED)

Experiments Allocated to Principles	Value	Rank	
Experiments			
What happens when a small amount of water is heated in a flask or a thick-walled test tube which is corked?.......	19	1	D
How does a cutaway model of a reciprocating steam engine operate "to convert heat energy to mechanical energy?"................................	16	2	D
Can the wall of potato cells be broken by subjecting them to the temperature of boiling water?.................	15	3	X
Does a jet of steam directed against "blades" on a circular wheel cause the wheel (turbine) to rotate?.............	14	4.5	D
How does a toy steam turbine convert heat energy to mechanical energy?.......	14	4.5	D
Does a body of air expand or contract when it is heated? If the open end of a deflated balloon is placed over the only outlet to a flask of air, does the balloon become inflated when the flask of air is heated?.....................	12	6	D
Does the air in a flask expand or contract when heated? When cooled? If an inverted flask of air with a glass tube through the stopper dips into water, does the water inside the tube move down to indicate expansion of the air or up to indicate contraction of the air when a warm hand is held on the flask? When a cloth wet with cold water is placed on the flask?.............................	10	7.5	D
Does a body of air expand or contract when it is heated? When it is cooled? Is there more or less than a flaskful of air after an inverted flask, fitted with a delivery tube which extends through a vessel of water into an inverted drinking glass entirely full of water, is heated with a Bunsen flame? After the air in the flask is cooled?....... :......	10	7.5	D

TABLE IV (<u>CONTINUED</u>)

Experiments Allocated to Principles	Value	Rank
153. The amount of heat which a constant mass of liquid or solid acquires when its temperature rises a given amount is identical with the amount it gives off when its temperature falls by that amount.		
<u>Experiments</u>		
If warm water is poured into about the same amount of cold water in a calorimeter how does the number of calories of heat lost by the warm water compare with the number gained by the cold water and the calorimeter?..............	19	1 L
What are the relative specific heats of copper, brass, lead, iron, and aluminum as determined by taking cylinders of equal weights from boiling water and placing them on a block of ice to observe the respective degrees of settling? Placing them in equal weights of water to observe the respective rises in the temperature?..	17	2 X
154. The charges on a conductor may be separated through the influence of a neighboring charge.		
<u>Experiments</u>		
Can an electroscope be charged negatively if a charged glass rod is held near the knob, the knob is touched with a finger, and the finger is removed before the rod is removed?....................	19	1.5 D
Can the top plate of an electrophorus be charged by induction, that is, if the lower plate of an electrophorus is rubbed with fur, the top plate is set on the lower plate and grounded with a finger, and the finger and then the top plate are removed, can a spark be drawn from the top plate by placing a finger near it or are the leaves of an electroscope moved apart when the plate is touched to the knob?....	19	1.5 D

TABLE IV (CONTINUED)

Experiments Allocated to Principles	Value	Rank
When a charged body is brought near a neutral body, is the opposite kind of electricity developed (induced) on the nearer side of that body and the same kind on the remote side, that is, if a positively charged rod is held near one end of a neutral body does a proof-plane touched to the end of the body near the rod attract or repel a positively charged pith ball? Does a proof-plane touched to the remote end of the body attract or repel a positively charged pith ball?..............................	18	3.5 D
If a suspended uncharged pith ball is grounded with the finger while a charged rubber rod is under, but not touching the ball, is the pith ball more or less strongly attracted by the rod than before touching the ball with the finger? Does a charged glass rod attract or repel the pith ball, that is, when a negatively charged object is used to charge a body by induction, what charge results in the body?..............	18	3.5 D
If a positively charged metal ball is suspended by an insulating thread in a metal vessel, are the inner and outer surfaces of the vessel neutral, positive or negative (as shown by using a proof-plane), that is, are charges of opposite kinds induced on opposite surfaces of a conductor by a charged body on one side of the conductor?......................	17	5 D
If each end of a neutral "conduction cylinder" is touched by a suspended neutral pith ball, do the pith balls move away from the cylinder when a charged rod is brought near one of its ends?.........	16	6 D

TABLE IV (CONTINUED)

Experiments Allocated to Principles	Value	Rank	
Does a large tack (lightning rod) set on top of a low tin can (house) between two parallel metal plates (cloud and earth) connected to a static machine prevent on electric discharge from the upper plate directly to the can?...............	12	7	D
Are spark discharges less likely from a point or a knob on metal standards of the same height placed between two insulated metal discs connected to a static machine?...................................	10	8	D
If a highly polished tin can, connected to an electroscope, is charged positively by induction, does the electroscope (and the can) hold the charge for a long time? What happens to the leaves of the electroscope (and the charge on the can) after a red-hot piece of metal is brought very close to the can?.........	8	9	D

155. The products of reacting substances may react with each other to form the original substances.

Experiment

	Value	Rank	
Do mercury and oxygen from heated mercuric oxide recombine to form mercuric oxide?......................	18	1	L

156. Equal volumes of all gases under similar conditions of temperature and pressure contain very nearly the same number of molecules.

157. Rocks may be formed by the cooling and solidifying of molten material.

Experiments Allocated to Principles	Value	Rank
Experiment How are granites (chiefly light-colored minerals, especially quartz) and gabbros (chiefly dark-colored minerals, but no quartz) --- two great classes of igneous rocks --- alike and different in general appearance, type of groundmass, and size of crystals?	11	1 D

Principles Having a Total Assigned Value of Seven

158. The amount of momentum possessed by an object is proportional to its mass and to its velocity.

Experiments

Is a block of wood moved farther when hit by a large or by a small steel ball rolled across a table with about the same speed?........................ 17   1   X

If two steel balls of different sizes and mass are suspended side-by-side as pendulums and each is separately pulled out to the same height and released while the other remains stationary, is the stationary ball of smaller or larger mass moved farther?..................... 16   2   D

What difference is felt by the hand which catches a heavy and a light pendulum at the bottom of its arc when the pendulums are released from the same position? From a short distance and from a greater distance out on the arc?..... 11   3   L

If seven heavy balls of the same size and weight are suspended side-by-side in one straight line, what happens when the ball on one end is drawn back in the same line and released? What happens when two balls are drawn back together and released simultaneously? 10   4   D

TABLE IV (<u>CONTINUED</u>)

Experiments Allocated to Principles	Value	Rank	
159. The free surface of a liquid contracts to the smallest possible area due to surface tension.			
Experiments			
Do surface films contract to made the surface area as small as possible? If a wire ring containing a loop of thread is dipped in soap suds and the film inside the thread is then punctured, what happens to the thread? The film between the thread and the ring?...............	19	2	D
If an oil drop is placed in alcohol floated on water in a glass cylinder, what happens to the oil drop, that is, what shape does a liquid that is free from a distorting force assume?........	19	2	D
Will a soap film across the mouth of an inverted funnel remain there or travel up to the narrowest point? Will a bubble blown on the funnel decrease forcing air out rapidly enough to deflect a candle flame?.................	19	2	L
Do drops of water placed on a thin layer of vaseline on a glass plate flatten out or tend to maintain a spherical shape? How does touching a little powdered castile soap to a drop affect the shape of the drop?...........	16	4	X
What happens when a drop of soap solution or alcohol is placed between two matches or toothpicks floated about an inch apart on water?.................	13	6	X
Are the hairs on a camel's hair brush drawn together as the brush is raised slowly from water?..............	13	6	X
What is observed when small particles of camphor are placed on water? At the rear end of a match (boat) on water?....	13	6	X
Can water be carried in a kitchen strainer that has been well greased?....	12	9.5	D

APPENDIX B

TABLE IV (CONTINUED)

Experiments Allocated to Principles	Value	Rank	
If five narrow slits are cut in one end of a small narrow rectangular piece of paper pointed at its other end, what happens when a drop of iodine solution (or alcohol) is placed across the slits at their closed ends and is then dropped horizontally on fresh water?............	12	9.5	X
When a glass tube is placed in water and in mercury is the liquid elevated or depressed?.........................	12	9.5	D
Is a liquid surface convex or concave if the liquid wets the container? Does not wet the container?.............	12	9.5	D
Is a liquid film elastic and contractile, that is, can a metal wire connecting the two sides of a U-shaped wire enclosing a soap film be moved back and forth without breaking the film?.....	11	12.5	D
What is observed when a layer of olive oil about two millimeters thick is slowly poured upon the surface of water in a beaker? When alcohol is added to the oil little by little?............	11	12.5	D
160. Sound waves are reflected in a direction such that the angle of incidence is equal to the angle of reflection.			
Experiment			
If a watch is held at the focus of a concave reflecting disk, can a person in different parts of a room hear the ticking of a watch better when the concave side of the reflector faces him or is turned away?.................................	14	1	D
161. When parallel light strikes a concave spherical mirror the rays, after reflection, pass directly through the principal focus only if the area of the mirror is small compared to its radius of curvature.			

Experiments Allocated to Principles	Value	Rank	
Experiment If a candle or a landscape and a screen are on separate arms of a V with a concave spherical mirror at the vertex, what is the appearance and location of the image formed on the screen by the mirror?...............................	10	1	D
162. An induced current always has such a direction that its magnetic field tends to oppose whatever change produced the current; whenever a change is made in an electrical system there is brought into existence something which opposes that change.			
Experiments If a flat stationary coil of wire is placed parallel to a similar lightweight coil suspended from a high point and free to move, is the suspended coil attracted or repelled by the stationary coil when direct current in the latter is started? Stopped? Is the direction of the current induced in the movable coil always such as to produce a polarity for the movable coil which will oppose the building up and dying out of the magnetic field of the stationary coil, that is, whenever a change is made in an electrical system is there always brought into existence something which opposes that change (Lenz's law)?	20	1	D
Is any difference noticed in the amount of energy needed when turning a magneto on an open circuit and on a closed circuit with an electric lamp in series?..............................	12	2	D
Does a lamp in series with a small motor on a lighting circuit glow brightly or become dim when the armature is slowed down by an extra external load? When the extra external load is taken off the armature?..............................	11	3	D

Experiments Allocated to Principles	Value	Rank	
163. Whenever a high frequency oscillating current produces in the field around it oscillating electric and magnetic fields, energy in the form of an electromagnetic wave is transmitted through space.			
Experiment			
Does the operation of an electric razor or the production of an electric spark produce "static" in a radio receiver?..............................	13	1	X
164. Electrons are emitted from any sufficiently hot body.			
Experiments			
Are electrons liberated from an incandescent metal, that is, do the leaves of a positively charged electroscope collapse when a red-hot iron wire is brought near the knob of the electroscope?.................................	20	1	D
Does a small flashlight bulb become dark on the inside after being placed on an 110-volt A.C. circuit?...............	16	2	D
If a highly polished tin can, connected to an electroscope, is charged positively by induction, does the electroscope (and the can) hold the charge for a long time? What happens to the leaves of the electroscope (and the charge on the can) after a red-hot piece of metal is brought very close to the can?...........	13	3	D
If three circuits (filament, plate, and grid) of a radio tube (201-A radiotron) are in operation, how is the current from the filament to the plate (plate current) affected by increasing the current through the filament (the temperature of the filament)? By increasing the positive potential of the plate (plate voltage)? By increasing the positive (and then the negative) voltage on the grid?..............................	10	4	D

Experiments Allocated to Principles	Value	Rank	
Do small variations in the electrical charge on the grid of a radio tube produce small or large changes in the plate current? If an "A" battery is connected in series with a slide rheostat and the filament of a radio tube and a "B" battery has its negative terminal connected through the rheostat to the filament but has its positive terminal connected through a galvanometer to the plate of the tube, is a small or a large change produced in the plate current when a charged rod merely approaches a wire leading to the grid? Does the plate current increase or decrease when the negative charge on the grid is increased by touching a negatively charged rubber rod to a wire leading to the grid?...........................	9	5	D

165. The speed of chemical reaction is increased by increasing the concentration of any of the reactants; and is decreased by decreasing the concentration of any of the reactants.

Experiments
   Does a red-hot iron picture wire, a glowing splinter, or a burning piece of wood or sulfur burn with greater brilliance in air or in oxygen?............ 19 1 X
   How is the speed of burning, affected by blowing additional air along with a fuel (cornstarch) into a flame?...... 11 2 D

166. Non-metals comprise a group of elements whose atoms tend to gain or share electrons and whose compounds, when dissolved in polar solvents, are capable of forming negative ions.

TABLE IV (CONTINUED)

Experiments Allocated to Principles	Value	Rank	
Experiments			
If direct current is passed through a saturated solution of sodium chloride in a U-tube, do red and blue litmus paper indicate a base, an acid, or a bleaching agent at the anode? Cathode?...........	12	1	D
Can the silver halides be precipitated by adding a soluble halogen salt such as sodium chloride to a solution of silver nitrate?...............................	10	2	L
167. Every chemical element when heated to incandescence in a gaseous state has a characteristic glow and a characteristic spectrum which can be used to identify very small quantities of the element and which is related to the molecular and atomic structure of the gas.			
Experiments			
What color is imparted to a non-luminous Bunsen flame by salts of Na, K, Li, Ca, Sr, and Ba, respectively, on a platinum or nichrome wire?..............	16	2	L
What color flames are observed when the borax-bead test is applied to compounds of Co, Cr, Cu, Mn, Fe, and Ni, respectively?.........................	16	2	L
What color flames are observed when the cobalt nitrate test is applied to compounds of Zn, Al, and Mg, respectively?	16	2	L
168. All chemical reactions which start with the same quantities of original substances liberate the same amounts of energy in reaching a given final state, irrespective of the process by which the final state is reached.			

TABLE IV (CONTINUED)

Experiments Allocated to Principles	Value	Rank	
Experiment As direct current is sent through a small lead cell consisting of two bright lead plates separated by a dilute solution of sulfuric acid, does one plate become unlike the other? When the two plates are disconnected from the direct current source and connected to a small electric bell (or buzzer), does the bell ring? Do the plates become more alike or more unlike as the bell rings (cell discharges)?..........................	11	1	D
169. A few elements are inert or chemically inactive because their atoms are so constructed as to be complete in themselves; i.e., their outer electron rings have no tendency to gain or lose electrons.			
170. Igneous rock may be formed from extruded magma and materials intruded into other rocks.			
Experiment How are granites (chiefly light-colored minerals, especially quartz) and gabbros (chiefly dark-colored minerals, but no quartz) --- two great classes of igneous rocks --- alike and different in general appearance, type of groundmass, and size of crystals?......	13	1	D

Principles Having a Total Assigned Value of Six

171. The frequency of the vibration of a stretched string is inversely proportional to its length, diameter, and square root of its density, and directly proportional to the square root of the stretching force.		

APPENDIX B

TABLE IV (<u>CONTINUED</u>)

Experiments Allocated to Principles	Value	Rank	
<u>Experiments</u> How does the frequency or pitch of a vibrating string or wire on a sonometer vary with its length? Tension? Diameter? Mass per unit length?...........	20	1	X
If a strong string runs horizontally from the clapper of a vibrating door bell over a pulley to a weight holder, does increasing the weight (tension) increase or decrease the number of vibrating loops? How can the string be made to vibrate as a whole (one loop, the fundamental), then in two loops (the first overtone), and finally in three loops (the second overtone)?............	11	2.5	D
If a light string attached to the vertical clapper of a vibrating door bell is pulled down upon gradually, does the number of loops in the vibrating string increase or decrease as the tension is increased? Can the string be in resonance with the clapper and produce standing waves for a number of different tensions?................................	11	2.5	D
172. All rays passing through the center of curvature of a mirror are reflected upon themselves.			
173. Forces within the earth may cause breaks to appear in the earth's crust.			
<u>Experiments</u> If three sets of six differently colored thick layers of cloth are placed side by side, where are faults, synclines and anticlines produced when the set on the left is raised from its bottom near the junction with the middle set? When both the middle set and the set on the right are raised simultaneously from their bottoms near their junction?.............	14	1	D

TABLE IV (CONTINUED)

Experiments Allocated to Principles	Value	Rank
Do eruptions similar to those of geysers occur when a funnel is inverted in a beaker of water heated with a low Bunsen flame?...............	12	2 X
What are some of the features of a region of former volcanic activity (Crater Lake Quadrangle)?.............	8	3 L

174. Under the high pressures which occur in the earth's interior, materials that usually are solid have the capacity to flow slowly and thus bring about equalization of pressure differences on the surface.

175. Glacial conditions are as a rule approached by increasing latitudes or altitudes.

Experiment

What is the appearance of some of the features of a glaciated area (terminal moraine, outwash plain, kame, esker, drumlin, shape of valley)?......	9	1 D

Principles Having a Total Assigned Value of Five

176. Gases may be converted into liquids and liquids into solids by reducing the speed of their molecules or removing the faster molecules.

Experiments

How is ice made in a commercial plant (a field trip)?......................	18	1 D
Can a liquid be separated from a solution by distillation and condensation? If common salt is dissolved in water can the water be obtained from the solution by heating the solution in a flask and condensing the vapors with a Liebig condenser or by passing the vapors into a test tube set in ice?...................	16	2 D

TABLE IV (CONTINUED)

Experiments Allocated to Principles	Value	Rank	
If cold water, in a watch glass or shallow metal lid resting over a flat dish of sulfuric acid, is under a small bell jar from which the air is being evacuated, does the water freeze (to ice) as it boils rapidly?.....................	15	3	D
Does moisture collect on the outside of a glass (or a polished metal cup) soon after it is filled with ice water?.......	14	4	D
Can fractional distillation and condensation be used to separate two miscible liquids (alcohol and water) which have different boiling points?.................	12	5	L
What is the dew point for the air in the classroom, that is, at what average temperature does moisture first appear on and disappear from the outside of a drinking glass (or polished metal cup) after ice (and later warm water) is added to water in the cup?.....................	10	6	D
Does cold water poured over an inverted closed flask of steam and water near the boiling point cause vigorous boiling action in the flask?.............	8	7	D

177. Electrons will always flow from one point to another along a conductor if this transfer releases energy.

Experiments

	Value	Rank	
Does a small electric bell ring when its two terminals are connected to the zinc (amalgamated) and copper (or carbon) electrodes, respectively, of a Voltaic cell containing dilute sulfuric acid as the electrolyte? Does the bell ring when the two electrodes are the same element?...................................	20	1	L

APPENDIX B

TABLE IV (CONTINUED)

Experiments Allocated to Principles	Value	Rank	
Is an electric current produced in a closed circuit when two dissimilar elements are immersed in an electrolyte? Does a galvanometer register current when connected to an iron nail and a copper wire sticking in a lemon? To a penny and a dime separated by a piece of blotting paper which has been dipped in salt water?......................	19	2	X
Is a current of electricity through a conductor the movement of electric charges (electrons), that is, do the leaves of an electroscope at one end of a long copper wire separate when a negatively charged rubber rod (or proof-plane from an electrophorus) is touched to the other end of the wire?..........	17	3	D
How is a simple telegraph system connected, and what happens to the relay and sounder when the key is depressed and released?......................	16	4	X
If a flat iron and a lighted electric lamp in parallel are connected in series with an ammeter and a source of 110-volt A.C., is there an increase or a decrease, when the iron is turned on, of the current in the main line, the voltage across the lamp, and the brightness of the lamp?..........................	9	5	X

178. No chemical change occurs without an accompanying energy change.

Experiments
Does oxygen burn? Does oxygen support combustion, that is, does wood or sulfur burning in air continue to burn in oxygen? What effect is observed when a glowing wooden splint or a red-hot picture wire is moved from air into oxygen?................................. 19 2.5 L

APPENDIX B

TABLE IV (CONTINUED)

Experiments Allocated to Principles	Value	Rank
What evidence is there of a chemical change when a match is burned?..........	19	2.5 L
Does magnesium ribbon burn with an intense white flame?..................	19	2.5 D
Are much heat and light produced when a new photoflash lamp is used? Do the materials in the lamp undergo a marked change?..............................	19	2.5 D
As direct current is sent through a small lead cell consisting of two bright lead plates separated by a dilute solution of sulfuric acid, does one plate become unlike the other? When the two plates are disconnected from the direct current course and connected to a small electric bell (or buzzer), does the bell ring? Do the plates become more alike or more unlike as the bell rings (cell discharges)?...........................	18	6 D
When concentrated sulfuric acid is poured on sugar in a beaker is a large honeycomb-like mass pushed up by a gas? Is heat produced?.....................	18	6 D
Does burning thermite produce much heat?................................	18	6 D
What evidence is there of a chemical reaction when a few drops of sulfuric acid are added to a test tube of water held in the hand?....................	17	9.5 L
If a lump of quicklime is placed into enough water to cover it does the container get warm?..............	17	9.5 D
Can a chemical change be produced by synthesis (heating iron and sulfur)? By decomposition (heating mercuric oxide)? By single replacement (hydrochloric acid on "mossy" zinc)? Double replacement (solutions of silver nitrate and sodium chloride)? By oxidation and reduction (heating sodium nitrate with lead)?.................................	17	9.5 L

TABLE IV (CONTINUED)

Experiments Allocated to Principles	Value	Rank	
Is an electric current produced in a closed circuit when two dissimilar elements are immersed in an electrolyte? Does a galvanometer register current when connected to an iron nail and a copper wire sticking in a lemon? To a penny and a dime separated by a piece of blotting paper which has been dipped in salt water?...................................	17	9.5	L
Is much heat produced when a mixture of powdered sulfur and powdered zinc are ignited?................................	15	12.5	D
Does powdered antimony or iron burn with a sparkle when dropped into chlorine gas?..........................	15	12.5	D
Is a chemical change promoted by stirring sodium bicarbonate with potassium bitartrate? By heating ammonium dichromate? By exposing a silver chloride to bright light? By sending direct current through a solution of sodium chloride? By adding manganese dioxide, a catalyst, to hydrogen peroxide?....................	11	14	L
Can the compound copper sulfide be synthesized from its elements by heating?	10	15	L
Does a small electric bell ring when its two terminals are connected to the zinc (amalgamated) and copper (or carbon) electrodes, respectively, of a Voltaic cell containing dilute sulfuric acid as the electrolyte? Does the bell ring when the two electrodes are the same element?..............................	8	16	D
179. Non-metals may be arranged in an activity series according to their tendency to pass into ionic form by gaining electrons.			

Experiments Allocated to Principles	Value	Rank	
Experiment What is the relative order of activity of chlorine, bromine, and iodine for a replacement series of the halogens, that is, will chlorine water liberate bromine from sodium bromide? Iodine from sodium iodide? Will bromine water liberate chlorine from sodium chloride? Iodine from sodium iodide?........................	16	1	D

Principles Having a Total Assigned Value of Four

	Value	Rank	
180. The amount of heat developed in doing work against friction is proportional to the amount of work thus expended.			
Experiments How does rubbing the hands together vigorously affect the temperature of the palms of the hands?......................	16	2	L
Does a stout wire held firmly with both hands close together become hot as the wire is rapidly bent back and forth?	16	2	L
What effect does hammering a wire placed on a hard surface have on the temperature of the wire?................	16	2	L
181. In the northern hemisphere great volumes of air revolve in a counter-clockwise direction, and in the southern hemisphere, they revolve in a clockwise direction.			
Experiment What are the effects on the weather of a given locality of the movement of lows and highs across it as determined by studying daily weather maps?.........	16	1	L

TABLE IV (<u>CONTINUED</u>)

Experiments Allocated to Principles	Value	Rank
182. Luminous vapors and gases emit only certain kinds of light producing bright-line spectra.		
Experiments If light from a "colorless" Bunsen flame passes through a slit and a glass prism to a white screen, what is observed on the screen when a platinum wire is held in the flame? When a platinum wire dipped in a solution of sodium chloride is held in the flame? If an iron pan containing sodium chloride is placed between the slit and the prism and heated enough to vaporize the sodium, but not enough to make it luminous, does a dark line replace a yellow line on the screen?........................	17	1 D
183. Magnets depend for their properties upon the arrangement of the metallic ions of which they are made.		
Experiments If a test tube almost filled with iron filings is given polarity by stroking it in one direction with one end of a bar magnet, is the polarity destroyed by shaking the tube vigorously?	20	1 L
Does heating a magnetized needle destroy enough of its magnetism to prevent it from picking up iron filings?...	19	2 L
Can a rod of soft iron be magnetized if held pointed toward the south-magnetic pole (down from the north-geographic pole) and tapped repeatedly on the end? Can the polarity of a soft iron rod be reversed by similar tapping when its south pole is pointed toward the south-magnetic pole? Does a magnetized rod of soft iron lose nearly all of its magnetism when held in an east-west line and tapped repeatedly?........................	17	3 D

APPENDIX B

TABLE IV (<u>CONTINUED</u>)

Experiments Allocated to Principles	Value	Rank	
Is a steel knitting needle magnetized (given polarity) by stroking it in one direction with one end of a bar magnet? If a magnetized steel knitting needle is cut into several pieces are there always at least two opposite kinds of poles for each piece?...............................	15	4	L
Is the polarity of the ends of a nail held near one end of a bar magnet reversed when the magnet is reversed?...	12	5	L
Can a watch spring (or a steel bar) be demagnetized by slowly withdrawing the watch (or bar) from a coil of wire carrying an alternating current?........	7	6	D

184. An electric current will be produced in a closed circuit including two strips of different metals if one of the junctions is heated or cooled.

<u>Experiments</u>

If two different kinds of wire, alumel and chromel (or copper and iron), are fused together at the ends, is the needle of a galvanometer inserted in one of the wires deflected when one junction is heated with a Bunsen flame and the other junction is cooled with ice water (thermocouple)? Does increasing the difference in temperature of the two junctions increase the deflection of the galvanometer needle (pyrometer)?...................... 19 1 D

Can the temperature of boiling water be measured fairly accurately with a homemade pyrometer?...................... 15 2 D

185. Elements may be changed into other elements by changing the number of protons in the nucleus.

TABLE IV (<u>CONTINUED</u>)

Experiments Allocated to Principles	Value	Rank
186. Since the earth rotates from west to east, the exact time (Arlington time) at which the sun is nearest overhead, grows continually later as one travels westward around the earth's surface.		
187. In every sample of any compound substance formed, the proportion by weight of the constituent elements is always the same as long as the isotopic compositions of each element is constant.		
Experiments		
Can hydrogen and oxygen be obtained by passing direct current through an acid solution of water in a Hoffman or similar apparatus? What gas bubbles "rise" from the anode? Cathode? What is the ratio of the volume of the gas collected at the anode, that is, what is the composition of water by volume?.......................	17	1 D
Does heated copper unite with oxygen in a definite proportion by weight?......	16	2 D
Does copper combine with sulfur in a definite proportion by weight? If copper gauze of known weight is heated in the fumes of boiling sulfur, removed, held in a blue Bunsen flame until all the free sulfur is burned off, and again weighed, what is the ratio of the weight of copper (original weight) to the weight of sulfur (amount of increase in weight)?..	14	3 D
When iron burns does it combine with a definite amount of oxygen?.............	12	5 X
What is the percentage of oxygen in potassium chlorate?....................	12	5 L
Does the law of definite composition hold true for hydrates? What are the percentages of water of crystallization and hydration, respectively, determined by heating to constant weight in separate crucibles equal weights of crystallized barium chloride?.......................	12	5 D

TABLE IV (CONTINUED)

Experiments Allocated to Principles	Value	Rank	
188. Carbon atoms form a number of "type groups" of compounds which are determined by the elements present and by the structural combinations of the atoms within the molecules. Experiment What is the structure of common hydrocarbon molecules and of various classes of hydrocarbon derivatives shown by using a set of molecular model materials?........................	18	1	D

Principles Having a Total Assigned Value of Three

	Value	Rank	
189. Freezing point depression and boiling point elevation are proportional to the concentration of the solution. Experiment When a substance (solid or liquid) is dissolved in water is the freezing point lowered in proportion to the quantity of material dissolved?........	20	1	X
190. Harmonious musical intervals correspond to very simple frequency ratios. Experiment Does the sense of hearing, when comparing different tones, depend on the ratio of the frequencies of the tones? When a jet of air is directed at holes in a siren disk, does the outer row of forty-eight holes give a pitch an octave higher than that of the inner row of twenty-four holes regardless of the speed of the disk? Do successive rows from the inner part to the outer part always give a different or the same sequence of tones?..............	18	1	D

Experiments Allocated to Principles	Value	Rank
191. Two sound waves of the same or nearly the same frequency will destructively interfere with each other when the condensations of the one coincide with the rarefactions of the other provided that the directions of propagations are the same.		
Experiments		
If two tuning forks of the same pitch are both struck, do their sounds blend into one sound which is louder than either one alone? Does a weight fastened on a tine of one of the two forks cause the sound to alternately grow loud and then weak? Are the beats repeated faster as the weight on the tine is increased to make a greater difference between the pitch of the two forks?..............................	18	1 D
Can beats be produced by adjusting a load on the tines of one of two vibrating tuning forks held over the same resonance jar?.....................	16	2 D
What is heard when a sounding tuning fork is rotated close to the ear?.......	12	3 L
Can beats be produced by "singing tubes" of variable length?.............	11	4 D
192. When a sounding body is moving toward or away from an observer the apparent pitch will be higher or lower, respectively, than the true pitch of the sound emitted.		

TABLE IV (CONTINUED)

Experiments Allocated to Principles	Value	Rank	
Experiments Does the pitch heard by a man standing still increase or decrease as an automobile approaches with its horn blowing? As the automobile goes away?	20	1.5	D
If as two cars approach and pass each other the horn of one car is sounded continuously, how does the pitch heard by the driver of the other car change on approach and separation?.....	20	1.5	D
Does the pitch of a train whistle rise or fall as the train approaches? Recedes?	19	3	D
193. The amount of heat produced by an electric current is proportional to the resistance, the square of the current and the time of flow.			
Experiments What is the efficiency of an electric grill or heater as determined by calculating the heat absorbed (heat output) by a known weight of water in a weighed container and the heat input by measuring the average ammeter and volt-meter readings and the time of operation for the heating device?.................	15	1	D
What is the electrical equivalent of heat energy, that is, how many watt-seconds (Joules) are required to produce one calorie of heat when an electric bulb or heating coil is used in water?...	10	2	D
194. Atoms have great sub-atomic energy.			
195. Atoms or molecules may lose electrons when struck by high speed electrons or ions.			

Experiments Allocated to Principles	Value	Rank
196. Suspended particles of colloids have a continuous, erratic movement due to colloidal, molecular, or ion impacts.		
Experiments		
What is the nature of the movement of particles of smoke as observed in a Brownian movement adapter used with a microscope and a strong light?.........	17	1.5 D
Are particles of chalk dust in the path of a beam of light in a darkened room visible to the naked eye? Do the dust particles exhibit random motion?...	17	1.5 D

Principles Having a Total Assigned Value of Two

197. The height to which a liquid rises in a capillary tube is directly proportional to the surface tension of the liquid and inversely proportional to the density of the liquid and to the radius of the tube.		
Experiments		
Does water rise higher in tubes of larger or smaller internal diameter?....	18	1 D
If a rubber band is placed vertically around a small glass plate near one edge and a similar glass plate is held against the first one by a horizontal band near the top of the plates, how does the height to which liquid rises in the wider part of the opening compare with the height in the narrower part when the two plates are set vertically in water colored with ink?..............................	14	2 D
198. The distortion of an elastic body is proportional to the force applied provided the elastic limit is not exceeded.		

Experiments Allocated to Principles	Value	Rank	
Experiments If weights are hung on a screen door spring suspended vertically at the side of a measuring stick, what is the relation between the elongation produced (strain) and the force (stress) that causes it, provided the elastic limit is not exceeded?............................	20	1	L
If weights are placed in a pan on the free end of a long glass tube (or a piece of "quarter-round") which is clamped at its other end, what is the relation between the amount of bending produced (strain) and the force (stress) that caused it?................................	16	2	D
Are household spring balances or scales accurate throughout their range?	15	3.5	D
When increasingly larger weights are hung on a vertical weighted rubber band and then removed before the next weight is added, does the rubber band always go entirely back to its original length?...	15	3.5	D
Does a coiled wire spring lengthened by an excessive force remain longer than its original length, that is, can a coiled wire spring be stretched beyond its elastic limit?.........................	14	5	D
Does a long horizontal glass rod bent by weight at its center straighten again when the weight is removed?..............	13	6	D
If an iron rod with one end securely fastened and the other resting on a sharp edge has another rod connected at a right angle by a clamp at its midpoint to the free end of the first rod, what is the relationship between the amount of weight hung on one end of the second rod (stress) to the torsion (strain) of the first rod as measured by the movement of the free end of the second rod across a scale?................................	10	7	D

TABLE IV (CONTINUED)

Experiments Allocated to Principles	Value	Rank	
Can a copper wire be stretched to almost twice its original length before it breaks (ductility)?..................	7	8	D
199. A spinning body offers resistance to any force which changes the direction of the axis about which the body rotates.			
Experiments			
Does a gyroscope resist a change in motion?................................	14	2	D
Does a gyroscope precess, that is move at right angles to a force attempting to move its axis?...................	14	2	D
If a person holding a spinning gyroscope by the outer gimbal ring sits on a swivel chair with his feet off the floor, what happens if an attempt is made to move the gyroscope in some direction that will change its spinning axis?.....	14	2	D
200. The rate of osmosis is directly proportional to the difference in concentration on opposite sides of the membrane.			
Experiment			
Does osmosis proceed faster in the direction from the less to the more concentrated solution or _vice versa_?...	20	1	D
201. The pressure of a saturated vapor is constant at a given temperature, and increases with an increase of temperature.			

Experiments Allocated to Principles	Value	Rank
Experiments		
Does the amount of gas which a liquid can hold decrease as the temperature rises? Do bubbles of gas appear on the inside of a glass of ice water which is permitted to stand for some time in a warm room? Does gas escape more rapidly from a warm bottle of soda pop or from an ice cold bottle of the same beverage? From heated household ammonia or from ammonia at room temperature?.....................................	17	1 X
Does ether introduced above the mercury in a barometer exert sufficient vapor pressure to push the mercury downward?..................................	15	2 D
202. Substances which expand upon solidifying have their melting points lowered by pressure; those which contract upon solidifying have their melting points raised by pressure.		
Experiments		
If weights are suspended by means of a copper or an iron wire over a cake of ice, does the wire cut its way downward through the ice without leaving two separate pieces of ice?............	20	1 D
Do two pieces of ice unite firmly when pressed together? When touching without added pressure?................	16	2 D
203. In a plane mirror a line running from any point on the object to the image of that point is perpendicular to the mirror.		

Experiments Allocated to Principles	Value	Rank
Experiment If an arrow or triangle (object) is drawn obliquely to a plane mirror, how does the image compare with the object in respect to size? Shape? Position? Distance from the mirror? Is a line from any point on the object to the image of that point perpendicular to the mirror?.....................	18	1 L
204. Incandescent solids and liquids emit all wave lengths of light and give a continuous spectrum.		
Experiment If light from a "colorless" Bunsen flame passes through a slit and a glass prism to a white screen, what is observed on the screen when a platinum wire is held in the flame? When a platinum wire dipped in a solution of sodium chloride is dipped in the flame? If an iron pan containing sodium chloride is placed between the slit and the prism and heated enough to vaporize the sodium, but not enough to make it luminous, does a dark line replace a yellow line on the screen?	12	1 D
205. Gases conduct electric currents only when ionized.		
Experiments Do the ions produced in gases by heat conduct electrical charges, that is, do the leaves of a charged electroscope collapse when the gases surrounding a Bunsen flame are collected by a funnel and directed against the knob of the electroscope? Do the leaves collapse if the Bunsen burner is turned on but not lighted?.................................	17	1 D

Experiments Allocated to Principles	Value	Rank	
What color is produced when an electric current is passed through a clear glass tube containing neon? Argon? Mercury vapor? A mixture of neon and argon gases with mercury vapor? The same mixture in an amber glass tube?	16	2.5	D
Does an electrical discharge occur more readily across a long path in a tube from which air is removed or across a much shorter path in air when an evacuated tube is connected in parallel with an air gap in the secondary of an induction coil?.........................	16	2.5	D

206. Condenser capacitance varies directly with the area of the plates, and inversely as the thickness of the insulation between them.

Experiments
What is the relationship between the capacitance of a condenser and the area of one plate? The distance between the plates? If plate B is grounded and clamped about one-half inch above plate C on a leaf electroscope, do the leaves diverge much less (because plate C holds more of the charge) for the same number of applications of charge from a proof-plane when the area of plate C is decreased or increased? In order to cause equal divergence of the leaves, must more applications of charge from a proof-plane to plate C be made (because plate C will hold more charges) when the distance between the two plates is decreased or increased? When glass replaces some air between the plates?......................

	Value	Rank	
	20	1	D

Experiments Allocated to Principles	Value	Rank	
Does a battery produce electric charges? If the terminals of a battery (at least forty-five volts) are connected to two metal discs (separated by shellac) on top of an electroscope, what happens to the leaves of the electroscope when the upper disc is removed after the lower disc is disconnected from the battery?................................	7	2	D

207. Alternating current charges a condenser twice during each cycle inducing opposite charges on the two plates with the result that a current appears to flow through the condenser.

Experiments
　　　If a condenser and a light bulb are in series does the light seem to glow continuously or merely flash momentarily when connected to an alternating-current source? When connected to a direct current source?......................

(light bulb series)	19	1	D
Does a condenser across contact points in an electrical circuit (induction coil) reduce the amount of sparking?................................	8	2	D

208. Electro-magnetic waves may produce electrical oscillation in a condenser circuit which is so adjusted as to oscillate naturally with the same frequency as that of the incoming waves.

TABLE IV (CONTINUED)

Experiments Allocated to Principles	Value	Rank	
Experiments			
If a radio receiver with a self-contained loop antenna is tuned to a broadcasting station, what variation is noticed in the strength of reception when the face of the loop antenna is parallel to and then perpendicular to a straight line from the loop to the broadcasting station?...............................	14	1	D
If a variable air condenser is connected across the secondary coil of a tuning transformer in series with a crystal detector and earphones, can radio programs picked up by the antenna-primary-ground circuit be separated for the earphones by turning the movable plates of the condenser between the fixed plates?..............	12	2	X
How is a crystal-type radio receiver constructed and operated?..............	10	3.5	L
How is a one-tube radio receiver constructed and operated?..............	10	3.5	L
Can a circuit consisting of a group of parallel condensers (0.02, 0.05, 0.1 and 0.2 microfarad) in series with a thirty Henry choke coil and a ten watt lamp be tuned to the frequency of an 110-volt 60-cycle alternating current by putting condensers in and out of the circuit?.................................	9	5	D
209. Atoms may be broken down by bombarding the nucleus with highspeed particles such as protons, alpha particles, or neutrons.			
210. Radioactive emission involves nuclear changes.			

Experiments Allocated to Principles	Value	Rank	
211. At a definite temperature and pressure, the relative combining volumes of gases and of gaseous products may be expressed approximately in small whole numbers.			
Experiments			
What is the ratio by volume in which hydrogen and oxygen combine in an eudiometer to form water?.....................	18	1	D
Can hydrogen and oxygen be obtained by passing direct current through an acid solution of water in a Hoffman or similar apparatus? What gas bubbles "rise" from the anode? Cathode? What is the ratio of the volume of the gas collected at the cathode to that collected at the anode, that is what is the composition of water by volume?.........	15	2	D
212. Orderly arrangement of molecules, atoms, or ions in crystals give crystals regular form.			
Experiments			
Can a large crystal of copper sulfate be grown by placing one well-shaped crystal of copper sulfate in a fresh (daily) saturated solution of copper sulfate for several weeks?..............	16	1	D
Can a crystalline solid (sodium thiosulfate or "hypo"; sugar; common salt) be obtained from its saturated solution by lowering the temperature?...	13	3.5	X
Can iodine be crystallized on the bottom of a dish of cold water set over a heated evaporating dish containing the oxidizing agent, manganese dioxide, with sodium iodide and sulfuric acid?........	13	3.5	D

Experiments Allocated to Principles	Value	Rank	
Do crystals form more rapidly when a supersaturated solution of sodium acetate or sodium thiosulfate ("hypo") in a flask is allowed to cool without moving the flask or when the solution is disturbed by stirring or by suspending a small crystal of the same substance on a string in the solution? Does the flask feel warmer or cooler as crystallization proceeds?.............	13	3.5	D
Will common alum crystallize out when potassium sulfate is dissolved in a solution of aluminum sulfate and cooled?	13	3.5	D
What form or shape is rhombic sulfur? Prismatic sulfur? Amorphous sulfur? Can rhombic or ordinary sulfur be prepared by dissolving sulfur in carbon disulfide and slowly evaporating the disulfide? Can amorphous or plastic sulfur be prepared by letting boiling sulfur flow into cold water? Can prismatic or monoclinic sulfur be prepared by slowly cooling sulfur heated until it just melts?...................	10	6	L

213. The properties of alloys are dependent upon the relative amount of their components, the extent of their compound formation, and upon the crystalline structure of the mixture.

Experiment

	Value	Rank	
How is Wood's metal made? How does the melting point of Wood's metal compare with the melting points of each of the four metals (tin, bismuth, cadmium, lead) used to make the alloy?.................	17	1	D

Experiments Allocated to Principles	Value	Rank	
214. Glacial abrasion occurs in proportion to the weight of the ice and the velocity of its movement. Experiment What is the appearance of some of the features of a glaciated area (terminal moraine, outwash plain, kame, esker, drumlin, shape of valley)?.......	17	1	D

APPENDIX C

THE EXPERIMENTS WHICH THE EVALUATORS DEEMED UNDESIRABLE
FOR INCLUSION IN AN INTEGRATED COURSE OF PHYSICAL
SCIENCE FOR SENIOR HIGH SCHOOL

<u>Physics: Mechanics.</u>

When a glass tube is placed in water and in mercury is the liquid elevated or depressed? Is the water and the mercury higher next to the tube or in the middle?

Will a roller which has the shape of a double cone roll "uphill" on a v-shaped track with the vertex at the lower end?

Are stains which can be removed from cloth with hot water readily removed if the hot water falls on the stain from a height of about one foot?

What is the horizontal velocity of a projectile shot by a spring gun or a blow gun?

What is the acceleration of a falling body as determined by using a falling vibrating fork with a stylus to trace a wavy pattern on special paper?

How long does it take a free falling steel ball to drop a measured distance as determined by using an improved form of a Whiting's pendulum?

What is the acceleration due to gravity as measured by using a Packard's inclined plane apparatus for studying projectiles?

Can the motion of the moon around the earth as the earth revolves around the sun be shown by a person holding his fist (the moon) in front of him as he (the earth) revolves counterclockwise at the same time that he moves to his left around a rectangular table with a bright lamp (the sun) at its center? If a finger is held between the nose and the light, is exactly, more than, or less than one revolution made to again bring the nose, finger and light in line as the body rotates on its axis while moving around the table, that is, is from noon to noon exactly, more than, or less than one day (or revolution)?

Can a north-south line or meridian (circle around the earth through the poles) be found at noon by pointing the hour hand of a watch at the sun and extending a line connecting the twelve and six on the watch? At any hour of the day by pointing the hour hand at the sun and, before drawing the line, going clockwise for morning and counterclockwise for afternoon that fraction of the circular face of the watch is the same that the number of hours before or after twelve o'clock noon is of twenty-four hours?

Do meteors observed on a starlit night (mid-July to mid-August; also, about October 20 and December 10) seem to come from one or many points of the heavens?

Have the common constellations advanced toward the east or the west after a lapse of two weeks?

Is the real motion of the earth clockwise or counterclockwise as determined by a "star-trail" photograph made by pointing a camera at the North Star?

If flat cardboard rings are placed one outside of the other on a horizontal wire frame around the center of a basketball (Saturn) suspended by a string, in what position is the north pole of "Saturn" with respect to the observer when the rings are most clearly seen?

Is the length of the year in days (366) equal to 1440 minutes per day divided by the average gain in time (minutes) of a star per day in crossing a stationary sight line to the east for several nights?

If two sharp edges some distance apart are lined up with the eye and the forward edge of the sun (or moon) when it is high in the sky, how many seconds are required for the entire sun (or moon) to cross the line of vision? What is the diameter of the sun (or moon) when seconds of time are converted into miles of diameter (time interval x 6760)?

Will a v-shaped wire truss supporting a vertical brace at its center prevent a long thin board supported at its ends from sagging under a weight which causes sagging when the truss is not used?

If a square cardboard (airplane wing) with the front edge near an electric fan higher than the rear edge is supported at its corners by slender wires about six inches above a heavier board placed on a platform of a counterpoised balance, what is the vertical lifting force on the "airplane wing" measured by the amount of weights necessary to rebalance the scales after the fan is turned on? What evidence is there that there is a component of the wind pressure which is parallel to the air stream? What is the lifting force on a model airplane determined in similar manner?

If a model airplane held firmly by a wire or rod to a platform balance about six inches below is counterbalanced and placed in the air stream from an electric fan, how does the lift on the wing vary with the angle of attack?

If thrust, drag, lift, and gravity are considered when a model airplane is held in position, what forces exceed what other forces when an airplane gains speed in level flight? Climbs? Glides?

How can an airplane pilot determine his location by signals from ground stations when flying by dead reckoning?

If an inclined plane is raised until a block of wood on it will continue to slide after it is pushed gently, what is the coefficient of sliding friction --- the ratio of the height of the elevated end to the base of the inclined plane instead of the forces parallel and perpendicular to the plane, respectively, in similar triangles?

In the air-wind-ground relationships for piloting an airplane, how do wind and course determine heading? How do wind and heading determine course? How can wind direction be determined from heading and track?

Will a solid model airplane stay in any position in which it is set using the two ends of any one of its three axes as points of support?

If a flat board of irregular shape with holes near its edges is hung by different holes on a horizontal nail and a line is drawn each time along a plumb line tied to the same nail, does the board remain balanced or rotate without assistance when placed on a horizontal nail through a hole at the point where the lines intersect (center or gravity)? When the nail is placed through holes away from the center of gravity, does the center of gravity always take the lowest possible position?

Is a cone or funnel on its base, on its side, and on its vertex, respectively, stable, unstable, or neutral equilibrium?

Does the mercury in a clinical thermometer move "upward" past a constriction in the capillary when placed in the mouth? Does the mercury move "downward" past the construction when cooled? Can the mercury be "shaken down" by a quick thrust of the arm and hand?

If a heavy metal ball suspended from the ceiling by a long steel wire is started swinging back and forth in one plane, will it continue swinging over one line or over different lines on the floor or soon stop (Focault's pendulum)?

When a table is struck a sudden blow with a hammer, which will move more the table or a small object on the table, that is, are the destructive effects of earth- quakes much worse on buildings fastened to bed rock or on buildings on loose material?

Does a marble projected horizontally hit the floor at the same time as or at a different time than one dropped vertically from the same height?

What force is exerted by an engine to accelerate a one-ton truck gradually from rest to thirty miles per hour?

If a toy electric train is on a circular track which is free to rotate about a vertical axis, what happens if the current is turned on when the track is still, but not held, and the train starts forward (and backward) from rest? What happens if the current is turned on after the track and the engine are rotating in the same direction that the engine heads? In the opposite direction from that toward which the engine heads?

If the ends of two similar blocks A and B face each other have a small section cut out so that a fire cracker fits snugly between the blocks, does an explosion of a firecracker move blocks A and B the same distance? How does placing a similar block C on top of block B affect the relative distances blocks A and B are moved?

Where along a baseball bat can the ball be hit the hardest with the least jar to the hands? If a meter stick is held in a horizontal position by a hand at one end, at what point can the stick be struck with a mallet without a sting being felt by the hand holding the stick, that is, where is the center of percussion of a meter stick?

Where is the center of percussion of a bar or rod? If a vertical meter stick is supported at its upper end between two boards by a weak wooden pin through a hole in the meter stick and resting on the boards, is the pin not broken (or the upper end displaced the least) when a sharp blow is struck with a hammer at a point two-thirds of the way down the meter stick or at some other point?

Is the propeller a source of thrust as determined by doubling the number of turns of a propeller blade used to wind up the rubber band on a model airplane and comparing the distances of the respective flights?

Can a small pail of water held at arm's length be swung up and over the head without spilling the water?

If a weight hangs anywhere along a rope whose ends are fastened to a crossbar, is the tension in any part of the rope as shown by a spring balance less than, equal to, or greater than the weight?

Is the propeller a source of thrust as determined by the change, if any, in the length of a rubber band held stretched in line with the shaft of a motor and fan mounted on a board and suspended?

If a wooden propeller mounted loosely over two pins set in the top of a spool is spun around a stationary vertical spindle by pulling on a string wound around the spool, does the propeller or "helicopter" rise and leave the propulsion device?

How can the weight of a golf club, baseball bat or tennis racket be found by using string, an overhead support, and a known weight?

How can a person determine the weight of a plank of wood by using only the plank, a stick, a shoe, and his own weight?

If a person pulls gently on a thread (or rope) coming from the bottom side of a small spool (for thread or a larger one for wire), does the spool roll toward or away from him as he pulls vertically? Almost horizontally? Is there some place between the horizontal and the vertical at which a pull will cause the spool to slide instead of roll?

Can a person standing with heels against the wall pick up a small object on the floor about a foot from the toes without moving the feet or bending the knees?

Can a paper clip placed on a stable paper glider upset the weight distribution enough to cause the glider to fall in an irregular path?

Will a solid model airplane stay in any position in which it is set using the two ends of any one of its three axes as points of support?

If a wing of cardboard with one aileron up and the other down is glued on a straw held in an air stream does the half of the wing with the aileron up move up or down?

How is the elevator (horizontal stabilizer) on an airplane adjusted to cause the tail to move up and down?

How is the rudder (vertical stabilizer) on an airplane adjusted to cause the tail to move to one side and then to the other?

Does dihedral (raising of the wings at the outer ends) increase the lateral stability of a model airplane?

How does the stability of straight wings compare with those having dihedral and those having sweepback?

Why does the pointer on a barograph move up or down with a change in pressure?

What are the different methods for finding the mechanical advantage of a train of gears?

What is the rotational energy of a disk on an axle rolling down on inclined plane?

What are the functions of the various parts of the automobile?

What is the mechanical equivalent of heat as determined by having one kilogram of lead shot fall one hundred times through a cardboard tube one meter long and dividing the number of gram-meters of work done by the number of calories of heat developed (the product of the change in temperature of the lead shot, the weight of the shot in grams, and the specific heat of lead)?

What is the mechanical equivalent of heat, that is, how many gram-meters of work are required to heat one gram of water one degree Centigrade as determined by using a frictional machine (Jouler)?

Do safety matches prepared from potassium chlorate and sulfur in mucilage ignite when scratched on sandpaper covered with a mixture of red phosphorus in dilute glue?

With the same pressure at the faucet, does more water flow out of a long tube or a similar shorter tube in the same elapsed time, that is, is there sufficient friction between water and the interior of a tube through which it flows to decrease the amount of water which can be forced out under constant pressure in a unit time?

If a block of wood is pulled with uniform velocity along a table top with a spring scale or if a cord extends from a wooden block on a horizontal surface over a pulley to a weight pan and sufficient weights are placed in the pan to cause the block to slide slowly toward the pulley once it has been given a start, what is the coefficient of sliding friction --- the ratio of the force used to overcome friction to the weight causing friction?

If glass T-tubes are inserted as manometers along a horizontal glass tube (pipe) connected to a reservior, does the pressure remain the same, increase, or decrease along a "supply" pipe at points farther and farther from the water reservoir when water flows? When water does not flow?

What deflection of wind currents is caused by the rotation of the earth? If less than a test tube of water is poured on a slate globe as it spins rapidly in a counterclockwise direction, does the water curve to the right or to the left (of a meridian) north and south of the equator when the globe is stopped suddenly?

When two hands are pressed together and one hand is turned, does the other hand turn (clutch)?

If one of two pie plates, each on separate shafts in line, is spinning, can the other plate be started to spinning by bringing it in touch with the first one (clutch)?

What is the relative viscosity of water, molasses, and a lubricating oil as determined by the number of seconds necessary for the same volumes of each to flow from a funnel?

What relation exists between the S.A.E. rating of an oil and the number of seconds it takes a glass tube full of oil to drain into a beaker?

Does a marble fall from the top to the bottom of a cylinder of oil more rapidly if the oil has a low or a high S.A.E. rating?

Can a tarnished penny be polished by rubbing it with moistened precipitated chalk, an ingredient of toothpaste?

Does a paste made from neutral soap, glycerine, household ammonia, hot water and precipitated chalk clean silver without scratching it?

What effect does rotation have on mercury and water in a bowl?

Does a body similar to the earth (hard-boiled egg) spin more readily or less readily if it has a liquid interior (fresh egg) than if it has a solid interior (hard-boiled egg)?

How does a tachometer record the revolutions per minute made by an engine?

How does a bank indicator work?

If a nail at the upper end of a string passing down through a tube is swung horizontally in a circle by moving the tube, how does the centrifugal force vary with the radius of curvature as judged by the number of nails required on the bottom end of the string to balance the centrifugal force? How does the centrifugal force seem to vary with the velocity?

What is the percentage of butterfat in a sample of milk or cream as determined by using a Babcock centrifuge?

About what percent of lemon extract is lemon oil as determined by using the Babcock centrifuge?

Can the insoluble suspended matter in milky lime-water be separated rapidly from the liquid by whirling the limewater in a centrifuge?

Can the direction in which an airplane is headed be read from a compass card mounted on the outer gimbal ring of a directional gyroscope?

How is a gyroscope used for an artificial horizon to indicate a banked position of an airplane? To indicate a pitched position?

If vertical copper, lead, and iron wires (no. 36) of the same length have more and more weights hung on them until they break, which wire breaks last, that is, has the greatest tensile strength? .

How does the tensile strength of the same kind of wire vary with its cross-sectional area (nos. 28 and 25 copper wire)?

What are the relative tensile strengths of a piece of cotton string and a fishing line of the same size? Of pieces of silk, linen, cotton and rayon?

How are cotton, linen, wool, silk and rayon distinguished from each other by the strength test, the burning test, the sodium hydroxide test, the hydrochloric and nitric acid tests, and the ink or the oil test?

Are "outside paints" more elastic than "inside paints"? Which paint chips and peels and which stretches with a metal strip on bending? If a painted surface is scratched with a sharp knife are the edges of the scratches clear-cut or ragged?

What is the effect of earthquakes on L-shaped buildings as determined by rocking a laboratory earthquake platform so that a model L-shaped building fastened securely to it is shaken first lengthwise and then sidewise?

Does a meter stick placed across two separated supports bend less if the stick is on its edge or on its flat side?

What is the coefficient of elasticity of a metal rod as determined by the method of bending?

If a piece of solder wire is placed straight through a small hole of the same size bored through two blocks of wood, what happens if the blocks are moved away from one another while the surfaces are in close contact and the ends of the wire are held firmly (shear stress)?

Can two things occupy the same space at the same time? Can water flow into a flask unless air can get out? Is some space still occupied by air after an inverted drinking glass is pushed down in a vessel of water?

Is the odor of oil of wintergreen (methyl salicylate) evident when salicylic acid, methyl alcohol, and concentrated sulfuric acid are warmed together?

If an electric light bulb and a much smaller solid weight are counterpoised on a platform balance under a bell jar, what is observed as the air is evacuated from the bell jar?

What fractional part of a floating body will sink into water as determined by placing a glass tube with one end closed in a tall jar nearly filled with water and loading it with shot until it floats upright?

What is observed when a layer of olive oil about two millimeters thick is slowly poured upon the surface of water in a beaker? When alcohol is added to the oil little by little?

Is hydrogen lighter or heavier than air?

Do soils contain air? Do gas bubbles come to the surface as soil is placed in water?

Does a cork (or an airtight metal chamber) with a wire stem projecting through the cap of the gasoline tank of a small airplane record the fractional part of the volume of the tank which is filled with gasoline?

How can the principle of fluid drive be demonstrated by using two electric fans facing each other? If fans A and B face each other, will fan B start rotating when fan A is turned on? If the speed of fan A is increased or decreased is the speed of fan B similarly affected?

May a hydraulic press have a mechanical advantage?

What happens to a balloon after a small piece of dry ice is placed in the balloon and the opening is tied?

What is the volume of a bolt as determined by finding its apparent loss of weight in water?

Does water sink or float when it is poured on the surface of a body of gasoline?

If ground coffee is sprinkled on the surface of a glass of cold water, do some solids (adulterants or over-roasted coffee) sink? Do some solids (pure coffee) float?

What is the specific gravity of a liquid? If air is taken at the top from a long branched tube of glass dipping into two separate beakers containing water and another liquid, respectively, is the specific gravity of the other liquid equal to the height of the water column divided by the height of the column of the other liquid or vice versa?

What is the approximate density of oil as determined by the height of an oil column in a straw, set alongside a ruler flush with the bottom in a glass of water, at the instant oil dropped into the straw begins to come out at its bottom?

If water flows from a rubber tube connected to a higher reservoir, what is the ratio of the amount of water which flows in a given time from a tube with a head of one foot, four feet, and nine feet, respectively, that is what is the relation between the head (height above outlet) and the velocity (pressure) of water at the outlet?

If water extends up about eight feet in a glass tube set in a small balloon, does the balloon burst?

What is the pressure of the gas at a jet in the classroom as determined by using a water manometer?

How much lung pressure can be exerted as measured by using a water manometer?

Does the addition of four drops of glycerine to a saponin (soap) solution permit the bubbles to be deflated and reinflated more easily? Does the addition of sodium oleate to the saponin-glycerine solution greatly increase the elasticity of the bubbles?

Does water pass more readily through sand or clay?

Can petroleum be extracted from oil sand by shaking the sand with ether followed by decantation and evaporation of the liquid on a watch glass?

What is observed when three similar glass tubes filled, respectively, with dry loose loam, dry sand, and packed dry clay are placed in a container of colored water?

Does methyl alcohol, denatured alcohol, glycerine, or ethylene glycol have the lowest capillarity or "seepage"?

Will red ink enter cracks and unblemished surfaces of dinnerware?

Can a needle or a safety razor blade be made to float on water?

Why does soap help to soften a beard? When a drop of soap solution is put on water near a floating razor blade (or needle), does the water wet the blade enough to cause it to sink?

Is considerable force needed to pull apart two clean flat surfaces of lead pressed firmly together?

What is observed when small particles of camphor are placed on water? At the rear end of a match (boat) on water?

Can glass tubing be cut? Bent? Drawn? Blown? Fire-polished?

Does water sink or float when it is poured on the surface of a body of gasoline?

Do butter and oleomargarine melted separately on the surface of hot milk solidify, on cooling, into dispersed granules or into one single mass?

Does paint prepared from zinc oxide, linseed oil, manganese dioxide, and turpentine spread easily and dry readily?

Does lampblack dispersed in water settle more readily after soap is added?

If a horizontal glass plate, attached to one arm of a beam balance and counterpoised, has a surface of water barely brought in contact with its lower surface, is the same, more or less weight necessary to maintain the balance, that is, is some force necessary to overcome the cohesion of water molecules?

Can a chair with a smooth wet seat be lifted by a rubber suction cup?

Can two classmates pull a set of Magdeburg hemispheres apart more easily before or after most of the air is pumped out of the hemispheres?

Does air exert pressure? If a test tube or glass brimful of water has a sheet of paper pressed against the glass all around the edges and is inverted with a hand against the paper, what happens when the hand below the paper is removed?

Is atmospheric pressure sufficient to sustain the water in an inverted fruit jar full of water and almost raised out of the water?

What happens to the water in a short glass tube lifted vertically from under water after the thumb is placed over the upper end?

What conditions are necessary in order that water may be siphoned from one vessel to another? Must the short arm and the long arm of a siphon always be entirely full of water? Must the outlet and the intake always be under water? Does the water always flow through the siphon toward the vessel which has its water level at the greater or at the smaller height above sea level?

Does the hollow metal wafer of an aneroid barometer or barograph respond to increased and decreased pressure by a finger? As a bell jar in which the instrument is placed is evacuated and then filled with compressed air?

Does the altitude reading of an airplane altimeter increase or decrease as the air pressure around it is decreased and increased in a bell jar?

How does a Cape Cod barometer show atmospheric
pressure changes?

Does ether introduced above the mercury in a
barometer exert sufficient vapor pressure to push the
mercury downward?

What is the vapor pressure of gasoline at room
temperature as determined by introducing gasoline above
the mercury in a barometer?

Can wind direction at a high altitude be determined
by following a balloon with a telescope?

How is the operation of the Bourdon-tube pressure
gauge similar to the "carnival snake" when air is blown
into the coiled paper tube and then air (or water) into
the hollow tube of the gauge?

What happens to a tightly stoppered bottle (or a
closed "steel bomb" or pipe) filled with water after it
is placed under a mixture of salt and ice?

If an open U-tube with a long base containing colored water extends through holes in a board covered with a
rug, what happens to the water when an electric vacuum
cleaner is operated over one end of the U-tube?

Does carbon dioxide flow down or up an inclined
trough to extinguish a candle flame?

When "dry ice" is placed on water, what evidence
is there of a change from solid to gaseous carbon
dioxide?

If a test tube of hydrogen chloride gas is inverted
with the mouth barely in water, how high does the water
"rise" in the tube, that is, about how much of a volume
of hydrogen chloride gas dissolves in water?

Does increasing the velocity of air through a constricted area increase or decrease the pressure in that
area? If an air stream is directed horizontally between two large square pieces of cardboard suspended
side-by-side a short distance apart, what is observed?

If a half of a ping-pong ball at the end of a
broom straw is held facing the air stream from an
electric fan, is the deflection from a vertical position
greater when the wind strikes the concave or the convex
side of the hemisphere (ball), that is, does streamlining
an object increase or decrease its resistance to the flow
of a fluid (gas or liquid) past it?

If long threads hang down on both sides of the wing
of a model airplane when it is pointed upward, what difference is observed in the movement of the threads after
the plane is held in a horizontal position facing an air
stream from an electric fan or wind tunnel and a fine
wire is used to move the threads forward from the leading
edge of the wing?

If a white mist, generated by dry ice in a flask of warm water, is forced by an electric fan through a slightly larger homemade wind tunnel and over a model of an airplane wing, what difference is observed in the movement of the white mist past the upper and lower surfaces of the wing?

If a test thread is held horizontally just above the end of an airplane wing in front of an electric fan or wind tunnel, do the eddy currents tend to move the thread outward or inward from the wing tip when the tip is rounded? Square?

Physics: Sound

Does the appearance of different sounds on the screen of an oscilloscope indicate that the sources of the sounds are in vibration?

How does the frequency or pitch of a vibrating string or wire on a sonometer vary with its length? Tension? Diameter? Mass per unit length?

What is the velocity of sound in the metal rod of a Kundt's tube?

How does the pitch of a whistle, organ pipe, clarinet and trombone vary with the length of the vibrating column of air?

When air is blown sharply across the open ends of test tubes filled to different levels with water, what relation exists between the length of the vibrating air column and the pitch produced?

How does the pitch of an open organ pipe compare with its pitch when one end is closed?

Is an echo as loud as the original sound? If a watch is held at the focus of a concave reflector and the ear is placed at the larger end of a small megaphone which has its smaller end at the focus of a second such reflector facing the first one, how does the ticking heard as an echo from the second reflector compare in loudness with the sound heard at the same point with the second reflector removed?

Do the lungs and other air cavities seem to vibrate in unison with the vibrating vocal cords during speech?

As the notes of the scale are whistled going up and coming down, does the volume of the mouth cavity increase or decrease for the high notes? For the low notes?

If two friends whose lips cannot be seen are talking, can the individual voices be recognized easily?

Can standing waves be produced by resonance in a strong thread attached at one end to one tine of an electrically driven tuning fork with the other end held over a pulley by a hanging weight? How does increasing the weight (tension) increase the wave length? The number of loops?

Are there vibrations of low frequency which may be heard by some persons but not by others? Can all, only some, or none of the members of a class hear a sound produced when a stretched wire about fifteen feet long is plucked gently? When a meter stick is set to vibrating after it is moved farther and farther under a clamp at the edge of a table?

If seven points divide a sonometer string into eight equal parts and v-shaped paper riders are placed at the first five points, from which points are the paper riders thrown (antinodes) and at which points do they remain (nodes) when the string is touched gently at the sixth point as it is bowed at the seventh point?

If a string runs horizontally from the clapper of a vibrating door bell over a pulley to a weight holder, does increasing the weight (tension) increase or decrease the number of vibrating loops? How can the string be made to vibrate as a whole (one loop, the fundamental), then in two loops (the first overtone), and finally in three loops (the second overtone)?

What is heard when a sounding tuning fork is rotated close to the ear?

Can beats be produced by "singing flames"? Can harmony and discord be produced by varying the length of one of two glass cylinders set over two "singing flames"?

How is a soap film (ear drum) over the smaller end of a megaphone affected when the tone a-a-a-h is sounded in the larger end (outer ear)?

Is a building more likely to be damaged by earthquakes that shake at certain speeds than by those that shake at other speeds? If two narrow tall towers, one about twice as tall as the other, are fastened to a laboratory earthquake platform, which tower first begins to rock at the same speed as the platform? Is there a speed at which the other tower will rock back and forth? Is there any speed at which both towers rock?

Physics: Heat

After absorbent cotton wound on the bulb of a thermometer is removed from liquid ether, does the temperature (thermometer reading) rise, fall, or remain the same?

Does heat from a Bunsen flame quickly reach a finger covered with asbestos and held in the flame?

If water in a funnel barely covers the bulb of an air thermometer, is the liquid column of the thermometer lowered very much when alcohol on the surface of the water is burned?

Can a cigarette be put out by pressing the lighted
end on a handkerchief in the hand without scorching the
handkerchief, if a quarter is underneath the spot on the
handkerchief?
Will liquid air in a teakettle boil on a cake of ice?
What happens to a penny one-third of which is pressed into a piece of dry ice?
Are rubber tubing and flowers brittle after being
immersed in liquid air? Does mercury in a test tube in
liquid air become hard enough to be used as a hammer for
driving nails?
Does examination of a wool fiber under a microscope
reveal overlapping scales which may entrap air thus pre-
venting convection currents?
What is the principle of the Bomb Calorimeter? How
many degrees rise in temperature occur in a known quantity
of water when a mixture of starch and potassium chlorate
are ignited in a crucible floating on the water?
If a candle burning in a milk bottle goes out, can
the candle be kept burning by inserting into the bottle
a piece of metal with the lower end bent and slightly
above the candle flame?
At what temperature does the bellows of the thermo-
stat of an automobile cooling system expand to permit
circulation of water?
Is hydrogen lighter or heavier than air?
How can a gas (ammonia) that is soluble in water
and lighter than air, be collected in the laboratory?
Does hot water weigh the same as, less than or
more than an equal volume of cold water?
Does a radiometer placed at the focal point of one
of two concave mirrors facing each other rotate faster
after a metal weight placed at the focal point of the
other mirror is heated?
If a heated glass rod is held just above the bulb
of an air thermometer, is sufficient heat energy radiated
from the rod to cause the air in the bulb to expand and
push the liquid downward?
As the temperature of a glowing body is raised, does
the wave length emitted (color) shift toward the shorter
values (blue) or the longer values (red)? Does the color
of a piece of iron wire change toward the red or the blue
end of the spectrum as the wire is heated hotter and
hotter? When the colors of Betelgeuse and Rigel in Orion,
Aldebaran in the Hyades, Arcturus, Vega, and Sirius are
observed and compared with tables giving the surface
temperatures of stars, are the red or the blue stars the
cooler? The hotter?
Will a gram-molecule of sugar and a gram-molecule
of glycerol lower the freezing point and raise the boiling point of a given weight of water by the same amount?

If the right hand is taken from ice water and the left hand from hot water and both hands are then plunged into lukewarm water, does the temperature of the lukewarm water (taken with a thermometer) seem different to the two hands? Is a person's sense of temperature reliable, that is, do the sensations of "hot" and "cold" depend on other factors besides the temperature of the object touched?

What is the error approximately of a mercury thermometer at the freezing point of water and at the boiling point? If the bulb of a thermometer is placed in a beaker of finely cracked ice (or snow) with enough water to fill the spaces around the pieces of ice, what is the lowest temperature reached? What is the highest temperature reached when the thermometer is placed with its bulb in the steam just above the surface of boiling water in an open flask (or steam boiler)?

Is the main chemical compound in a commercial antifreeze methyl alcohol, ethyl alcohol, isopropyl alcohol, ethylene glycol, or glycerine?

Does gasoline or kerosene evaporate more readily from a watch glass?

What effect does temperature have on the viscosity of an oil?

At what temperatures do oil of different S.A.E. rating stop flowing?

If equal amounts of oils rated S.A.E. ten and S.A.E. thirty are placed in a clean pipette at 130 degrees Fahrenheit, which oil flows out of the pipette in the least time?

Can the solid, liquid, and vapor states of sulfur be produced by heating and cooling?

Can sulfur dioxide be liquefied by passing it into a vessel surrounded by a freezing mixture of ice and salt?

Can nitric acid be prepared by heating sodium nitrate and sulfuric acid in a retort and condensing the vapors?

Can liquid bromine be prepared by condensing the vapors resulting from heating a mixture of the oxidizing agent, manganese dioxide, with sodium bromide and sulfuric acid?

Does the unpurified gas produced by the destructive distillation of soft coal burn? Contain hydrogen sulfide? Ammonia? What residue remains after no more gas is given off?

Does smell indicate that ammonium hydroxide is or is not volatile at room temperature?

What is the percentage of capillary moisture (evaporates on exposure to air) in a sample of soil? Of hygroscopic moisture (evaporation occurs on heating air-dried material? Of organic material or humus?

What percent of the weight of whole milk is water and can be evaporated using a water bath?

What is the correct laboratory procedure for reading a graduate? Holding a test tube in a flame? Removing a stopper from a bottle? Pouring liquid from a bottle? Separating a precipitate from a liquid by filtration? Recovering dissolved material from solution?

Do sodium sulfate crystals, calcium chloride granules, and sodium hydroxide pellets readily gain or lose weight on exposure to air while counterpoised on a balance?

Can solid matter be separated from its solution by evaporation? If a clear solution of common salt in water is heated to dryness in an evaporating dish, is there a residue which tastes salty? If a colored solution of potassium permanganate is also evaporated to dryness, is there a residue which is colored?

Can crude oil be separated by distillation into "fractions" which vaporize at different boiling points within selected temperature ranges?

Which of two different fuel oils (or gasoline) will burn more readily as shown by the determination of curves for the vaporizing temperatures?

Do crystals of common salt grow larger if their saturated solution is evaporated slowly in air or more rapidly over a steam bath?

What is the nature of the tracks observed in the laboratory adaptation of the Wilson cloud chamber?

What is the effect of humidity upon the temperature of a moist object? If two bottles each with a three-hole stopper containing a thermometer with wet cotton on its bulb, a thistle tube and an outlet to an aspirator, but one with calcium chloride at its bottom and the other with water, does the temperature of the moist bulb, fall more rapidly in the bottle of low humidity (containing calcium chloride) or the one of higher humidity (containing water)?

Does an electric fan cool a small thermometer as well as it cools a large hand holding the thermometer in an air stream?

Does dew form more readily and remain longer on the outside of a glass of ice water when the humidity is high or low?

What is the relative humidity of the air in the classroom as determined by the use of tables for the thermometer readings taken from a sling psychrometer or a stationary wet--and dry-bulb thermometer?

If a test tube of ether is placed in a slightly larger test tube of water, does the water between the tubes freeze when air is bubbled through the ether?

How does the amount of sputtering and the amount of foam compare when butter and oleomargarine are heated gently?

If three holes in a stopper of a wide mouthed
bottle contain a thermometer, a thistle tube with a jet
at the bottom, and a tube connected to an aspirator,
does the temperature in the bottle rise, fall, or remain
the same if the aspirator is kept going until about
fifty cubic centimeters of chloroform has passed down
the thistle tube? (refrigeration)

What is the vapor pressure of gasoline at room
temperature as determined by introducing gasoline above
the mercury in a barometer?

If a "blinker button" is placed under a light bulb
in a socket, how does the light act?

How does a sunshine recorder work, that is, when
mercury is heated does it expand and close an electric
circuit?

Can a bottle be cut into two parts by directing a
flame from a blowpipe upon a narrow space between two
bands of several thicknesses of wet paper toweling?

Does an increase in temperature near a maximum and
minimum thermometer cause expansion of a liquid (alcohol)
which moves the mercury in a U-shaped column and which,
in turn, moves a small iron index above the mercury, and
vice versa? After the mercury falls leaving the iron
index at its maximum height, can the iron index be moved
back to the mercury by means of a small U-shaped magnet?

Does a jet of steam directed against "blades" on a
circular wheel cause the wheel (turbine) to rotate?

Is the amount of expansion of different gases (air
and cooking gas) about the same for the same rise in
temperature? If two test tubes, one containing air and
the other cooking gas, set in warm water each have glass
delivery tubes extending vertically downward into water,
does the water rise to about the same height in each
glass tube after no more bubbles appear and the test
tubes are set in cold water?

What is the coefficient of volume (cubical)
expansion of air? If a Charles' law tube (air enclosed
in the closed end of an open tube of uniform bore by a
globule of mercury) is placed in cracked ice and then in
steam, what fraction of its volume at zero degrees
Centigrade does the enclosed air expand when heated one
degree Centigrade under constant (atmospheric) pressure?

If the same pressure is maintained, how does the
volume of an enclosed gas vary as its temperature is increased and decreased? If a little mercury is near the
middle of an open horizontal glass tube which has one end
connected through a one-hole stopper to a flask of air set
in a water bath, is the mercury moved in a manner to indicate an increase or a decrease in the volume of the confined air as the temperature of the water bath (and the
confined air) is raised? Lowered?

If the temperature is kept constant, how does the volume of an enclosed gas vary as the pressure upon it is increased and decreased?

What is the relative effectiveness of fire extinguishers of the soda-acid, foam, and liquid carbon-dioxide types and water in putting out a paper fire? An oil or gasoline fire?

Will a spray of strong solution of copper sulfate extinguish burning phosphorus?

Will gasoline vapor in a stoppered container explode violently when mixed with air and ignited by an electric spark?

What happens when a blazing splint is moved near a hole in the lid of a tin can containing acetylene mixed with air?

When concentrated sulfuric acid is poured on sugar in a beaker is a large honeycomb-like mass pushed up by a gas? Is heat produced?

When biscuit dough is placed in a hot oven, is the dough raised?

What is the relative increase in size after fifteen minutes of balls of dough made using different types of baking powders and also sour milk and baking soda?

When a small piece of sodium is placed on the surface of water is hydrogen liberated? Does the residue give a basic or acid reaction with litmus paper?

Does gelatin dissolved in boiling water change from the sol phase to the gel phase, or vice versa, on cooling? On reheating?

What is the heat of combustion of a gas, that is, how many British thermal units of heat are produced when one cubic foot of gas is burned in a Bunsen burner?

Is the temperature of water constant, raised, or lowered when sal ammoniac, ordinary salt, or potassium iodide is dissolved in it? How is the temperature of the solution affected by adding salt to ice?

Does a freshly made "solution of hypo" feel colder or warmer than the water used in making the solution? If a flask one-third full with crystals of "hypo" is shaken with water (enough to just cover the crystals) until most of the "hypo" has dissolved, do the temperature readings indicate that the water has taken heat from the "hypo" or given heat to it while the "hypo" was dissolving?

What is the thermal capacity or specific heat (number of calories of heat needed to raise the temperature of one gram of the substance one degree Centigrade) of a metal (a solid piece, or pellets, of lead, copper, aluminum or iron) as determined by the "method of mixtures?"

What is the approximate temperature of a gas flame
as determined by placing in water nails heated in the
flame?

What is the temperature of a red-hot iron ball as
determined by the "method of mixtures?"

Is ice a better cooling agent than ice water? Does
a pound of ice cool two pounds of boiling water more or
less than a pound of ice water at zero degrees Centigrade
cools two pounds of boiling water?

How much longer does it take to vaporize a given
quantity of water than it does to bring that same
quantity from the freezing point to the boiling point?

When water is at its boiling temperature does
adding more heat increase its temperature?

Physics: Light

What is the complimentary color of red which appears
after gazing intently at a small square of red paper on a
sheet of white paper and then blowing the red paper away?
What is the complimentary color for green? Yellow? Blue?

What is the complimentary color of red light as determined by cutting red from a spectrum before a prism
recombines the spectrum into one color?

If paper of different colors is folded and held over
an electric lamp above a light meter, which color increases the reading of the light meter most and should
be used on the inside of shades for reading lamps?

Do equal quantities of different white paints have
different degrees of opacity or covering power when used
over a black stripe?

Does the color of an object change as the size of
the particles in that object change?

Is the intensity of the heat energy on a hand held
about six inches from a Bunsen flame (or electric light)
increased or decreased when the radiant heat energy must
pass through window glass instead of through space?

Does a true solution and a colloidal solution contain particles large enough to reflect light and show the
Tyndall effect? Is a strong beam of light highly diffused
and therefore easily observed from the side as it passes
through a true solution (pure water or a clear solution
of salt)? As it passes through a colloidal suspension
(gelatin in boiling water)?

What is the candle power of an electric lamp
measured by using a grease-spot (Bunsen) photometer and
a lamp of known candle power (Assume a forty-watt lamp
to be thirty-two candle power.)?

How are photographic negatives and prints developed
and fixed?

How does a periscope permit one to see around a
corner or over an opaque object?

If a small piece of paper between a large light
and the eye is brought closer to the eye until the
light can barely be seen, is the shortest line from
the eye to the light curved or straight?

If several metal balls are suspended in line,
can energy be transmitted from ball to ball with little
motion of the balls themselves?

Does lycopodium powder in a long glass tube show
the effect of standing air waves produced by moving a
piston back and forth after a brass rod connected to a
disk closing the other end is set in vibration?

Does radiant heat energy from a source (Bunsen
burner or electric lamp) at the focal point of one
concave reflector increase the reading of a thermometer
at the focal point of a similar reflector five feet away?

Does a metal "Maltese" cross intercept cathode rays
and prevent fluoresence of the glass in the shadow behind
the metal cross?

Does a thermometer held just beyond the red color of
the spectrum of sunlight show that heat rays are present
in this infra-red portion of the spectrum?

What is the index of refraction of glass measured
by using a square glass plate and pins? Is the light ben
toward or away from the normal after it has passed
obliquely into a medium of greater density (air to glass)
and into a medium of less density (glass to air)? Is
the emergent ray parallel or at an angle to the incident
ray?

What is the index of refraction of glass measured
by using a flat triangular glass prism and pins? Is the
light bent toward or away from the normal after it has
passed obliquely into a medium of greater density (air
to glass) and into a medium of less density (glass to
air)?

If one triangular glass prism bends an incident ray
from pins, can a second prism placed alongside the first
one cause that same ray to emerge in a line straight with
or parallel to the incident ray?

If stiff paper on a vertical board extending across
the inside of a battery jar and upward to the left has a
pin near the center at a point one-third down in the jar,
a second pin near the right edge and one-third up in the
jar, and water up to the level of the first pin, what is
the index of refraction of water based on measurements
taken after a third pin at the upper left is placed in
line with the other two pins?

What is the index of refraction of water (or olive
oil) as determined by placing rulers inside and outside
a glass of water and dividing the real depth by the
apparent depth?

If a candle or a landscape and a screen are on separate arms of a V with a concave spherical mirror at the vertex, what is the appearance and location of the image formed on the screen by the mirror?

Is a well lighted picture inside a box projected on a screen when at the focal length of a double convex lens in the opposite side of the box?

How are a convex and concave lens arranged as an opera glass?

What is the magnifying power of a double convex lens used as a reading glass or simple microscope?

How may two convex lenses be arranged to act like a compound microscope? What is the magnifying power of a compound microscope?

How is an astronomical (refracting) telescope set up and what is its magnifying power?

What is the wave length of sodium light as measured by using a diffraction grating?

Can hydrogen spectra be produced by passing an electric current from an induction coil through an evacuated glass tube containing hydrogen?

Do some minerals exhibit fluorescence when placed under an ultra-violet lamp bulb in a box blackened on the inside?

Do cathode rays cause crystals of certain chemicals to fluoresce?

Do cathode rays produce sufficient mechanical energy to drive a wheel with vanes along a track in a cathode ray tube?

Do cathode rays produce an intense heat effect when they bombard a tungsten target?

What color is produced when an electric current is passed through a clear glass tube containing neon? Argon? Mercury vapor? A mixture of neon and argon gases with mercury vapor? The same mixture in an amber glass tube?

Does an electrical discharge occur more readily across a long path in a tube from which air is removed or across a much shorter path in air when an evacuated tube is connected in parallel with an air gap in the secondary of an induction coil?

Can an electric arc be produced by separating two carbon arc rods after their pointed ends are touched together in a closed electrical circuit?

Physics: Electricity.

How is a candle flame affected when placed opposite a sharp point (and a round knob) connected to one terminal of a static machine?

Are spark discharges less likely from a point or a knob on metal standards of the same height placed between two insulated metal discs connected to a static machine?

Do smoke particles settle from a chimney (long glass tube about an inch in diameter) when a charged wire connected to the secondary of an induction coil (or to one terminal of a static machine) runs the length of the chimney at its center (working model of Cottrell precipitator?

Does a neon wand used in testing spark plugs flash when an electric discharge from a static machine is passed through the wand?

In what direction does an electric whirl rotate when connected to one end of a static machine? Is a "brush discharge" visible at the points?

Are electric charges more readily conducted from a charged rod to an electroscope by a copper wire or by a silk thread?

If a freshly polished zinc plate, connected to an electroscope, is made negative by sandpapering, do the leaves of the electroscope collapse (due to the electrons leaving the surface of the plate) when the plate is exposed to light from a carbon arc?

If charges of opposite kinds are induced on the inside and outside surfaces of a metal vessel (as shown by using a proof-plane) by suspending a positively charged metal ball in the vessel and the ball is then touched to the inner surface and withdrawn from the vessel, is the ball, the inner surface, and the outer surface, respectively, neutral, positive or negative (as shown by using a proof-plane), that is, do charges on an isolated conductor tend to reside on the outside surface?

How does a tungar-bulb rectifier operate on an 110-volt A.C. circuit to charge a storage battery?

Does an electrolytic cell of aluminum and lead electrodes in borax change alternating current to direct current?

How is a dry cell constructed? Is there any evidence of chemical action on the carbon rod and the zinc in a dry cell which has been used?

How is a commercial lead storage cell constructed as shown by a "cut-away view"?

Does the voltage reading drop (or the sound of an electric bell become weaker) as bubbles accumulate around the copper (or carbon) electrode of a Voltaic cell which stands on a closed circuit for several minutes? What is the effect on the bubbles and the voltage reading (or the sound of the bell) as chromic acid solution is introduced near the bubbles?

Is the Daniell cell a polarizing or a non-polarizing cell, that is, does its voltage reading drop or does the sound of an electric bell connected to the cell decrease in intensity with use?

What weight of copper will a current of one ampere deposit in one second on a copper cylinder in a copper plating solution?

Do particles collect around the positive and negative electrodes when direct current is passed through a colloidal suspension of arsenious sulfide prepared by passing hydrogen sulfide through the filtrate from arsenious oxide in boiling water?

Does a car, airplane, ship or other base supporting a floating compass rotate around the compass needle?

How is a dynamic and a magnetic speaker constructed and operated?

How does a radio receiver (old battery or all-electric set) attached to a microphone (magnetic type) operate as a public address system?

What is the temperature coefficient of resistance of copper (increase in the resistance of one ohm of the metal per degree Centigrade rise in temperature) as determined by measuring the resistance of a copper temperature coil when immersed in cold water and in boiling water?

Does a solid body expand or contract when it is heated? Does a long "horizontal" iron wire expand and sag or contract in length when the temperature of the wire is increased by sending 110 volts A.C. through the wire? Decreased by turning off the current?

What is the resistance of the following automobile circuits based on ammeter readings taken when the engine is not running and the voltage of the storage battery; two head-lights, two parking lights, horn?

Which allows the more current to pass through it, an electric toaster or an electric iron?

What is the resistance of a coil of resistance wire (or an electrical appliance) as determined by using a Wheatstone bridge of the slide-wire type? (resistance determined by the Wheatstone bridge method)

If a small unknown resistance in series with one dry cell and a galvanometer causes a certain deflection, what resistance must be used in a resistance box substituted for the unknown to obtain the same deflection of the galvanometer? (resistance determined by the substitution method)

What is the resistance of a coil of resistance wire as determined by using an ohmmeter (resistance determined by the ohmmeter method)?

Is the electromotive force of an old dry cell measured by using a potentiometer greater or less than the voltage of the cell obtained with a direct-reading voltmeter?

What is the internal resistance of a dry cell as determined by the voltmeter-ammeter method?

Does the voltage (and also the current) of a non-polarizing cell increase, decrease, or remain the same as the plates are moved closer together? Are decreased in size by slowly lifting them to the surface?

Can the wind direction be read directly from a voltmeter calibrated north, east, south, and west because it is in series with a source of direct current and a rheostat, the resistance of which is varied due to a contact which slides around the circular rheostat as the weather vane to which it is connected turns?

How are dots and dashes sent and received through a short telegraph line?

Do direct and alternating currents carry the voice satisfactorily in telephone circuits as determined by using in series with a transmitter and receiver (or earphones) a six-volt storage battery and then replacing it with the secondary of a six-volt transformer connected to an 110-volt A.C. circuit?

Does the mere vibration of a disc in a telephone receiver set up sufficient induced current to deflect a galvanometer needle?

Does a horizontal bar magnet set whirling above a copper disc mounted on a pivot cause the disc to follow the magnet (principle of the induction motor)?

Must a synchronous motor be turned at a certain speed before it will continue to run?

Can a stream of cathode rays (electrons) be deflected by moving a magnetic field (U-shaped or bar magnet) across the stream?

What is the efficiency of a quarter-horsepower direct-current shunt- or series-wound motor at half and full load, that is, what is the ratio of the mechanical output to the electrical input (Prony brake)? Does the current supplied to the motor increase or decrease as the resistance in the starting box is cut out and the brake load is increased?

If a finger is held lightly against the armature of a St. Louis motor to feel how much power the motor has at starting, how does the starting power and acceleration of a shunt-wound direct-current motor compare with that of a similar series-wound motor?

If a galvanometer is in series with a crystal detector and a coil of wire in which a magnet is rotated on the same shaft as the rotating dippers of an anemometer, can the galvanometer be calibrated in miles per hour by holding the anemometer outside a moving car and recording the galvanometer reading with the corresponding speedometer reading?

How are A.C. and D.C. voltmeters and ammeters constructed and operated?

Do two pieces of soft iron suspended inside of a coil of wire remain together or separate when the current passing through the coil is direct current? Alternating current (The A.C.-D.C. meter)?

Does the reading of a galvanometer increase, decrease or remain the same for the same current when a low resistance shunt is connected across its terminals (making an ammeter)?

What is the cost of electrical energy for a home for one month?

How is a wattmeter constructed and how does it operate? If a small coil of fine insulated wire (the secondary of a radio audio transformer), connected in parallel with a heating element in series with a larger coil of heavy insulated wire, a switch and an 110-volt A.C. circuit, is suspended in front of the larger coil with the axes of the two coils at right angles to each other, what happens to the position of the coils (wattmeter) when the switch is turned on?

What are some of the characteristics of a transmission line? If a transmission line connected to an 110-volt A.C. circuit has voltmeters across a switch at each of its ends and a parallel-lamp bank with an ammeter in series at the "far" end, how do the following factors change as the load is increased by turning on more lamps: load resistance, line resistance, power consumed by load, total power delivered?

What is the true power (watts) consumer in an 110-volt A.C. circuit having a "choke coil" of high inductance (electromagnet) in series with a parallel-lamp bank? How does the presence of the soft iron core in the coil effect the current?

What part of the electric power apparently used (product of the ammeter and voltmeter readings) in an inductive circuit (one containing a coil of wire such as the primary of a bell-ringing transformer) is true power (reading of wattmeter), that is, what is the power factor of a given inductive circuit?

If a lamp rheostat (lamps connected in parallel) is used, along with a voltmeter and an ammeter, in the secondary circuit of a bell-ringing transformer which has a wattmeter in its primary circuit (110-volts A.C.), what is the percent efficiency of the transformer when different numbers of lamps are lighted?

How may an ammeter be calibrated by the volume of hydrogen resulting from the electrolysis of water for a certain length of time?

How may an ammeter be calibrated by the weight of copper deposited in a certain length of time (copper coulometer)?

What characteristics does a light in the secondary coil around the closed "keeper" of a large electromagnet exhibit when a switch in the primary is closed? Is opened? Remains closed?

Does a "choke coil" in series with a lamp in an ordinary house circuit dim the lamp? If a soft core is pushed farther and farther into the "choke coil" does the lamp grow dimmer and dimmer or brighter and brighter?

Can an induction coil increase the voltage of an intermittent direct current in its primary sufficiently to produce a spark across a gap in its secondary?

If one terminal of two dry cells in series is connected to a coarse steel file and the other terminal is drawn along the file, are the sparks produced larger with or without an electromagnet in the circuit?

If a large coil of wire with an iron core (electromagnet) and a battery and light bulb of about six volts are connected in parallel to a source of direct current, what is observed as the circuit is closed and opened? As the circuit is closed and opened with a condenser in series and parallel?

Is any difference noticed in the amount of energy needed when turning a magneto on an open circuit and on a closed circuit with an electric lamp in series?

Can a secondary circuit be tuned with a variable condenser so that a spark or the flash of a flashlight bulb is produced in resonance with a spark in the primary circuit?

Does increasing the capacitance in a buzzer oscillator with battery power increase or decrease the volume of the tone heard in the earphones? Does a vacuum tube audio oscillator with similar power provide a better tone than a buzzer oscillator?

Does varying the resistance and capacitance in the grid circuit of an audio oscillator cause the frequency heard to vary?

How is a radio-frequency amplifier constructed and tuned?

Can two electrical circuits separated from each other as in Lodge's resonant Leyden jars be tuned to each other so that a spark occurring in one circuit will produce one in the other circuit?

Can something which oscillates be produced by charging a Leyden jar and then discharging it through a coil of wire on a spool? By tilting a U-tube containing water, placing the thumb over the longer arm of water, and removing the thumb after the tube is returned to a vertical position? By pulling a pendulum to one side and releasing it?

Can alternating current be changed to direct current by means of a vacuum tube?

What is the frequency of an alternating current?

If one wire of an extension cord with an electric lamp in series is connected to a pie tin on which is placed a cloth soaked in a paste of potassium iodide dissolved in starch and the other wire has a nail at its end, what is observed where the nail is drawn lightly over the wet cloth for a time interval when the cord is connected to a source of alternating current? To the positive terminal of a dry cell after the lamp is removed?

Does varying the resistance and capacitance in the grid circuit of an audio oscillator cause the frequency heard to vary?

How is simple radio transmitting circuit constructed and operated?

How is a short-wave radio receiving set constructed and operated?

How is a radio-frequency amplifier constructed and tuned?

Is an 115-volt A.C. vacuum tube oscillator sufficiently powerful to operate several sets of earphones?

Does the operation of an electric razor or the production of an electrical spark produce "static" in a radio receiver?

Does a single triode audio amplifier amplify the imput from an audio oscillator sufficiently to operate earphones? A loudspeaker?

Does a three-stage voice amplifier amplify the output of a crystal or a carbon-button microphone sufficiently to operate a loudspeaker?

Chemistry

Is a chemical change promoted by stirring sodium bicarbonate with potassium bitartrate? By heating ammonium dichromate? By sending direct current through a solution of sodium chloride? By exposing a silver chloride solution to bright light? By adding manganese dioxide, a catalyst, to hydrogen peroxide?

Can hydrogen peroxide be prepared from barium peroxide and dilute sulfuric acid?

Does the addition of dilute acetic acid (an electrolyte) cause the coagulation and precipitation of colloidal casein in sweet milk?

Can ozone be prepared by the passage of an electrical discharge through oxygen or air? By exposing white phosphorus to oxygen or air?

What is a test for ozone, that is, does ozone liberate iodine from a solution of potassium iodide? What is the characteristic smell of ozone?

Will a mouse which has become unconscious in a sealed jar be revived by introducing oxygen?

How much oxygen will a person consume in a measured interval of time as determined by a basal metabolism test?

Will a burning stick plunged into liquid air continue to burn?

Which has dried or hardened more after one day, the surface on a wooden splint dipped in boiled linseed oil and placed in an air-tight sealed tube or the surface on a splint similarly dipped and left exposed to the air?

Which of the following oils are good drying oils which harden into a tough film: tung, linseed, cottonseed, mineral, corn?

Does a change in temperature occur in a piece of absorbent cotton saturated with a mixture of equal parts of boiled linseed oil, turpentine, and Japan drier?

Does hydrogen burn in air? Does a candle flame continue to burn when placed in hydrogen, that is, does hydrogen support combustion?

Can carbon monoxide be prepared by adding warm concentrated sulfuric acid to formic or oxalic acid?

Does carbon dioxide support combustion?

Is a fire extinguisher of the soda-acid type or of the foam type more effective in putting out a paper fire? An oil fire?

Do the vapors of carbon tetrachloride burn? Support combustion? Flow downward to displace air?

Will sand extinguish an oil or gasoline fire?

Is carbon dioxide present in greater amount in a bottle of oxygen or a bottle of oxygen in which charcoal has been burned?

What color does carbon monoxide produce in a color detector tube containing iodine pentoxide?

Does the breaking of a bomb containing liquid carbon dioxide permit the carbon dioxide to evaporate and push water out the nozzle of the fire extinguisher?

How is the speed of burning affected by increasing the surface area of the fuel as determined by comparing the rate of burning of a piece of wood and an equal weight of its shavings?

Does a Bunsen burner give more heat with a yellow flame or a blue flame?

What change occurs in the color of a Bunsen Flame when the air vent is opened?

Does a yellow Bunsen flame contain more or less unburned carbon than a blue flame?

Where does combustion occur in a flame?

Are there enough acids and water present in different brands of lubricating oil to cause polished copper and iron to corrode?

What are some conditions which cause metals to rust
or corrode, that is, what happens to tin cans and galvanized iron scratched and exposed to dry and moist air,
respectively; to bright copper exposed to dry and moist
carbon dioxide, respectively; to painted or oiled strips
of iron scratched to the surface of the metal and exposed
to moist air?

If equal weights of magnesium powder are placed on
sand on opposite platforms of a balance, how does the
magnesium powder on one platform change in weight while
burning?

Does the weight of fine iron powder decrease or
increase on being heated in air?

Does heating copper turnings in air cause an increase in their weight?

If a candle under a lamp chimney containing
potassium hydroxide is balanced on a pan of a beam
balance, does the pan go up, go down, or remain stationary as the candle burns? Do the products formed by burning the candle weigh more than the burned part of the
candle?

Will a bright surface of a piece of lead become dull
when in air for a few minutes?

What change in appearance occurs when small thin
sheets of bright aluminum, copper, tin, lead, and zinc,
respectively, are heated in a Bunsen flame? Left in air
for days?

How are substances "burned" that require high
temperatures such as tin, zinc, copper, head, and aluminum

Can arsenic trioxide be reduced to arsenic by heating
wood charcoal covering the trioxide? Can arsenic be
oxidized to arsenic trioxide by warm air?

Does a heated copper wire (copper oxide) plunged
into methyl alcohol convert the alcohol to formaldehyde?

Can water gas be made by passing steam over hot
charcoal in an iron pipe?

Does guncotton or ordinary cotton burn more readily?

What happens when a flame is applied to a teaspoonful
of gunpowder prepared by mixing sulfur, charcoal, and
potassium nitrate?

Is concentrated nitric acid a strong oxidizing
agent? Does hot charred sawdust in an evaporating dish
take fire instantly when concentrated nitric acid is
poured on it or does a glowing piece of charcoal dropped
into nitric acid continue to glow after it touches the
acid?

Can silver nitrate be prepared by dissolving silver
in nitric acid and evaporating the solution?

Is nitrous oxide a good oxidizing agent, that is, do
substances such as sulfur and iron burn almost as
brilliantly in nitrous oxide as in oxygen?

Is nitrous oxide a good oxidizing agent, that is, do substances such as sulfur and iron burn almost as brilliantly in nitrous oxide as in oxygen?

Can nitrogen be prepared by heating ammonium chloride and sodium nitrate? Does nitrogen burn? Support combustion?

Can almost pure nitrogen be prepared by passing air over hot copper gauze which combines with oxygen?

Does burning white phosphorus in air leave nitrogen?

What is a decisive test for nitrogen, that is, is the odor of ammonia present after water has been added to the compound formed by heating magnesium?

Does ammonia contain nitrogen set free by passing dried ammonia gas through a tube containing hot copper oxide?

Can nitric acid be prepared by heating sodium nitrate and sulfuric acid in a retort and condensing the vapors?

Can nitric acid folowing down through the stem of a clay pipe be decomposed by heat into water, nitrous oxide and oxygen?

Can nitric oxide be prepared by the action of dilute nitric on copper turnings?

Does oxygen unite with nitric oxide to form reddish-brown nitrogen dioxide?

Can nitrous oxide be prepared by heating ammonium nitrate?

Can ammonia gas be prepared by heating ammonium hydroxide or a mixture of ammonium chloride and slaked lime?

Does smell indicate that ammonium hydroxide is volatile at room temperature?

When ammonia is passed into water is the product neutral, a base, or an acid?

How may fertilizers be tested for some common elements (potassium, phosphorus, nitrogen as nitrates, and ammonium compounds) which are essential to plant growth?

Does ammonia contain hydrogen set free by passing dry ammonia gas through a tube containing heated magnesium?

What color change occurs as blue copper sulfate is heated gently? Does the color change reverse itself after water is added?

Does cupric sulfide result from the action of hydrogen sulfide upon a solution of copper sulfate?

Can sulfuric acid be prepared by using potassium permanganate to oxidize sulfurous acid prepared by burning sulfur in a bottle of air and dissolving the product, sulfur dioxide, in water?

Does concentrated sulfuric acid dehydrate sugar, wood, paper, or cotton leaving carbon as a residue?

Does the solution made by adding potassium dichromate
crystals to concentrated sulfuric acid clean glassware
readily?

Is much heat liberated when solid sulfur trioxide
is placed in water?

Does sulfur dioxide bleach moist colored flowers
or red apple skin? Does hydrogen peroxide restore the
color?

What is a test for sodium sulfite, an adulterant,
in meat? If hamburger to which sodium sulfite, powdered
zinc, and hydrochloric acid are added is boiled in a
flask covered with filter paper saturated with lead
nitrate, what color does the filter paper turn? Do dried
fruits give a similar reaction?

Does a surface of white lead paint or one of paint
containing zinc oxide discolor less when exposed to
hydrogen sulfide gas?

Does a solution of hydrogen sulfide in water form a
precipitate of sulfur on being treated with chlorine
water?

Does hydrogen sulfide in the interior of its own
flame decompose to leave sulfur on a dish held in the
flame?

Can hydrogen sulfide be prepared by the action of
dilute hydrochloric or sulfuric acid on iron sulfide?

Is black lead sulfide precipitated by the action of
hydrogen sulfide on a soluble lead salt such as lead
acetate?

Is hydrogen sulfide a reducing agent, that is, when
hydrogen sulfide is bubbled through hydrogen peroxide is
the latter reduced to water? Is sulfur precipitated?

What color precipitates are thrown out of solution
when hydrogen sulfide is passed into separate solutions
of compounds of copper, lead, silver, and mercury?
Arsenic and cadmium? Antimony? Zinc?

Does a solution of hydrogen sulfide in water form
a precipitate of sulfur on being treated with chlorine
water?

What effect does the length of exposure of photographic print paper, by light passing through a negative,
have on the darkness of the final print, other factors
being equal?

How are photographic negatives and prints developed
and fixed?

In photography, what observable effect does the
developer have on the precipitate (silver bromide) resulting from mixing equal volumes of solutions of silver
nitrate and potassium bromide if the precipitate has not
been exposed to ordinary light? Has been exposed to
ordinary light? What is observed after the "hypo" (fixer)
is added?

Can silver nitrate be prepared by dissolving silver
in nitric acid and evaporating the solution?

How are household mirrors silvered?

Can a satisfactory fountain pen ink be prepared by
mixing a five percent solution of ferrous sulfate with a
ten percent solution of tannic acid with and without the
addition of some blue dye or household bluing?

Can an iron ink be made by adding solutions of
ferrous sulfate and tannic acid? What color change
occurs sometime after the ink is used?

Does blue ink made using tannic and gallic acids
and ferrous sulfate turn black on exposure to air?

Does invisible writing done with cobalt nitrate
become visible when heated?

Can a satisfactory drawing ink be prepared by
stirring a mixture of orange shellac and lamp-black
in alcohol?

Can liquid bromine be prepared by condensing the
vapors resulting from heating a mixture of the oxidizing
agent, manganese dioxide, with sodium bromide and
sulfuric acid?

Is the odor of iodoform evident when ethyl alcohol
is warmed with iodine in the presence of potassium?

Can chlorine gas be prepared by passing direct current through hydrochloric acid in a Hoffman or similar
apparatus?

Can chlorine gas be prepared by treating bleaching
powder with sulfuric acid?

Can chlorine gas be prepared by using manganese
dioxide to oxidize hydrogen chloride as the latter is
made by heating a mixture of sodium chloride and sulfuric
acid?

Will bleaching powder liberate its chlorine when
heated or when acted upon by weak acids?

Is mercurous chloride precipitated by adding sodium
chloride to a solution of mercurous nitrate?

Does a candle of hydrogen gas continue to burn in
chlorine gas?

Does dry chlorine bleach strips of a bright colored
cotton cloth or some highly colored flowers best when it
is dry, slightly moist or thoroughly wet?

Will chlorine water bleach colored cloth?

Will sodium hypochlorite bleach cotton goods?

Does hydrogen peroxide bleach black hair? Does a
paste of bleaching powder bleach colored cotton cloth?
Does straw from an old discolored straw hat bleach when
placed in a closed bottle with a mixture of sodium sulfite and dilute hydrochloric acid?

Does a solution of chlorine unite with the hydrogen
and liberate the oxygen from water more rapidly in strong
sunlight or in the dark?

Will chlorine gas "tear" hydrogen away from hydrocarbons such as turpentine leaving carbon and forming hydrogen chloride following a flash of light?

What is the test for an aluminum compound? What color appears when acetic acid and logwood extract are added to an aluminum compound?

Do deodorants contain aluminum chloride?

Does bluing spot or streak clothing from which soap is not thoroughly rinsed?

If a picture from a magazine is moistened in a solution of water, turpentine, and green soap, can the picture (face down) be transferred to white paper by rubbing?

Does pure and imitation lemon extract form an emulsion with water?

Does a depilatory (paste of starch and sodium sulfide) dissolve hair?

Is the emulsion formed by shaking a mixture of kerosene and water more permanent if a little soap is added?

Does an emulsion made by shaking olive oil with water last longer if a teaspoonful of yolk of egg (or a little pancreatin) is added before shaking?

Can a protective colloid such as egg yolk prevent an emulsion of corn, olive or cotton-seed oil and vinegar from separating (mayonnaise)?

Will solutions of ferric chloride and calcium hydroxide react to form an insoluble jelly-like precipitate (ferric hydroxide) which carries solid particles (sand or sewage sludge) with it as it settles?

Does hard water (containing calcium or magnesium sulfate) form more suds with soap solution before or after the water is passed through a "zeolite" (Permutit; Decalso)?

Can both temporary and permanent hard water be softened by boiling? With borax? With washing soda? With "zeolites," and "Permutit" system?

What common impurities are present in drinking water, that is, what are tests for the following in drinking water: color, odor, ammonia, sulfates, calcium, chlorides organic matter?

Does a solution of calcium carbonate or one of calcium bicarbonate deposit a precipitate ("boiler scale") on being boiled?

How is water tested for the presence of soluble chlorides? Soluble sulfates? Calcium compounds?

Are phosphates, carbonates, or borates present in commercial water softeners?

Does a saturated solution of common salt coagulate a colloidal dispersion of soap in water which settles on standing?

Does the addition of four drops of glycerine to a
saponin (soap) solution permit the bubbles to be deflated
and reinflated more easily? Does the addition of sodium
oleate to the saponin-glycerine solution greatly increase
the elasticity of the bubbles?

What is the effect of carbon dioxide and water on
limestone (or marble), that is, if carbon dioxide (from
dry ice) is passed for ten minutes into a test tube of
cold water containing a little pulverized limestone, is
there a residue when the filtrate from the contents of
the test tube is evaporated to dryness? What is the
effect of carbon dioxide and water on iron rust treated
in the same manner?

What is observed when small particles of camphor are
placed on water? Are placed at the rear end of a match
(boat) on water?

Does a soap contain free fat? If soap shavings are
dissolved in ether or gasoline and filtered into a beaker
is a greasy residue left in the beaker after the liquid
evaporates?

What is the relative hardness of different samples
of water obtained by comparing the amount of standard
soap solution required for the formation of suds with
the amount an equal volume of distilled water requires?

How is an analysis of soil made to detect the
presence of nitrates? Sulfates? Ammonium compounds?
Chlorides?

Is more insoluble matter suspended in muddy water
removed by passing the muddy water through a sand and
gravel filtration bed of the gravity type before or
after the addition of a coagulant?

Is the size of the pigment particles different in
different paints? Do some particles, which remain after
a solvent removes the oil from paint, settle more rapidly
than others in water?

Does the solute of a true solution (invisible salt
in water) and of an ordinary suspension (visible flour in
water or muddy water) settle on standing? Can the solute
of a true solution and of an ordinary suspension be
separated from the liquid by filtration?

What is the effect of hydrochloric acid on lime-
water? On a piece of mortar?

Can a colloidal dispersion of a metal be prepared
by setting up an electric arc between two wires of the
metal under water?

After hot saturated solutions of sodium nitrate and
potassium chloride are poured together, can sodium
chloride be filtered out? Can potassium nitrate be
crystallized out?

What is a test for the presence of water, that is,
what change in color occurs when a strip of cobalt
chloride paper is moistened with water?

Can boneblack be made by the destructive distillation of animal bones followed by treatment with an acid to dissolve mineral matter?

Does the unpurified gas produced by the destructive distillation of soft coal burn? Contain ammonia? Hydrogen sulfide? What residue remains after no more gas is given off?

Does the unpurified gas produced by the destructive distillation of wood burn? Contain hydrogen sulfide? Ammonia? What residue remains after no more gas is given off?

Can quicklime (calcium oxide) be prepared by heating a lump of limestone in the hot part of a Bunsen flame?

Can limewater be made from quicklime?

Can precipitated chalk be prepared by mixing solutions of a calcium salt (calcium chloride) and a soluble carbonate (sodium carbonate)?

Can liquid bromine be prepared by condensing the vapors resulting from heating a mixture of the oxidizing agent, manganese dioxide, with sodium bromide and sulfuric acid?

Can hydrofluoric acid be made by heating calcium fluoride with sulfuric acid and passing the resultant gas through water?

Can ferrous chloride be prepared by heating iron and hydrochloric acid in the absence of air? By boiling ferric chloride with iron wool?

Can ferric chloride be prepared by treating ferrous chloride with chlorine water?

Can stannous chloride be made by dissolving tin in concentrated hydrochloric acid?

Does a sample of soil contain available aluminum, iron, and manganese?

Does a sample of soil contain calcium or magnesium carbonates?

Does a plant contain water? Carbon? Ash? Nitrogen? Starch?

Does a sample of soil contain available potassium?

Does a mixture of a saturated solution of lead acetate and imitation vanilla (and pure vanilla) clear on standing?

Will a mixture of powdered casein and borax solution "set" to form a plastic?

Can phenol crystals and hexamethylene tetramine be heated together and cooled to form a plastic of the bakelite type?

What is the test for phosphates, that is, if a "phosphate" is mixed with an acid solution of ammonium molybdate and warmed slightly what color precipitate is formed?

Does a sample of soil contain available phosphates?

Can an acid phosphate used in fertilizer be prepared
by mixing bone ash and sulfuric acid?

How may fertilizers be tested for some common elements (potassium, phosphorus, nitrogen as nitrates and
ammonium compounds) which are essential to plant growth?

Do laxatives contain phenolphathalein? Magnesium
compounds?

Is a precipitate formed when solutions of potassium
sulfate and barium nitrate are mixed? Aluminum chloride
and silver sulfate?

How is an analysis of soil made to detect the
presence of nitrates? Sulfates? Ammonium compounds?
Chlorides?

Can the yellow pigment for paint (lead chromate or
chrome yellow) be prepared from equal parts of solutions
of lead acetate and potassium chromate?

Can the artist's "cadmium-yellow" be made by passing
hydrogen sulfide through a solution of cadmium nitrate?

Does a baking powder contain a carbonate, tartrate,
sulfate, starch, phosphate, ammonium compound, aluminum
compound and calcium compound?

Can baking soda be prepared by passing carbon
dioxide through a solution of ammonium carbonate, sodium
chloride, and ammonium hydroxide?

How does the weight of common salt prepared from a
weighed amount of baking soda compare with the weight
that theoretically should be obtained?

Does concrete made from mixing sand and gravel with
cement and water harden on standing?

Does mortar made from mixing sand with slaked lime
and water harden and form calcium carbonate on standing?

How can rayon be made by the copper-ammonium process?
Nitrate process? Acetate process? Viscose process?

Is zinc stearate present in baby powders? Does
fatty material (stearic acid) remain after a beaker
containing baby powder and dilute hydrochloric acid is
heated over a water bath?

Does glass remain clear or become opaque where it
comes in contact with hydrofluoric acid?

Can insoluble suspended matter (calcium carbonate,
sand, or flour in water) be separated rapidly from the
liquid by filtration (pouring the liquid containing the
suspended matter through a porous substance such as
filter paper)?

Can kerosene, mixed with sulfuric acid, be separated
from the acid by letting the mixture stand in a separatory
funnel and drawing off the lower liquid?

What is the relative value of Fullers' earth and
charcoal as an adsorbing material?

Can liquids such as brown sugar solution and cider
vinegar be decolorized by filtering them through boneblack or activated carbon?

Can more color be removed from a solution of brown sugar by mixing the heated solution with boneblack (adsorption) before filtration than by filtration of the sugar solution alone?

Does activated carbon adsorb bromine vapor? Ammonia gas?

Can the odor of a dilute solution of hydrogen sulfide be decreased by shaking the liquid with activated carbon?

Can Bentonite clay adsorb enough water to form a sticky mass?

What is the effect of carbon dioxide and water on limestone (or marble), that is, if carbon dioxide (from dry ice) is passed for ten minutes into a test tube of cold water containing a little pulverized limestone, is there a residue when the filtrate from the contents of the test tube is evaporated to dryness? What is the effect of carbon dioxide and water on iron rust treated in the same manner?

Can silverware be cleaned electrolytically by placing it in a boiling solution of baking soda and table salt in an aluminum vessel?

Can brass, bronze and copper be cleaned by rubbing them with precipitated chalk moistened with ammonia? With salt and vinegar?

Does dilute sulfuric acid show a cleaning action on metals such as a rusted nail?

Is starch changed to glucose (Fehling's test) by saliva? By pancreatin? By diastase?

Can silver nitrate be prepared by dissolving silver in nitric acid and evaporating the solution?

Does considerable effervesence occur when a mixture of lye and small pieces of aluminum are placed in water?

What is the combining weight of magnesium? How many grams of magnesium are needed to liberate one gram of hydrogen from hydrochloric acid?

Can a "silver tree" be produced by suspending a strip of copper in a dilute solution of silver nitrate for several hours? Can a "lead tree" be produced by suspending a strip of zinc in a dilute solution of lead acetate?

Can the artist's "cadmium-yellow" be made by passing hydrogen sulfide through a solution of cadmium nitrate?

Do some foils used as wrappers for chewing gum, candy, and other products react with nitric or hydrochloric acid as tin, lead, or aluminum does?

Can a precipitate be peptized or forced into a colloidal state by adsorption of ions?

Can deep-red colloidal ferric hydroxide be prepared by adding a solution of ferric chloride drop-by-drop to a beaker of boiling water? Is a cloudy effect produced followed by precipitation when dilute sulfuric acid is added drop-by-drop to the deep-red solution?

How is a ferric salt distinguished from a ferrous salt, that is, what color is characteristic of a ferric salt with potassium ferrocyanide? With potassium sulfocyanate? Of a ferrous salt with potassium ferricyanide?

Does a solution of chlorine unite with the hydrogen and liberate the oxygen from water more rapidly in strong sunlight or in the dark?

Can a hole be burned through a sheet of galvanized iron with a oxyhydrogen torch?

Does the reaction between crystals of lead nitrate and sodium chloride occur more rapidly when the crystals are dissolved separately in water and then mixed or when the crystals alone are mixed?

Do plants grow better with their roots in a well-balanced nutrient solution (no soil) through which air is bubbled or in ordinary soil?

Is the conductivity of a solution a minimum with excess acid or excess base or when neutralization is complete (sulfuric acid from a burette into a solution of barium hydroxide)?

What positive and negative ions in a given unknown salt are identifiable by the following tests applied in respective order: flame, bead, cobalt, nitrate, carbonate, chloride, sulfate, and nitrate tests?

Is methyl alcohol, ethyl alcohol, isopropyl alcohol, glycerine, or ethylene glycol the poorest electrolyte (conductor of electricity)? Does the poorest electrolyte cause the worst corrosion on iron (automobile block) and copper (brass radiator) placed in the electrolyte for one week? What commercial anti-freezes are poor electrolytes? Corrode iron and copper placed in them for one week?

What is the test for the sulfate ion, that is, does a solution of barium chloride added to a solution of any sulfate or of sulfuric acid give a white precipitate which is insoluble in hydrochloric acid?

What is the test for a sulfite ion, that is, is sulfur dioxide liberated when hydrochloric acid is added to a sulfite (calcium sulfite)?

What is the test for the sulfide ion, that is, is hydrogen sulfide liberated on the addition of sulfuric acid to the substance tested?

Does a brown vapor appear (to indicate the presence of the nitrate ion) when concentrated sulfuric acid is added to sodium nitrate and heated with copper?

What is the brown-ring test for the nitrate ion, that is, does a dark brown ring form at the interface between a solution of ferrous sulfate with sodium nitrate, and heavier concentrated sulfuric acid poured down the side of a slanting test tube containing the solution?

Is the silver nitrate test a test for chlorine or
for a chloride ion? A chlorate ion?

What is the characteristic taste and feel of very
dilute acids? Of very dilute bases?

Does a solution of sugar or alcohol in distilled
water ionize and change blue litmus to red, or vice versa

Does a soap contain free alkali? Does a deep red
color appear when an alcoholic solution of phenolphthalei:
is placed on a small piece of soap heated gently to dryness or is mixed with a solution of soap in alcohol?

If the white of an egg is thoroughly mixed with cold
water, does coagulation occur on setting? On heating?
On the addition of two or three drops of dilute nitric
acid (an electrolyte)?

Can a colloidal dispersion of sulfur be prepared by
dissolving sodium thiosulfate (hypo) in water and adding
dilute hydrochloric acid? By adding distilled water to
a solution of sulfur dissolved in alcohol?

Does a firm jelly (gel) form when two or three drops
(not more) of concentrated hydrochloric acid is added to
a solution of water-glass (sodium silicate)?

Is a sample of soil acid, that is, does a paste of
the soil turn blue litmus red or does a red color appear
when a sample of dry soil is added to a solution of
potassium thiocyanate dissolved in alcohol?

Is a given sample of soil acid or alkaline? What is
the approximate ph of the soil as determined by a color
chart?

Do different electrolytes (solutions of sodium
carbonate, common salt, hydrochloric acid, sulfuric acid)
in a Voltaic cell produce different voltages?

Can a solution of a base of unknown concentration be
neutralized by titration against a solution of an acid of
known concentration, and vice versa?

What is the percent of acetic acid in a sample of
"white" vinegar as determined by titration against sodium
hydroxide?

What percent of actual ammonia is present in two
different brands of household ammonia as determined by
titration against hydrochloric acid?

Can soap be prepared by heating salad oil with a
solution of sodium or potassium hydroxide followed by
the addition of a saturated solution of common salt?

What is the relative amount of acid in different
brands of lubricating oils as determined by the neutralization number representing the amount of potassium
hydroxide needed to neutralize the acids in one gram of
oil?

What is the xanthoproteic or nitric acid test for
proteins in a solid? What color appears when nitric acid
added to the white of a hard-boiled egg is neutralized
with ammonium hydroxide? What is the Biuret test for
proteins in solution or colloidal suspension? What color
change is produced when solutions of sodium hydroxide
and copper sulfate are shaken with liquid egg white?

Can the color produced by a dye (safranine; fast
green) be made different by using different cloth
(cotton, wool)? Different mordants (water solutions of
sodium and aluminum sulfate)? Different solutions (acid,
alkaline, neutral)?

Does the use of a mordant (water solution of alumin
sulfate) increase the permanency of a dye (alizarin)
which washes out of unmordanted cotton cloth?

If similar pieces of cloth, one white and the other
dyed with Congo red, are rolled together and boiled in
water, does the addition of common salt to the water
prevent the color from "bleeding" or "running" into the
white cloth?

Does the same dye (alizarin) give the same color on
mordanted (water solution of aluminum sulfate) and non-
mordanted cloth?

Does congo red dye cotton cloth without the use of a
mordant (direct dyeing)?

Is a basic dye (safranine) used with a mordant
(sodium sulfate in water) on cotton cloth "fast" to washing with laundry soap?

Can the color produced by a dye (safranine fast gree
be made different by using different cloth (cotton, wool)
Different mordants (water solutions of sodium and aluminu
sulfate)? Different solutions (acid; alkaline; neutral)?

Does white cotton cloth soaked in a colorless solution of indigo (vat dye) change to insoluble (color-fast)
blue indigo on exposure to air?

How does concentration of the dye bath, temperature
of the dye bath, and length of time in the dye bath,
respectively, affect the depth of color imparted to
bleached muslin?

Are different samples of cloth color-fast to sunlight? Washing? Perspiration?

What are the percentages by weight of moisture
content, volatile matter, ash content and fixed carbon
in soft coal? Hard coal? Coke?

Do common substances such as copper, glass, rubber,
lead, wood, steel exhibit the properties of hardness,
luster, malleability, and elasticity to different degrees

In what proportion by weight do hydrogen and oxygen
combine to form water as determined by the Dumas method
in which dry hydrogen is passed over heated cupric oxide
and then through calcium chloride?

How does the volume of hydrogen in water compare with the volume of oxygen as determined by analysis (electrolysis)? By synthesis (eudiometer)?

Do particles collect around the positive and negative electrodes when direct current is passed through a colloidal suspension of arsenious sulfide prepared by passing hydrogen sulfide through the filtrate from arsenious oxide in boiling water?

Can a compound be prepared if the table of solubilities lists the compound as insoluble and solutions of two different soluble compounds are mixed to furnish the positive and negative ions desired?

If a test tube of hydrogen chloride gas is inverted with the mouth barely in water, how high does the water "rise" in the tube, that is, about how much of a volume of hydrogen chloride gas dissolves in water?

Can chlorine gas be collected by the displacement of water? Of air?

What is the silver nitrate test for the presence of a chloride? Is a white precipitate formed when clear solutions of silver nitrate and sodium chloride are mixed?

Is greater effervescence produced when hot or cold water is added to baking powder?

Is chicory more readily soluble in cold water than coffee?

When ammonia is passed into water is the product neutral, a base, or an acid?

Does an "hydrogen chloride fountain" show hydrogen chloride to be slightly or extremely soluble in water?

Does the solution made by adding potassium dichromate crystals to concentrated sulfuric acid clean glassware readily?

Can the sulfides of copper, iron, and potassium, respectively, be precipitated in either acid or alkaline solutions?

What colors are exhibited by the following metallic sulfides precipitated from solution by hydrogen sulfide: arsenious sulfide, cadmium sulfide, antimony tri-sulfide, cupric sulfide, zinc sulfide, lead sulfide?

How is a qualitative analysis run to detect the presence of silver, lead, and mercury ions (Group I) in the same solution?

How is a qualitative analysis run to group the acid radical ions (barium chloride group, silver nitrate group, soluble group) and to identify some common acid ions in each group?

What unknown salt is present in a given solution?

How may fertilizers be tested for some common elements (potassium, phosphorus, nitrogen as nitrates and ammonium compounds) which are essential to plant growth?

What substances are contained in plant tissues?

Do depilatories contain a sulfide?

Does a soap contain free alkali? Does a deep red color appear when an alcoholic solution of phenolphthalein is placed on a small piece of soap heated gently to dryness or is mixed with a solution of soap in alcohol?

Is free chlorine present in drinking water, that is, what coloration appears when orthotolidine is put in distilled water containing chlorine?

Does the plastic mass formed when powdered plaster of Paris is moistened with water harden gradually?

Can a colloidal dispersion of sulfur be prepared by dissolving sodium thiosulfate ("hypo") in water and adding dilute hydrochloric acid? By adding distilled water to a solution of sulfur dissolved in alcohol?

Which sulfides (copper sulfide) are insoluble in dilute acid? Are soluble (zinc sulfide) in dilute acids and insoluble in an alkaline solution? Are soluble (sodium sulfide) in water, in dilute acids, and in an alkaline solution?

How is the presence of a soluble bromide detected, that is, what color does bromine, released by mixing carbon tetrachloride and chlorine water, impart to carbon tetrachloride?

What test distinguishes between a chloride, a bromide, and an iodide, that is, what colors appear when a bromide, an iodide and a chloride are placed in separate test tubes of carbon tetrachloride?

Can hydrofluoric acid be made by heating calcium fluoride with sulfuric acid and passing the resultant gas through water?

Does glass remain clear or become opaque where it comes in contact with hydrofluoric acid?

Does hydrochloric acid liberate carbon dioxide from a carbonate (marble)? A bicarbonate (baking soda)?

Is the size of the pigment particles different in different paints? Do some particles, which remain after a solvent removes the oil from paint, settle more rapidly than others in water?

Can common shellac be prepared by dissolving dry shellac in wood alcohol?

Is saccharin used in the place of sugar in a food? Do saccharin and sugar dissolve in ether?

Do laxatives contain phenolphthalein? Magnesium compounds?

What physical and chemical tests distinguish cotton from linen? What are the similarities and differences in the reaction of cotton and linen to the following tests: burning, litmus, lead acetate, sodium hydroxide, hydrochloric acid, fuchsin, ink or water spot, glycerine or oil spot, and microscope?

What physical and chemical tests distinguish wool, silk, and rayon, respectively? What are the similarities and differences in the reaction of wool, silk, and rayon to the following tests: burning, litmus, copper sulfate, lead acetate, nitric acid, sodium hydroxide, hydrochloric acid, moisture, acetone, and microscope?

Are cotton and rayon (dissolves in sulfuric acid) present in a sample of "woolen" cloth? Is reclaimed wool (no scales)?

What is the percentage of wool (dissolves in sodium hydroxide) in a sample of mixed cotton and wool cloth?

How can rayon be made by the copper-ammonium process? Nitrate process? Acetate process? Viscose process

Can raw wool be cleaned by washing it with soap and sodium carbonate followed by immersion in hot dilute acid and a rinse water containing sodium carbonate?

Does a spot of oil or fat on brown paper grow larger when heated? Is the spot transparent, translucent, or opaque? Can fat be obtained from peanuts by crushing them in carbon tetrachloride which evaporates?

Is a furniture polish made from carnauba wax, oleic acid, borax, and triethanolamine water-insoluble?

Can a face cream (cold, cleansing, vanishing, brushless shaving) be prepared by emulsification of an oil or fat in water?

Can an eyewash be prepared by adding boric acid crystals to hot water until no more crystals will dissolve?

Can lanolin lotion be prepared by heating together stearic acid, lanolin, triethanolamine, and water?

Can acetylene gas be prepared by adding water drop-by-drop to calcium carbide? Are black particles evident after acetylene, not mixed with air, is ignited?

Can methane gas be prepared by heating fused sodium acetate with soda lime? Is methane combustible? Does it support combustion?

Is the odor of ether evident after shaking ethyl alcohol with a concentrated sulfuric acid?

Can ethyl acetate (an ester) be prepared by the action of acetic acid on ethyl alcohol?

Can acetaldehyde be prepared by using ethyl alcohol, hydrochloric acid and potassium dichromate? What color appears when formaldehyde is heated with Fehling's solution?

Is sugar converted into alcohol and carbon dioxide when yeast is placed in a solution of corn syrup or molasses and kept warm?

Can a hydrogen of benzene be replaced with bromine in the presence of iron?

Can nitrobenzene (odor from shoe polish) be prepared by adding benzene drop-by-drop to a mixture of concentrated sulfuric and nitric acids? Is much heat evident? What liquid goes to the bottom on standing?

What are the products of the burning of gasoline?

What color precipitate, if any, results when Fehling's (or Benedict's) solution is heated with glucose (corn syrup)? Sucrose (cane and beet sugar)?

Can dextrin be prepared by heating starch in an evaporating dish until the starch begins to turn light brown? Is dextrin sweet or tasteless? What color appears when iodine is added to a solution of dextrin?

Does "canned heat" (alcohol gel) prepared by mixing ethyl alcohol with a saturated solution of calcium acetate ignite from a lighted match?

Will bromine vapor which is heavier than air diffuse upward?

Will sufficient hydrogen diffuse downward through a porous membrane or cup to force bubbles out through water?

Does a true solution or a colloidal diffuse faster through a gel (Alexander's Patriotic Tube)?

Can copper chromate rhythmic banding (colored rings) be formed by permitting time for the diffusion of copper ions downward from copper sulfate into a gel made of sodium silicate, acetate acid, and potassium·chromate?

Do a colloid (Pour starch paste into boiling water, let settle, and use the clear liquid.) and a crystalloid (common salt in solution) pass through a cone of parchment paper or a cellophane bag set in a beaker of distilled water (dialysis)?

If a drop of formic acid in the eye of a needle is deposited under the surface of a solid gelatin (salad), Does swelling similar to that caused by a bee sting occur over-night around the place where the acid was inserted?

Does pepsin change the appearance of chopped egg white (digestion of protein) to which a little dilute hydrochloric acid is added?

Can a vegetable oil be hydrogenated by passing natural gas through cottonseed or corn oil in the presence of nickel?

Is more starch produced in green leaves (geranium; begonia) when they are placed in bright sunlight or when they are in darkness?

Is oxygen liberated from fresh green leaves placed in sunlight under water saturated with carbon dioxide?

Does paint prepared from zinc oxide, linseed oil, manganese dioxide, and turpentine spread easily and dry readily?

Does water sometimes act as a catalyst? Does chemical action begin in baking powder, a mixture of chemicals, as soon as water is added?

Will pure zinc or impure mossy zinc replace hydrogen from hydrochloric acid more rapidly?

Is sugar converted into alcohol and carbon dioxide when yeast is placed in a solution of corn syrup or molasses and kept warm?

Can sulfur trioxide be prepared by passing sulfur dioxide over asbestos dipped in platinic chloride and then ignited over a Bunsen flame?

Can crystals of aspirin be prepared by mixing salicylic acid, acetic anhydride, concentrated sulfuric acid, and glacial acetic acid?

Can white crystals of caffeine be obtained from coffee by drawing off the chloroform from a mixture of chloroform and coffee solution, evaporating the chloroform, dissolving the residue in ethyl alcohol and evaporating the alcohol? How does the amount of caffeine in regular coffee compare with that in coffee advertized as having the caffeine removed? Does a soft drink contain caffeine?

Are aminopyrine, phenacetin, acetanilide, aspirin, and an alkalizer present in a headache remedy?

After hot saturated solutions of sodium nitrate and potassium chloride are poured together, can sodium chloride be filtered out? Can potassium nitrate be crystallized out?

Does a chemical garden, made by pouring water glass over crystals of various salts (chlorides of aluminum, cobalt, copper, iron, nickel and manganese) scattered over the bottom of a beaker change color? Appear to grow in size?

Can particles of colloidal size be formed by condensation or aggregation of particles which are less than colloidal size?

Geology.

Do eruptions similar to those of geysers occur at regular intervals when cold water from a reservoir flows down through rubber tubing, containing a constricted glass tube, into a flask where it is heated and pushed upward through a glass tube deep in the flask and out a glass nozzle with a diameter of the constriction in the supply tube and level with the water in the reservoir?

How are the washing, the heating and cooling, and the humidity of air controlled in an air-conditioning unit (cutaway model or a field trip)?

Do maps of trade winds show that winds, in general, have a more constant direction on land or on water?

What is the relation of principal ocean currents to prevailing winds?

What is the relation between climate and the life zones on the earth?

THE EXPERIMENTS WHICH THE INVESTIGATOR WAS UNABLE TO
ALLOCATE TO ANY OF THE 214 PRINCIPLES JUDGED
DESIRABLE FOR INCLUSION IN THE INTEGRATED
COURSE OF PHYSICAL SCIENCE FOR
SENIOR HIGH SCHOOL

<u>Physics, Including Meteorology and Astronomy.</u>
What are some relationships between the English and
the metric systems of measurement in length? In volume?
In weight?
What is the volume of a steel ball using a micro-
meter gauge? Of a solid metal cylinder using a vernier
caliper?
What is the value of g (the acceleration of gravity)
as measured by using a simple pendulum?
What is the effect on the number of vibrations of
a simple pendulum in one minute of change in mass?
Change in amplitude? Change in length?
What is the maximum horsepower developed by a
person running up a flight of stairs as fast as possible?
If one person pulls a given weight to a given
height as fast as he can, and two other persons pull the
same weight to the same height as fast as they can is
the same or different amounts of power expended?
Is there any relation between the work done in
lifting a body and the work done in dragging it the same
distance? Does time have any effect on work done? On
power?
If a loaded car is drawn by a spring balance along
a smooth table top with uniform motion, is more force
required to overcome the friction when only the rear or
all four wheels are prevented from turning, that is, do
four-wheel brakes have an advantage over rear wheel
brakes alone?
May two bodies have the same mass but different
volumes?
What is the volume of an irregular shaped body as
determined by the volume of water displaced by the body
in a graduated cylinder or a weighed over flow can?
What is the density of a block of wood as determined by using a meter stick and scales?
What is the density (mass per unit volume) of a
liquid more (and less) dense than water?
What is the weight of a given volume of air taken
from a hollow metal sphere or round-bottomed flask?
What is the density of that air using the volume obtained
by filling the sphere or flask with water?

What is the water pressure at a given time as determined by directing the water vertically upward from a garden hose to secure the height to be substituted in an equation? (neglect air resistance)

How do the lift and drag of a model airplane change as the angle of attack becomes steeper?

What is the pressure of air in terms of inches of a mercury column it will hold up?

How does the atmospheric pressure read from a homemade mercurial barometer compare with the reading taken from a Fortincistern barometer?

What is the weight of one liter of air at room temperature and pressure?

What is the forecast for the weather for two days in advance based upon the following for two days past: barometer reading, temperature changes, clouds, wind velocity and direction, relative humidity, weather maps for the past week?

What types of clouds accompany the various types of weather?

How much precipitation occurs during a given period of time, say one month?

Does the hair in a hair hygrometer increase or decrease in length as the relative humidity increases?

What are the weather conditions over a state as determined by interpretation of a weather map? What weather conditions have taken place at four widely separated cities during a twenty-four hour period?

What is the sequence of conditions in cold, warm, and occluded fronts as shown by placing diagrams of them on boards which can be moved across a horizontal wire in front of a class?

What is the height of a cloud base as determined by using a clinometer?

How does the temperature vary throughout the United States in July and January as shown on isothermal charts?

Can matter exist in three states, namely, solid, liquid and gas?

Do solids, liquids, and gases have a definite shape and a definite volume?

What is the cost of heating one quart of water from room temperature to the boiling point with a gas burner when the vessel is covered? Not covered? What is the efficiency of a Bunsen burner?

What is the frequency of a tuning fork as determined by tuning a stretched piano wire (no.6) to unison with a tuning fork of known frequency, measuring its length, then lengthening or shortening the wire until it is in unison with the fork of unknown frequency, and setting up an inverse proportion between the respective frequencies and lengths?

What is the frequency of a tuning fork taken from the smoked record of a vibrograph?

If a page on a wall is lighted by an unshaded lamp between the wall and a reader, can the print be read more easily before or after a book is placed almost between the reader's eyes and the lamp? If a mirror, replacing the printed page, is moved about on the wall, are there places where distinctly more light is reflected into the reader's eyes?

If a coin is placed between two mirrors making a right angle (and then a sixty degree angle), are multiple images produced?

How does the size, shape, and position compare for an object and its image using a convex lens and the parallax method?

What are the characteristics of the images produced by a double convex (and concave) lens compared with the object with respect to kinds, size, and location when the object and the lens are apart by less than the focal length, exactly the focal length, greater than the focal length but less than twice the focal length, exactly twice the focal length, and greater than twice the focal length?

What are the characteristics of the image produced by a concave mirror with respect to kind, size, and position if the object (a candle) is between the mirror and its principal focus? Between the principal focus and twice the principal focus? At a distance greater than the principal focus?

Using a plane mirror, a convex mirror and a concave mirror, the latter with the object both inside and outside the focal point, what is the size of the image in relation to the size of the object? The distance of the image from the mirror compared with the distance of the object from the mirror? The nature of the image, whether erect or inverted? The apparent position of the image, whether behind or in front of the mirror?

If first a convex and then a concave lens is held in a hole at one end of a shoe box, for which type of lens must a ground glass be moved farther back or forward in the box to achieve focus when viewed from the open end opposite the lens?

If a camera is made by placing long-focus and short focus-lenses in one end of a shoe box and sliding a ground glass back and forth through the other (open) end to achieve focus, does the long-focus lens make images on the ground glass larger or smaller than those produced by the short focus lens (telephoto lens)?

What is the focal length of a double convex lens using an optical bench?

What is the focal length of a concave mirror?

If an inverted bouquet of flowers hidden from view in a box which opens toward a concave mirror is strongly lighted, can a person facing the mirror and standing in line with the mirror and a vase on top of the box see a bouquet of flowers in the vase? What happens when the person steps out of line?

If an inverted duck hidden from view in a box which opens toward a concave mirror is strongly lighted, can a person facing the mirror and standing in line with the mirror and a glass dish on top of the box see a duck on water in the dish? What happens when the person steps out of line?

Where is the principal focus of a converging lens and what is the relation between the focal length and distances to conjugate foci?

Does the eye produce astigmatism as shown by observing the spokes on an eye chart?

If a light bulb is held below the edge of one side of a table and the eye is below the opposite edge, what is observed as the eye looks at the under surface of water in a jar placed midway between the bulb and the eye (critical angle)?

Does total internal reflection occur in glass for a beam of light whose angle of incidence is greater or less than the critical angle for glass?

If light is sent into one end of a bent tube of Lucite, does the light "escape" through the clear edges or the other end of the tube?

Is total reflection secured in a periscope by the use of right-angle prisms?

What is the relation between the entering and the emerging beam of light for a right-angle prism?

What is the index of refraction of a glass prism as measured by observing the critical angle?

Will a transverse wave in a rope pass through a vertical slit in a board representing a polarizer? A horizontal slit representing an analyzer?

Do the letters on a printed page appear double when viewed through a crystal of Iceland spar (calcite)? If a crystal of Iceland spar is placed over one dot and rotated, does another dot appear to rotate around the stationary dot?

Can light alternately be stopped and transmitted by rotating one of two tourmaline crystals? One of two polaroid discs?

Does light pass through two tourmaline crystals when corresponding axes of the two crystals are in the same plane? Are turned at right angles to each other?

Can print or objects be seen through polaroid which is "crossed"?

Can two polaroid discs which overlap be rotated so
that little or no light passes through the overlapping
portions of the discs?

Are Newton's rings produced by a thin film of oil?
Of soap solution? By two pieces of glass placed together
and pressed in the middle?

Can black interference bands be observed where light
from a sodium flame is reflected from two glass plates
placed at a small angle to each other? What difference
is observed where light produced by inserting sodium
chloride in a Bunsen flame is reflected from a clear
piece of glass placed flat on a table near the burner
and from an adjacent wedge of two pieces of glass one on
top of the other but held apart at one edge by a piece
of tissue paper?

Can a dark (Fraunhofer) line be seen if a beam of
white light is passed through a sodium flame and then
into a spectroscope?

Will minerals such as calcite, flourspar, or
willemite fluoresce under strong ultra-violet light?
Under ordinary light?

What is the commercial efficiency (watts per candle
power) of a tungsten filament lamp?

What is the intensity of illumination of different
parts of a classroom as measured by a light (foot-
candle) meter?

Can distance to an object be estimated accurately
with only one eye?

How can the meaning of "variation east" and
"variation west" be demonstrated by using colored strings
on a large map of North America?

Is the alternate lighting of electric lamps in
quadrants one and three with those in quadrants two and
four similar to the alternation of the fields from the
"A" antenna and the "B" antenna of a loop-antenna radio
range station?

If a card is held between the knobs of a static
machine as it sparks, does the appearance of the holes
punctured in the card show that the sparks passed in
only one or in both directions, that is, is the discharge of Leyden jars oscillatory?

If a lighted 100-watt lamp (the sun) is across
the room from a very small steel ball (the earth),
does the "earth" get a very large or a very small
amount of the light given off from the "sun"?

How are the following located in the heavens with
the aid of a constellation map: the Big Dipper, Ursa
Minor, the North Star, Orion, Cassiopeiae's Chair, Vega,
the future pole star, and Sirius, the brightest star in
the heavens?

What is the relative size of the earth and the
sun with the distance between them on the same scale?
If a cardboard disk four and one-half feet in diameter
(model of the sun) is placed 160 yards from a marble
one-half inch in diameter (the earth), can a person see
the "earth" from the "sun"? How big does the "sun"
appear from the earth as measured by the length on a
pencil held vertically at arm's length in the visual
angle bounded by the edges of the model of the sun?
     Is the latitude of a given place equal to the
angle between the horizon and the North Star as determined by using a level, a straight plank in sighting,
and a protractor?
     What is the latitude of a place, that is, what is
the angle of elevation of the North Star above the
horizon at night as determined by attaching a plumb line
to the center of the horizontal portion of a protractor
and reading the angle of elevation directly after one
edge of the protractor is turned up and pointed toward
the North Star?

Chemistry
     Can any article be placed in water without causing
a rise in its level, that is, does matter occupy space?
     Can flocculation (coagulation) of a colloid be
caused by heat?
     Can a silicic acid gel be prepared by mixing equal
volumes of normal acetic acid and sodium silicate solution of high density?
     What is the "thread count" of a sample of cloth?
     Does sodium sulfite or potassium nitrite restore
the fresh, red color to discolored hamburger meat?
     Can sodium bicarbonate be prepared passing carbon
dioxide through a mixture of solutions of ammonium
carbonate, ammonium hydroxide, and sodium chloride?
     How does the amount of gas liberated by equal
weights of sodium bicarbonate and various "alkalizers"
compare?
     Does smoke burn?
     Can a simple gunpowder made from potassium nitrate,
powdered charcoal and powdered sulfur be ignited?
     How are the following produced: lime, plaster of
Paris, mortar, cement?
     Can carbon monoxide be prepared by adding warm
concentrated sulfuric acid to formic or oxalic acid?
     In the test for borates, what color change occurs
in tumeric paper moistened by a solution of "borax" in
hydrochloric acid followed by a drop of sodium hydroxide?
     What is the percentage of water vapor in air as
determined by forcing a known volume of air through
calcium chloride?

Does the addition of a common ion force a reaction
to go to completion? When hydrogen chloride gas is passed into a saturated solution of sodium chloride, will
some sodium chloride be precipitated?

Is microscopic animal life, obtained by letting
barnyard manure and dry grass stand in water in a warm
place, killed by chlorine gas?

Do impurities collect on the unglazed porcelain in
a Pasteur or a Berkefeld household filter attached to
a faucet?

At what temperature does an alloy, made by melting
together one part of tin, four of bismuth, one of cadmium,
and two of lead, melt as water is warmed?

What is the weight and volume of hydrogen which can
be displaced from dilute hydrochloric acid by a given
weight of magnesium?

Will the addition of sodium chloride to freshly
made soap cause the soap to separate from the water?

Will the addition of salt make a dye less soluble in
water and cause more of it to unite with the fabric?

What is the molecular weight of oxygen?

Can "canned heat" be prepared by adding eight parts
of concentrated solution of calcium acetate to one part
of alcohol?

Will sodium chloride precipitate as its solution is
concentrated by evaporation?

Is the flavor of meat better preserved if the meat
is first placed in boiling water or in cold water for
boiling?

Do some laundry soaps and toilet soaps contain
rosin? Is a purple coloration produced when concentrated
sulfuric acid is added to soap dissolved in acetic acid?

Can a different color be developed in cotton cloth
with primuline dye by diazotizing the dye in a solution
of sodium nitrite and hydrochloric acid followed by
"developing" in a solution of resorcinol?

Does high quality writing paper made from rags turn
yellow when treated with a water solution of aniline?
Does newspaper or wrapping paper?

What is the tendering effect of the common mineral
or organic acids upon the common fibers: cotton, linen,
silk, and wool?

What is the quality of different samples of silk
and cotton fabrics as determined by tests for the
following: strength, thread count, weighting (ash left
on burning), color fastness (boil in water)?

What is the percentage of "weighting" in a sample
of silk cloth?

How is cotton cloth mercerized?

What percentage of a face cream are water, mineral
oil, and vegetable and animal oil, respectively?

Can "gray goods" (unbleached cotton muslin) be bleached by dipping the cloth, in order, in hot chloride of lime, cold water, cold dilute hydrochloric acid, and "hypo" followed by rubbing in a mixture of soap, water, and bluing?

Can a face powder be prepared by mixing talc, kaolin, precipitated chalk, zinc oxide, and zinc stearate with coloring matter and perfume?

Can lipstick be prepared from ceresin, lanolin, mineral oil, and carmine?

How may a mouthwash be made?

Can hair dressing be prepared by shaking olive oil, glycerine, and alcohol together?

Can a finger-waving lotion be prepared using gum tragacanth, glycerine, alcohol, and water?

Can a glycerine hand lotion be prepared using gum tragacanth, witch hazel, glycerine, boric acid, and water?

Can a fingernail polish be prepared by mixing camphor gum, alcohol, and collodion (new skin) with carmine?

Can a nail-polish remover be prepared by mixing ethyl acetate, acetone, and olive oil?

Is a fifteen percent solution of aluminum chloride or a saturated solution of a mixture of equal parts of boric acid and baking soda a satisfactory deodorant?

How is a "dry-bright" linoleum polish prepared?

Can an effective fly-and-mosquito spray be prepared by mixing odorless kerosene and pyrethrum?

Can an anti-sunburn ointment be prepared from phenyl salicylate, liquid petrolatum, and lanolin?

Can a toothpaste be prepared by mixing powdered sugar, precipitated chalk, castile soap, glycerine or "karo" syrup, and oil of peppermint or wintergreen?

What color change occurs in a paper flower covered with a solution of cobaltous chloride as the air becomes more moist? Less moist? Does the solution used as an ink become visible on heating?

What is the relative sweetness of saccharin and sugar?

Can a lacquer paint be prepared by mixing a dye (carmine) with equal volumes of amyl acetate and collodion?

What are the general characteristics of organic acids, alcohols and esters?

Do different fertilizers have a different effect on the growth of the same plants?

Does the addition of vitamin B-one to soil containing tomato plants improve the yield and condition of the flowers or fruit? The condition and amount of the root system?

What is the effect of antiseptics and germicides on the growth of bacterial colonies?

Do colonies of bacteria develop on a culture medium exposed to the air? To a finger? To a drop of milk?

Does pasteurization delay the spoiling of milk?

What color appears when starch comes in contact with a solution of iodine?

Does milk contain protein? Fat? Sugar?

Does a soft drink contain a vegetable dye or a coal-tar dye? Is white woolen cloth not colored (vegetable dye) or colored (coal-tar dye) when placed in water in which a piece of white woolen cloth previously boiled in a soft drink, rinsed, and dried is boiled?

What is the purity of cocoa as determined by the percentage of solids (ash) which does not volatilize?

Does jam contain an artificial acid dye or a vegetable dye?

Is starch used as an adulterant in bulk sausage?

What is the test for borax and boric acid, an adulterant sometimes found in crackers and wafers?

What are tests for the presence of benzoic acid (or sodium benzoate) and salicylic acid sometimes used as a preservative in catsup, jams, and jellies?

What is a test for the presence of cotton seed oil? What color is produced when cottonseed oil is treated with Halphen's reagent?

Is a sample of olive oil pure? What color changes occurs as pure olive oil and nitric acid are shaken? Heated?

What is a test for the presence of formaldehyde? What color ring appears at the interface of sulfuric acid and the distillation from an acidulated solution of milk containing formaldehyde to which gallic acid in alcohol was added?

Can a "cast" of a dime be made by cooling type metal poured over a dime?

Is a red hot steel bar made harder by cooling slowly in air than by cooling rapidly in water?

How is the temper drawn from a steel needle and restored?

Will a green solution of chlorophyll (obtained by dissolving green leaves in ether) fluoresce, giving a blood-red color, under strong ultra-violet light? Under ordinary light?

Is precipitation prevented in an iron ink by including or excluding hydrochloric acid?

Geology.

How is a profile of a section of a contour map constructed?

How is a contour map constructed when the elevations of a sufficient number of points are known?

What is the meaning of some of the conventional
signs used on topographic maps?

What type of house construction, balloon or
Western, better withstands the shaking on a laboratory
earthquake platform?

What are the features of a recently submerged
coast (Boothbay Sheet)?

How do the thickness of the earth's crust, depths
of oceans, heights of mountains, and thickness of the
atmosphere compare with the distance from the center of
the earth to its surface as shown by striking an arc
with chalk at the end of a string to represent the surface of the earth? An arc two-thirds of an inch closer
and one the same distance beyond the "surface" to represent the deepest oceans and the highest mountains
respectively? An arc thirteen-sixteenths of an inch
closer than the "surface" to represent the bottom of
the earth's crust? An arc three feet beyond the "surface"
to represent the upper limits of the atmosphere?

Miscellaneous.

May classmates hold certain ideas which may or may
not be true? Which has more air space, a jar filled
with small pieces of coal or a similar jar of larger
pieces?

How is a controlled laboratory activity carried on
to solve a problem scientifically? What factors affect
the rate of evaporation of alcohol?

How is error and percentage of error computed?

Is there a limit to the divisibility of substances
such as eosin dye?

How does the articulated connecting-rod assembly
of a radial engine work?

How can a lamp cord be correctly repaired?

In what respects does the Mercator map show the
earth's surface correctly and in what ways is it in-
correct?

If a yardstick which touches San Francisco on a
globe intersects a vertical ruler above Kansas City,
what evidence is there that the surface of the earth
curves?

Is the shortest distance between two points on a
parallel (a small circle) a great Circle route or the
arc of the parallel?

Has lack of knowledge of some fact been a serious
handicap in a critical situation? How can chewing gum
be removed from fur? How can the flame of fat burning
in a frying pan be extinguished?

How are a transit and a tridirectional protractor
correctly used?

How are angles measured by means of a protractor?
How many board feet in some lumber?

Date Due

JUN 2 0 '52		
JUL 3 1952		
JUL 8 '52		
AUG 6 '52		
JUL 2 9 1954		
MAR 6		
OCT 8 196		
OCT 7		
MAR 1 9		
C # 11 c		
C 4 A		
June 1)		
FEB 15 '70		
MAR 16 7		
MAY 1 8 '76		

85